"Drawing on poignant personal stories, Jewish life and traditions, and a spiritual letter from Einstein to a grieving father, Naomi Levy's book outlines an inspiring guide on how to live a meaningful and connected life."   —Alan Lightman, author of *Einstein's Dreams*

"Read about Naomi Levy's spiritual journey at the risk of having her take you deeper into yourself. *Einstein and the Rabbi* takes you on the journey of journeys."   —Norman Lear

"Rabbi Naomi Levy has done something extraordinary. Inspired by one of the most famous letters written by Einstein, she has, through meticulous research uncovered the utterly unexpected background to Einstein's letter, words written to a saintly rabbi who had just undergone the worst suffering a parent can experience. Naomi Levy, who decades earlier had undergone the worst suffering a child can experience, has united the words of Einstein, the story of Rabbi Robert Marcus, and of herself and her own father in a way that makes us all realize that the soul truly can see what eyes cannot. With Naomi Levy as our guide we too can learn to see with our souls, and thereby bless the lives of those around us and our own lives as well."
    —Rabbi Joseph Telushkin, author of *Jewish Literacy*,
    Rebbe, and *Words That Hurt, Words That Heal*

"Levy offers us a blessing—which indeed comes true as one travels through her luminous book: 'I am praying that something sacred will happen to you. Something unexpected. A turning. An awakening.' And it does; all of that and more."
    —Abigail Pogrebin, author of *My Jewish Year* and *Stars of David*

"In these bewildering and often implausible times, Naomi Levy's book provides a vital and necessary antidote. Without stooping to easy remedies or spiritual jargon and drawing on centuries of Jewish thought,

Levy shows us a soulful way to navigate a materialist world. *Einstein and the Rabbi* is a heartwarming and lucid reflection on balancing your life and schooling your heart."   —Daphne Merkin,
author of *This Close to Happy: A Reckoning with Depression*

"A great read both for those who love the science of Einstein and the soul of the Zohar. The history of Einstein's correspondence with Rabbi Marcus is fascinating and brings together science and soul."
—Alan Dershowitz, author of *Taking the Stand: My Life in the Law*

"Rabbi Naomi Levy shares her loving spirit, her inspirational stories of Einstein and the rabbi whose grief he sought to assuage, and her lessons on hearing the voice of your soul. This remarkable book spoke to me as I am sure it will speak to you."   —Susan Cain,
author of *Quiet*

"Naomi Levy examines life's polarities: birth and death, love and loss, faith and doubt. With keen insight, she shows how each duality is connected by the vital force we call 'the soul.' This is a lovely, tender book that will illuminate and inspire."   —Jerome Groopman,
Recanati Professor, Harvard Medical School,
and author of *The Anatomy of Hope*

"'What is the soul?' This question has been on the tips of the tongues of seekers, saints, and prophets from the beginning of time. 'Are there words to describe the ineffable?' This question has been on the tips of the pens of poets across the ages and the continents. Rabbi Naomi Levy takes on these questions in *Einstein and the Rabbi*, and she does so with humility, mastery, and poetry in a book that reads like a mystery novel. I couldn't put it down."
—Elizabeth Lesser, author of *Broken Open* and *Marrow* and cofounder of Omega Institute

"It is the task of the rabbi to articulate the wisdom and power of the Jewish religion in all its profundity, mystery, and earthy relevance. Naomi Levy performs the task spectacularly; she speaks from deep within the Jewish soul and gives the spiritual gifts of Judaism not only to Jews but to the world at large. It is difficult to overestimate her contribution. *Einstein and the Rabbi* is worthy of the matriarchs from whom originated the blessing of Jewish womanhood and who continue, through such as her, to bless it still."   —Marianne Williamson, author of *A Return to Love* and *Tears to Triumph*

"Everyone needs to read this book. It is a book for the times we live in now, capturing the human spirit through historic journeys to present-day gestures of kindness and understanding. Naomi Levy writes with a clear, easy style that allows us to fall into her narrative, bearing witness to the soul life."   —Julianna Margulies, actor and producer

"With keen insight, an open heart, and the graceful, accessible wisdom for which she is widely known, Rabbi Naomi Levy has written a book that will be a balm and a provocation for all who read it. It made me cry. It made me think. To read it is to be gently guided into a deeper place."   —Dani Shapiro, author of *Devotion* and *Hourglass*

"Naomi Levy weaves together a series of stories from her perspective as a rabbi, her personal journey through illness, and a remarkable search for a letter to Einstein that results in describing the indescribable— the nature of our souls."

—Stephen Tobolowsky, actor and author of *My Adventures with God* and *The Dangerous Animals Club*

ALSO BY NAOMI LEVY

EINSTEIN

and the

RABBI

Searching for the Soul

NAOMI LEVY

FLATIRON
BOOKS
NEW YORK

READER'S NOTE: SOME SECTIONS OF THE BOOK APPEAR OUT OF SEQUENCE INTENTIONALLY.

EINSTEIN AND THE RABBI. Copyright © 2017 by Naomi Levy. All rights reserved. Printed in the United States of America. For information, address Flatiron Books, 175 Fifth Avenue, New York, N.Y. 10010.

Image on page 27 from the collections of the Jewish Museum in Prague. Illustration on page 155 created by Macmillan Cancer Support and reused with permission.

Sections from Chapter 30, "Turning Your Weakness into Your Strength," previously appeared in *Reform Judaism Magazine*. Sections from Chapter 38, "Treasuring Blessings That Can Never Die," previously appeared in *Jewish Journal*.

www.flatironbooks.com

Designed by Steven Seighman

The Library of Congress Cataloging-in-Publication Data is available upon request.

ISBN 978-1-250-05726-6 (hardcover)
ISBN 978-1-250-05872-0 (ebook)

Our books may be purchased in bulk for promotional, educational, or business use. Please contact your local bookseller or the Macmillan Corporate and Premium Sales Department at 1-800-221-7945, extension 5442, or by email at MacmillanSpecialMarkets@macmillan.com.

First Edition: September 2017

10 9 8 7 6 5 4 3 2 1

For Rob

I found the one my soul loves.

—Songs of Songs (3:4)

CONTENTS

You lead me beside still waters,
You restore my soul.

Psalm 23

SEARCHING
FOR THE
SOUL

1

Meeting the Soul

WAS YOUR FATHER A RABBI?

When I tell people that I wanted to be a rabbi from the time I was four years old they always ask me that same question. No, my father made women's clothing, but he was *my* rabbi. When I was a child my father would read me tales of biblical heroes and prophets, these were my bedtime stories. He taught me how to pray, to love the melodies of prayer, and how to sing in harmony with him as we'd walk hand in hand down the street. While my friends stayed home on Saturday mornings to watch cartoons in their pajamas, my father would take me to synagogue, and I would sit beside him and play with the strands of his prayer shawl.

When I announced in kindergarten that I wanted to be a rabbi everyone laughed. Some people scolded me: "Don't you know girls can't be rabbis!" But my father was rooting for me. "Nomi," he said, using my nickname, "keep dreaming and you're the one who will be laughing one day. Not from 'I told you so.' You'll be laughing from pure joy on the day you become a rabbi." So I held on to my dream even though it seemed like a fantasy.

My father kept teaching me and I kept learning. When it was time for my bat mitzvah, our family belonged to a synagogue that wouldn't allow girls to chant from the Torah or lead any part of the service on a Sabbath morning. Instead, girls were permitted only to offer a reading from the Book of Prophets on Friday evening. My father taught me how to chant from the Prophets. When I had mastered the reading, my father began teaching me how to lead a Friday evening Sabbath service, all the melodies and prayers. I soaked it all up with great eagerness and ease. The two of us sang together, creating beautiful harmonies to God. Then my dad went before the board of the synagogue to present our case. He was fighting for justice and he argued with passion and courage. In the end the board relented somewhat: they said I could lead certain Psalms, but I wasn't allowed to utter prayers or blessings to God. I loved this compromise. My bat mitzvah became a beautiful homemade service. It was just me and my dad on the pulpit. I chanted the Psalms, and whenever we came to a blessing he would offer up the blessing. It seemed so perfect to me to be leading a service together with him in that way.

Was the rabbinate my soul's calling? I never thought much about the soul one way or another as I was growing up. Yes, there were expressions like "touched my soul" that I understood to mean that the soul was a metaphor for a very deep place inside us. A place of emotional truth. I knew that music was a very soulful experience for me. I knew that love was soul territory too.

My parents were soulmates. Of that I was certain. They were inseparable, always in each other's arms. There was something rare about the way they interacted. Each morning as my father left for work they would grab each other with passion, as if it was a difficult parting, and each evening when my father returned home they would stand there just holding each other at the front door like lovers reuniting after a long separation. Did they somehow sense that their time together was limited?

Just two years after my bat mitzvah, when I was fifteen, my parents were walking down the street one night. A man approached them with a gun, demanded money, then shot my father.

My father died and my whole world came crashing down.

Suddenly that word "soul" kept coming up over and over again. People kept saying things to me about my father's soul. At his funeral the rabbi offered a prayer about his soul finding peace beneath God's sheltering wing. Was God a bird? All I knew was that my father was gone. I missed him so much. I felt so cut off from him. I wanted more than anything to talk to him, to sing with him, to pray with him, to sit beside him in synagogue. I wanted to study with him. Silence. There was nothing. I was alone. My father would never teach me again.

So many things died the day my father died. My mother died, at least the strong, vibrant woman who had raised me up to that day. Now she seemed so small and weak to me. The Sabbath died and all the holidays too. How do you sit at a holiday table when the person who always led those gatherings is missing? My friends died. They were still with me, of course, but how could they understand me? They were talking about acne and sweet sixteens and I was sleepwalking in a dark mist beside them but not with them. I died. The fifteen-year-old girl giggling and whispering with her friends about crushes on boys and our favorite rock stars. I was numb. Prayer died too. All those powerful discussions my dad and I had about God and faith and prayer seemed hollow now. What good was God? I stopped longing to be a rabbi.

Four years passed. I was in college, and one day I was minding my own business just walking along a path on campus and I felt my father. I felt his presence. It was unmistakable and very strong. It's hard to describe exactly what I felt. It was a deep knowing, like when you're sleeping and you suddenly have a strong sense that someone is standing over you, watching you. At first it was a bit frightening to sense my father's presence, but then it felt comforting. He was with me, walking with me.

I thought the feeling would pass, but I was wrong. My father wouldn't leave me alone, I couldn't shake him. I sensed him all the time.

I started to worry that maybe I was losing my grip on reality. One day after class I decided to tell my literature professor, Dr. Berk, about this problem I was having. He was my mentor and I needed to confide in someone. It was gray and cold outside. We sat down for coffee and I gathered up the courage to tell him about my father's visitations. I said, "I think I might be losing my mind." I wondered if I needed to be medicated.

Dr. Berk smiled and said, "Why would you think that? It's a gift!"

A gift? It felt like a burden. But that rainy afternoon Dr. Berk talked to me about *Hamlet* and *Wuthering Heights* and Irish folk tales and Gabriel García Márquez. We talked about sensing the pulsating rhythm in all things, the heartbeat of creation, about being attuned to mystery, about embracing life's magic instead of needing to control it all the time. He said, "Naomi, you come from a tradition of the great prophets, of Abraham and Moses and Deborah and Samuel—they were all touched by a Presence." I flashed on the Bible stories my father had read to me as a child. Dr. Berk reminded me that the word "psychology" does not mean the study of the mind or the heart—it is the study of the soul. He told me with confident assurance, "Trust me, you're not losing your mind. You're meeting your soul . . . and your father's soul too."

I walked back to my dorm that day together with my father. Instead of worrying about his presence I welcomed him. And I told myself, *So, mental illness is when you feel cut off and alone, and mental health is when you start sensing spirits you can't see.*

I had been mistaken when my father died and I felt so cut off from him. My grief had clouded my ability to hear and feel. Now I was walking with him and I was learning new lessons from the things he taught me long ago.

What if the soul isn't just a metaphor for a deep place inside us? What if the soul is a spiritual entity, a holy guide, an eternal messenger of God dwelling within us? What if the soul can see what our eyes can't perceive? What if the soul has longings and needs and wisdom to offer us about our higher calling and true love, and the very purpose of our lives? What if the soul lives on when we die? What if the souls of departed loved ones are closer to us than we ever imagined?

I began to study the soul—its place within us and its journey when it departs from us. I began to pray for the ability to know my soul, I began to meditate and to listen for the voice of my soul. Slowly, the longings of a four-year-old girl came alive with a passion I had never known before. My soul was calling me, it had always been calling me, to be a rabbi.

In my senior year of college the Jewish Theological Seminary in New York voted to admit women into its rabbinical school. When I heard the news I was overwhelmed with emotion, I was laughing and crying at the same time. I was in the first class of women to enter the seminary. It felt like coming home, like completing a circle. And on the day the dean of my seminary called me up to the pulpit and proudly spread a prayer shawl over my shoulders to bless me and ordain me as a rabbi, I knew my father was laughing too, laughing from pure joy.

Not long after my ordination I began delving into biblical texts, rabbinic interpretations, and mystical teachings about the soul. I started to see that the soul is not only the link to the afterlife, it is also the key to *this* life, here and now.

I learned that we live in what the Jewish mystics call the World of Separation, a place where we see only partial truths, where life seems disjointed and disconnected. I learned Jewish teachings about the Narrow Mind and the Expansive Mind. It's all intuitive wisdom, really. We tend to dwell in our smallness. We are petty and jealous. Our anger blinds us, our past hurts blind us, our lusts and desires and ambitions blind us. But there is an Expansive Mind available to us—that is the vision your soul has to offer you. It is our ability to see the unity, to see with eyes of compassion, to witness the beauty we so often ignore and the blessings that we've already been given. As we enter the state of Expansive Mind, the obstacles that have been keeping us frozen in place melt away. We see our way through them, over them, and beyond them. And then we are given eyes to behold the World of Unity, where all dualities melt away.

In my many years as a rabbi people have come to me with their life questions: *What should I do with my life? Is this the right person for me? How do I breathe excitement back into my marriage? How do I find my true calling?* I realized pretty early on in my rabbinate that most life questions are actually soul questions. We have a gnawing sense that the life we are living is not the life we are meant to be living. We know there is more to do, more expected from us, more to give and more to feel. And we are right!

We experience these longings because at some point we became separated from our own souls, from a voice within us that is here to guide us toward the very purpose of our existence. People will often describe their problems in terms of soul: "I feel like a lost soul." "I feel like there's a hole in my soul." The truth is, our souls are not lost at all, we have simply lost touch with them. If we can learn to reconnect with our souls, we will know the answers to the questions that have been plaguing us.

If the soul is so wise, then why do we stop listening to our souls? Because that's the challenge of being human. We have the power to choose what we want to listen to. The body has its desires, and the ego has its ambitions, and the world around us calls out to us with its distractions, temptations, and promises. The soul can't force you to listen, but it never gives up trying and it never loses hope in you. All through your life your soul tugs at you. That's where that empty feeling comes from. The hole you sense is the distance between where you are and where your soul knows you can be.

What can you say about your soul? Maybe you see the soul in secular terms, as a metaphor for a place of truth deep inside you. Perhaps religious answers come to mind—the soul is holy, divine, eternal. But what do you know of your soul? Can you describe what your soul needs? What it has to offer? Did you once feel deeply connected to your soul? When did you lose that connection? The tragedy of life is that your soul is so close, yet remains a stranger.

It's so easy to get lost and confused. Who among us hasn't felt that way? It's so easy for our senses to get dulled—sometimes by a hurt that causes us to shut down, but more often by our routines. We fall into predictable patterns, we get through our days without reaching and stretching and listening. And then you wake up one day and you realize you have drifted far afield from your own essence. You lost yourself while trying to please others. Your work no longer resonates with you. Your relationships feel superficial. With all your obligations and pressures you've stopped doing the things you love. We wander in exile hoping for a way to return to our essence.

Here is the good news: we are not doomed to remain cut off. There is a way back to our true selves. It hinges on our willingness to meet our souls, to access and to hear the voice of our souls. The soul is our own personal in-house consultant in matters of love and wisdom and guidance and strength. We have become experts at ignoring the soul, our challenge now is to learn to listen and to be receptive to its teachings.

Bring soul to the very places where you feel cut off and adrift, and watch how your life will open up before you. Bring soul to your relationships and you will learn the meaning of intimacy. Bring soul to your work and you will learn the meaning of calling. Bring soul into your house and you will come to understand what home is. Bring soul into your learning and you will acquire wisdom. Bring soul into your heart and you will experience the relief of vulnerability and a depth of love you never knew was inside of you. A love that will lead you to acts of kindness and selflessness. Bring soul to your fears and you will learn courage. Bring soul to your conscience and you will burn with a passion to help people you've never even met. Bring soul to your dreams and you will learn the joy of perseverance. Yes: the sheer joy of sticking with something.

Your soul wants to teach you about your strength. It wants you to believe in your abilities and your gifts. It wants you to lift up your head with pride and claim your birthright: the life that is yours to experience. Your soul wants you to follow it through times of darkness, through the fog and confusion. Your soul will lead you to heights and to loves and to kindness.

Your soul misses you. God misses you. Your soul never stops waiting for you. Yes, it is rooting for you and praying for you. So stop running and hiding and distracting yourself. Free yourself. Break away from the routines that keep your eyes closed and your head down. Welcome your soul back into your life. Take its hand. Let it lead you on a journey toward your true path.

Inviting soul into your life takes practice. It also takes a bit of madness. A sacred madness. A willingness to welcome and to follow a spiritual entity you cannot prove exists. On the other hand, we've spent so many years following other voices that no one can see—the voice of fear or worry or judgment or ambition. So welcome in the sacred madness.

Living with soul does not mean that all pain will disappear. It doesn't mean that all confusion will magically vanish. Sometimes we fail to meet our souls because we naively assume that meeting our souls will lead us to a state of internal peace or ecstasy. The truth is, the soul doesn't deal in satisfaction or in bliss. It deals in open eyes and discomfort. The soul wants you to be uncomfortable enough to strive for more, to grow and to learn and to see what needs fixing in this beautiful and broken world. Living with soul can keep you up at night. You suddenly start seeing the humanity in the eyes of strangers you were ignoring. Their problems come alive inside you. Living with soul can be painful. But it is the only way I know to live the life God has planted inside us.

I became a rabbi so that I could help people hear their souls and connect with the souls of others—the living and the departed. I've seen people experience remarkable changes when they set out to access their souls. Lifeless marriages regain romance, boring days take on new color, a lifelong sense of isolation is lifted, negative internal voices begin to soften, indecision gives way to clarity. Fear doesn't necessarily vanish, but it becomes less of a barrier. A new sense of belonging emerges—of connection to our inner truth and of union with others. People begin to uncover deeper purpose and meaning and long to turn work into calling. Love becomes less threatening, it enters and it flows more freely. Faith and hope seem less like aspirations and more like old friends. Death becomes less frightening and less final. We begin to sense that we are part of something, that we are connected to all of creation. People often tell me that getting to know their souls is like a home-coming to something new. And that sensing the presence of a departed loved one is a precious gift, as Dr. Berk taught me long ago.

Tonight, as I write these words, is my father's *yahrzeit*, the anniversary of his death. He has been gone for thirty-seven years, and he has never left me. On behalf of my father, I'd like to offer you a blessing from a lesson he taught me many years ago:

May you follow the call of your soul, and may you come to laugh with pure joy on the day your deepest yearning becomes a reality. Amen.

2

Einstein and the Rabbi

REVIVING SOULS

THREE YEARS AGO I BEGAN to feel the presence of another soul tugging at me. This time it wasn't the soul of a loved one, it was the soul of a man I had never even met. I didn't see it coming. I was just minding my own business . . .

I was doing research for a class called Oneness. I wanted to teach my students to see the ways we are all interconnected—the living, the dead, animals, rocks, all of creation. I was going to share with them the metaphor I used when I first taught my children about the soul and about what happens to the soul after death.

I'd say, "We're all part of a cosmic soup."

"A soup like chicken soup?" they'd say.

"No, thicker," I'd reply.

"Like a vegetable soup?"

"No," I'd say, "more like a stew."

That's been my metaphor for our place in eternity. I believe that the physical world we perceive is actually part of a spiritual world that is as close to us as our own breath. We are all part of a churning cosmic stew, surrounded by souls we cannot see. And that same stream of eternity runs through us and through everything around us.

One afternoon, as I was piecing together material for my class, I stumbled upon a description of our relationship to the universe by Albert Einstein:

A human being is part of the whole, called by us "Universe," a part limited in time and space. He experiences himself, his thoughts and feelings as something separate from the rest, a kind of optical delusion of his consciousness. The striving to free oneself from this delusion is the one issue of true religion. Not to nourish the delusion but to try to overcome it is the way to reach the attainable measure of peace of mind.

Einstein's exquisite words stopped me in my tracks. He was expressing everything I believed about our limited vision and about the oneness we have trouble seeing, but that we are all part of. Einstein was describing the mystical teachings I'd been studying for years—the Narrow Mind and the Expansive Mind, the World of Separation and the World of Unity that we all have access to. Yes, I thought, we are living in a state of blindness. When we feel alone, we are wrong. Einstein's words reaffirmed everything I'd come to see in my own experience. Einstein was saying that we are all part of a greater whole, all things. And it is our delusion of separateness that causes us so much pain and confusion and loneliness, when in reality all things are connected and intertwined.

Little did I know that this powerful teaching by Einstein about the universe would lead me to the soul of a stranger, and that I would feel compelled to follow the sacred thread of his story. I stumbled on a quote from Einstein, and it took me on a journey that would deepen my understanding of the soul and eternity.

I couldn't believe Einstein had written those words. His description of our place in the universe sounded like it could have come from a Zen master or from an ancient mystical text. But it came from a man who was speaking to us not as a Buddhist and not as a mystic, but as a physicist convinced of the unity of all existence, who saw the interconnectedness of matter, of time and space.

When I came upon Einstein's moving quote on the Internet, it was divorced of all context. I wanted to know where this quote came from, what Einstein was thinking about when he wrote those words. I needed to know who he was talking to.

That's where my journey began. As I dug deeper I discovered that Einstein had written those words in a letter to a man who had lost a child. I searched further and learned that Einstein's letter was addressed to someone named Dr. Robert S. Marcus, whose identity was of absolutely no interest to those who quoted Einstein's exquisite statement. Wherever I found Einstein's quote I would always see it accompanied by the same notation in parentheses: *(a letter Einstein wrote to a grieving father).* I needed to know more about this grieving father.

I wondered to myself, who was this doctor? What kind of doctor was he? And what did he say to Einstein to elicit this beautiful characterization of the universe that spoke so deeply to me?

I spent days and weeks searching, trying to learn more about Dr. Marcus. Then, one morning as I was sifting through archival documents, I discovered that Dr. Marcus was not a medical doctor. He was a rabbi!

It was *Rabbi* Robert S. Marcus, he was the grieving father who had written to Einstein. I felt an immediate closeness to this rabbi. People turn to their clergy when they are in pain, but who do we clergy turn to? I knew Rabbi Marcus must have been suffering and was searching for answers. *But why did he write to Einstein?* I wondered.

Thus began a three-year journey into books and letters, dusty attics and archives and scores of interviews. A quest that led me to New

York City and Cincinnati and to Jerusalem too. Slowly I began to peel back the layers of the mystery.

Rabbi Robert S. Marcus was born in 1909 in Jersey City, New Jersey. He was ordained as an Orthodox rabbi in 1931, and he earned a degree in law from NYU in 1935. He began his rabbinic career as a congregational rabbi, but he realized fairly quickly that he wasn't cut out for the pettiness or the politics of synagogue life. He felt called to work for the greater cause of the Jewish people in an era when Hitler's rise to power was threatening not only his own people's survival, but the very conscience of the world. Rabbi Marcus left his pulpit to serve alongside the renowned Jewish activist Rabbi Stephen S. Wise at the American Jewish Congress. When the United States entered the war, Rabbi Marcus immediately enlisted to become a Jewish chaplain in General Patton's army. The decision could not have been easy. He had a wife and two small sons back home, but he could not remain home when he knew he had a duty to encourage and comfort men in battle.

Rabbi Marcus shipped off in the spring of 1944 just in time for D-day. His wife, Fay, was pregnant with their third child. He wrote home to Fay almost every day of his deployment. Often at the bottom of those letters he would include a special note to Jay, his firstborn son, who was only five years old but already wise beyond his years. Rabbi Marcus seemed to share a deep, spiritual bond with Jay. The letters were a combination of encouragement, parental worry, and longing. "Dear Son, . . . Please be very careful not to get your feet wet when you go out because it is very easy to catch a cold that way . . . Your loving, Father." "Are you getting enough fresh air?" "I love you more every day." "Remember to be careful when you go swimming . . ."

In the letters, he often spoke to Jay as if he were talking to a much older child: "You must protect [little brother] Stephen and keep an eye on Mommy too." On D-day he wrote to Jay, "Today our armies invaded France to attack the Nazis . . . They have already killed 4 million of our Jewish men, women and children . . . I am sorry I cannot be home to celebrate your 6th birthday as I must stay with my very brave men who are fighting for all the children in the world. I must try to encourage them so that they should not be afraid. Even though I shall not be with you, I will be thinking of you and Stephie and Mommy."

Rabbi Marcus was a captain in the Ninth Tactical Air Unit, and was awarded six battle stars and the Bronze Star for meritorious service. He was there on the beaches of Normandy and then in southern France and in Germany, where he brought comfort and solace to frightened, wounded, and dying soldiers. I read the descriptions he wrote to Fay of young boys taking their last breaths in his arms. I also read letters full of compassion that Rabbi Marcus wrote to the parents of fallen soldiers promising them that their sons' souls would live on in "the house of everlasting life."

And then in April 1945 Rabbi Marcus was one of the first chaplains to enter the Buchenwald concentration camp and participate in its liberation.

As he walked through Buchenwald he saw the indescribable inhumanity. Corpses piled high, the stench of burning flesh. And then he came upon the living corpses. He cried out to one person after another: "You are free! You are free!"

As he walked deeper into this hellish world, he found children. This was an unbelievable sight. Children were the first to be sent to slaughter in the concentration camps. But amazingly, Rabbi Marcus discovered 904 Jewish boys who had been hidden and saved by the camp inmates. They were malnourished, but they were alive. Immediately Rabbi Marcus fired off a cable to the OSE, a Jewish children's welfare organization in Geneva: "Have found 1000 Jewish children in Buchenwald. Take immediate measures to evacuate them."

These youngsters became Rabbi Marcus's personal mission. Among them was a sixteen-year-old boy named Eliezer who looked more dead than alive. He is not known to most people as Eliezer, though. The world came to know him as Elie Wiesel.

Rabbi Marcus's colleague Rabbi Herschel Schacter was given a window into the state of mind of these children. He discovered a little boy named Lulek hiding in fear among a pile of corpses:

With tears streaming down his face, Rabbi Schacter picked the boy up. "What's your name, my child?" he asked in Yiddish.

"Lulek," the child replied.

"How old are you?" the rabbi asked.

"What difference does it make?" Lulek, who was seven, said. "I'm older than you, anyway."

"Why do you think you're older?" Rabbi Schacter asked, smiling.

"Because you cry and laugh like a child," Lulek replied. "I haven't laughed in a long time, and I don't even cry anymore. So which one of us is older?"

Little Lulek grew up to be Rabbi Yisrael Meir Lau, the chief Ashkenazi rabbi of Israel.

People who observed these boys noticed that, like Lulek, they looked like children, except two things stood out. First, it was their eyes. They weren't children's eyes, they were the eyes of adults who had seen far too much pain and suffering. And second, they didn't play children's games. They were drawn to the radio and the newspaper headlines and needed to know what was going on in the world.

It would take several weeks for the OSE to secure spaces in orphanages for these children. In the meantime, they remained in Buchenwald under the protection of Rabbi Marcus. It was his mission to let them be children again. He knew they had a long road ahead of them, but he was determined to restore some measure of innocence and laughter into their lives.

They were 904 orphans with no home to return to, no parents to come home to, and no outstretched arms waiting to embrace them. Rabbi Marcus took it upon himself to become their home, their father, their mother, their rabbi, their teacher, with arms wide enough and a heart big enough to embrace them all.

Of course, when he'd look upon the beautiful faces of these orphaned children he couldn't help but long for his own children, Jay and Stephen, back at home, whom he missed so terribly. And he desperately wanted to meet and hold his new baby daughter, Tamara, whom Fay had given birth to in August 1944.

But Rabbi Marcus stayed on in Buchenwald, committed to restoring these boys to health and to finding them a new life. He held personal discussions and led religious services. He wanted to revive their souls, to teach them to believe in a new day, to trust again, to hope again, to have faith again.

Rabbi Marcus was instrumental in establishing a farm on German soil to teach teenage boys and girls skills they would need to work the land in Palestine. It was called, of all things, Kibbutz Buchenwald. There they were learning to build a communal farming life. Rabbi Marcus wrote in June 1945: "They have cows, horses, sheep, oxen and tractors. They have learned to laugh again, to play and sing and to dwell on things of the spirit." Yes, Rabbi Marcus was helping to revive their souls.

After several weeks Rabbi Marcus succeeded in arranging safe passage for hundreds of the Buchenwald boys into France. He insisted on bringing them there himself.

On the eve of that trip, Rabbi Marcus stood proudly, smiling for a photo beneath a large banner that had been created for the children in honor of this joyous occasion. It read in Yiddish and in French: WE ARE STARTING A NEW AND FREE LIFE.

In the morning Rabbi Marcus escorted twelve railway cars filled with orphaned boys, including Elie Wiesel, out of Buchenwald. From the train the boys would shout at German passersby: "Nazi murderers, where are our parents?" After four sleepless nights Rabbi Marcus led his Buchenwald boys to a new life in France. He wrote, "My kids had been brought into the bright sunshine of a freer world—and I was happy."

When I learned that Elie Wiesel was one of Rabbi Marcus's Buchenwald boys, I reached out, hoping I could speak with him. I wanted to know what Elie remembered, what he thought of Rabbi Marcus, if he knew about the letter exchange between Rabbi Marcus and Einstein. Elie's assistant told me he wasn't available at that time, but she encouraged me to be patient and to keep checking back with her. I waited and I hoped, and I understood that time wasn't on my side. The Buchenwald boys were mostly in their late eighties and many of them were in poor health. Some suffered from memory loss and mental confusion. But I was fortunate to speak with Buchenwald boys who shared gems with me. Alas, not one of them had heard about Rabbi Marcus's letter to Einstein.

Henry Oster, a tall and distinguished man, who at the age of eighty-eight still practices as an optometrist in Los Angeles, characterized the journey with Rabbi Marcus from Buchenwald to France this way: "He was our Moses, leading us from slavery to freedom." Perry Shulman told me that Rabbi Marcus saved his life by rushing him to a hospital when his foot became infected during the train ride to France.

Three months after that train ride to France, Rabbi Marcus traveled back to Germany. He had miraculously managed to secure eighty tickets on a ship to Palestine, the S.S. *Mataroa*, and he was overjoyed to be personally escorting another group of child survivors to freedom—the young men and women from Kibbutz Buchenwald. One of the teenage passengers on that very ship was a seventeen-year-old girl who would grow up to become Dr. Ruth Westheimer, the renowned sex therapist.

Dr. Ruth spoke to me, remembering the hope that was in the air along that journey. She said it was a time of tremendous expectation and idealism. She told me that she and her friends sang and danced Jewish folk dances on the ship and how they gathered on the deck beneath the stars dreaming of a new day. She said, "The facilities were low, the idealism was high."

They landed in Haifa on Rosh Hashanah and Rabbi Marcus led High Holy Day services on the ship. The New Year prayers resonated with a depth that the passengers would remember for the rest of their days. Rabbi Marcus wrote about that momentous day: "The New Year was ushered in with an inspiring service under the clear Mediterranean skies . . . Never before in my life did it feel so good to be a Jew . . . The long and tortuous voyage from bondage to freedom is over. They are home at last."

The teens of Kibbutz Buchenwald would go on to found a kibbutz on Jewish soil, Netzer Sereni. I had the joy of visiting the kibbutz in the summer of 2014 and meeting with the surviving members of Kibbutz Buchenwald. They offered me their memories of the man who had cared for them with such compassion. I asked about the letter exchange between Rabbi Marcus and Einstein, but none of them had any information to share with me. They allowed me to read diaries from days long ago, they shared treasured photographs and precious letters.

Sara Feig, one of the teenage girls Rabbi Marcus saved, wrote him a letter from her new homeland asking him to preside over her wedding ceremony: "To my savior in times of trouble . . . I feel a spiritual connection to you, my rescuer and guide. You were my teacher, my rabbi. You cared for me with a fatherly devotion and a love without bounds . . . I don't have the words, there isn't enough ink or paper to thank you for all the good your hands have wrought me and for the way you led me with your strength to a life of joy and goodness."

Rabbi Marcus had witnessed horrors that defied description, but he was honored to know that he'd had a hand in restoring children's souls, and for that he was grateful.

When he finally returned to the United States, Rabbi Marcus was at last reunited with his wife, Fay, and their three children, Jay, Stephen, and Tamara. His days back home were precious indeed. Just the same, his experiences in the war and in the concentration camps hung over his head like a nightmare he couldn't shake. His soul burned with a passion for social justice. Soon he assumed a position as political director of the World Jewish Congress (WJC), where he fought tirelessly to help survivors remake their lives. He was not only fighting for the rights of Jews across the globe. He was fighting for the soul of humanity.

Rabbi Marcus became the WJC's key representative to the UN. He worked night and day to offer input for the framing of the UN's policies on human rights. The two issues that kept Rabbi Marcus awake at night, and which he poured all his energy into, are as alive and pressing today as they were in his own day: genocide and the status of stateless peoples. Read about the wholesale slaughter in Sudan and know that Rabbi Marcus was struggling to prevent such inhumanity. Worry over the fate of millions of Syrian refugees and remember that Rabbi Marcus foresaw their plight and fought for their rights in all the countries where they might find refuge.

In the summer of 1949, Fay and the children were spending August at a bungalow colony in the Catskills. It seemed like an ideal way to spend summer vacation together with other families. But suddenly an epidemic of polio struck and spread like wildfire among the children. All three Marcus children became infected. Rabbi Marcus was aboard a ship on his way to France to argue for better protection for Europe's remaining Jews. As soon as he heard the news, he raced home on the first flight he could take. But he was too late. Jay, his beloved eleven-year-old son, his firstborn, whose very soul was intertwined with his own soul, died of polio.

The grief and the guilt were overwhelming.

In his agony Rabbi Marcus reached out to Albert Einstein for help, and Einstein wrote him back with his beautiful description of the universe.

This was the man who wrote to Einstein and elicited that luminous conception of the universe. He was not some footnote in history. He was a great man who had dedicated his life to the cause of human dignity, who had protected and cared for so many children, but who could not save his own precious son.

What did Rabbi Marcus say to Einstein? What did he want? Why did a rabbi reach out to a man of science for comfort? I had no way of knowing, because I could not find the letter Rabbi Marcus had written to Einstein.

Eleven short months after receiving his response from Einstein about the unity of all things, on January 18, 1951, Rabbi Robert S. Marcus died of a heart attack. He was only forty-one years old. His wife, Fay, at thirty-five years of age, bereft of her eldest child and her husband, was left with two small children to raise and support on her own.

Once I learned of Rabbi Marcus's untimely death I thought that I could let him go, but I couldn't stop thinking about him. Still, I realized I had to let my search for his letter rest for a while. Perhaps with time a new door would open. In the meantime I turned my attention to the letter he had received from Einstein, the letter that had moved me so and resonated so deeply within me. I kept the letter taped to the wall beside my desk and meditated over the words daily.

Einstein never uses the word "soul," but in just four sentences he manages to paint a picture of an eternal life that exists in the here and now, an infinite life that we are blind to. According to Einstein, the ultimate goal of religion is to help us see and experience that greater whole we are all part of. He believed we have the power to free ourselves from the delusion that we are separate entities, when in truth we are all interwoven strands in an elaborate and infinite web. ✓

If the mission of Einstein's "true religion" is to help us see the underlying oneness of all things, then as a rabbi I consider it my mission to spread the word about a faith that can unite people of all religions and races. A meta-religion we can all agree upon and belong to. A religion of universal interconnectedness, a unity that holds us all together.

Every once in a while you catch a glimpse of that oneness—a sense that you are part of something infinite and wondrous that not only surrounds you, but flows through you. The key to detecting that unity, I believe, lies in our capacity to meet our own souls and the souls of others. I am not saying that Einstein believed in an eternal soul that survives death—in fact, he did not. I am saying that *I* believe in the existence of a divine soul within us that can teach us to experience the "whole" Einstein described so poignantly.

In the World of Separation our perceptions are limited. There are particles too small for our eyes to see, but they are still here. There are frequencies of sound our ears cannot hear, but our pets can sense them. There are vibrations we cannot feel, but they still affect us. We are limited by the confines of our bodies. But within us there is a soul that can guide us and teach us to experience the oneness that Einstein so beautifully described. Within us there is a force that can lead us to the fulfillment of our God-given potential. A force that can help us see connections between seemingly disparate and disjointed elements, even between the living and the dead. Knowing and heeding the soul can transform our lives, and it may indeed transform our world.

If we can learn to encounter the soul within us, we can begin to shatter the delusion of our separateness, and we may arrive at a vision of oneness and discover the soul within all things. We will greet the soul, the piece of eternity dwelling within us, and all around us. We will meet the souls of the dead and the soul hiding within everything we see. And we will learn to open ourselves up to the soul's timeless teachings.

Would I find the letter Rabbi Marcus wrote to Einstein? *Patience*, I told myself.

The soul's journey is never linear. It requires patience and perseverance. Just when you're ready to give up, a door opens and you are granted the opportunity to step inside if you wish. You are invited to explore new realms that were previously locked to you. Were those turns you took back there wrong turns? Were those dead ends you reached worthless? Or were they all part of the "whole" that Einstein was talking about? The whole that encompasses all paths, all choices, all people and all things. Was your hand being guided all along? Look back on your journey through the distance of time and you will come to see, that's a question only the soul can answer.

May you meet the soul inside you. May you welcome its timeless teachings and may you open your eyes to the world it sees and knows: a Oneness that encompasses us all. Amen.

3

Finding the Me Within me

LOCATING YOUR INNER ESSENCE

WHEN EINSTEIN WAS A YOUNG boy sick in bed, his father brought him a present. It was a compass, a toy to delight a child. But this compass marked the beginning of Einstein's inquiry into the workings of the universe. What force caused the needle to point north? Years later when Einstein wrote about that compass, he said he discovered that "something deeply hidden had to be behind things."

When we take the time to observe the workings of our own selves, I believe we may discover that there is something deeply hidden inside us, forever guiding us. I envision the soul as a compass that resides within us, always pointing us toward eternal things—love, beauty, wholeness, meaning, union, calling, God.

The soul has an uncanny sense of direction. It can point us toward our unique spiritual anatomy.

The soul has wisdom to offer us, answers to questions that haunt us. There is something that your soul knows that you've forgotten. But when we incline our lives and our hearts toward its call we receive tiny revelations. "A-ha" experiences. Feelings of déjà vu. You learn something new and reconnect with what you've always known. You meet someone new and understand the true meaning of reunion.

Invisible threads of connection run through us and through the entire universe. The soul's consciousness links us to the blade of grass beneath our feet and to the majesty of the high peaks and to the souls of the living and the dead. The collective soul of generations long gone echoes through us and reverberates in the rhythms of our daily lives. The soul perceives that those we have loved and lost are never far from us. Life may end, but the light of their presence continues to shine on us from the place of eternity.

Connecting to the soul is the key to a life of meaning and fulfillment. But where do you look for your soul? And how do you find it when you're not even sure what you're searching for?

Many of us wish we could have a visual construct of the soul that might help us envision the seat of God within us.

I had never seen a representation of the soul that resonated with me. And then I visited Prague and I entered the ancient Pinkas Synagogue in the Jewish Quarter. In one display case there were paintings and drawings made by children. It is a lovely exhibit—until you realize where those children had created that art, and what became of those innocent souls.

The children created those paintings inside the Theresienstadt concentration camp during the Holocaust. Yes, even in hell the soul can create beauty. My teary eyes moved slowly from drawing to drawing, and then I stood transfixed before one piece. I could not move. It was a simple line drawing of a man with striped pants. He had two eyes, a dot for a nose, a mustache, and a hat. No mouth, no arms. It seemed an expression of helplessness—no way to speak, no arms to reach out. All along the entire torso of the man there was another drawing. I looked more carefully. It was a picture of the same man in miniature taking up lodging within the lines of his body. What was the child who drew this picture trying to convey? What was this man within

"Soul and Body" by František Brozan

the man? And then I read the card associated with the picture. The work was titled "Soul and Body." A little ten-year-old boy in a concentration camp captured the soul. He was murdered in Auschwitz at age eleven. His name was František Brozan.

František asked us to see the soul with new eyes. I think he was saying the soul is the Me within me. It is the truest version of Me. The Me that we are given by God. The Me that cannot be taken away even when we are imprisoned. The Me that cannot be lost even when we lose our lives. It is the Me containing all the strength and potential God has placed inside us. We all pray that the awesome potential hidden inside us will find its way into the world. František Brozan was robbed of the opportunity to fulfill his awesome potential, but his piercing vision of the eternal soul lives on and beckons us to inhabit our days on earth with the fullness and the power of the Me within me.

May the Me inside you guide you and lead you to claim all your astounding God-given gifts. Amen.

4

Taking a Soulfie

IN THE SUMMER OF 2014 I was in Israel with a group of rabbis from the United States. We were invited to a retired rabbi's home for Sabbath dinner. Rabbi Stuart Geller had been a congregational rabbi in the United States for decades. He was a very slight man, bald, and he had a mischievous twinkle in his eyes. The first thing he said to us was, "Welcome, everyone! By the way, if an air raid siren goes off, you're all on your own."

Rabbi Geller was a funny guy. When we gathered around his courtyard to recite the blessing over the wine, he said, "I know you rabbis are all already worried about your High Holy Day sermons. Ha-ha, I'm retired. Good luck to you!" And then he added, "Actually, you're in luck. Tonight I'm going to give you a sermon."

I was sure he was going to offer us deep wisdom. We all waited with rapt attention. Then he looked at us and said, "Okay, are you ready? Here's the sermon: Selfie."

That was it! One word.

Everyone laughed. It reminded me of that moment in the movie *The Graduate* when Dustin Hoffman receives the sage advice, "Plastics." Then Rabbi Geller started to lead us in the blessing over the wine.

I had trouble concentrating on the blessing. *Selfie? That's all he had to say?* No one around me took him seriously. My colleagues all laughed it off, but I couldn't let it go. Where was the lesson in that one word, "selfie"? I couldn't get it out of my head.

On Sunday we were in our tour bus and I wasn't paying attention. The tour guide was talking into the microphone, and I was daydreaming about the word "selfie" while she was speaking. The next thing I knew the bus stopped and we were all getting out. We walked a little bit and then we arrived at a breathtaking scenic overlook.

Instantly I whipped out my iPhone and started to take photos. It was a gorgeous panoramic view of the Old City of Jerusalem. But I looked around and I saw that all of my colleagues were taking pictures of the opposite side of the street. They were all fixated on something behind me. I started worrying, *Did I miss something? Is this a special holy site? A famous ruin?* It just looked like a bunch of rubble to me. I was too embarrassed to ask my colleagues what they were photographing, so I came up with a plan: *I'll just take a picture of the rubble now and later I'll find a way to ask somebody on the bus secretly what it was that I took a picture of.*

I turned around and snapped a picture of the rubble, and suddenly I understood what I'd been missing out on. My rabbi friends were all taking selfies with the beautiful vista behind them.

Selfie. There was that word again. It was stalking me! Where was the sermon in a selfie?

We call the picture that we snap of ourselves a selfie, but it doesn't capture the self at all. It doesn't take in our interior world. It can't capture your mind, your soul, your longings, your feelings, your prayer. A selfie is all surface.

Selfies tend to exaggerate the amount of fun we are having. The trip I took with the rabbis was interesting, but it was rather somber. Mostly we sat around in meetings all day. But one of the rabbis took a selfie of our group and posted it on Facebook with the caption: "Rabbis in Israel," and it looked as if we were having a party the whole time. The trip wasn't like that at all! Selfies have a way of turning life into something more than it is.

A selfie is always a distortion of reality. The truth is, you are a tiny little speck in the face of a vast, magnificent expanse. But in a selfie we're always disproportionately large and the majestic vista looks like a tiny little speck.

Yes, selfies are narcissistic exaggerations of reality, but they're also fun. They help us remember important moments with people we love and places we've been. There's no harm in them. So where was the sermon in a selfie?

I was mulling it over, and all of a sudden I flashed on Rabbi Geller with his twinkling eyes, and I got my answer.

I believe that God is forever pleading with us, "Listen." Every day we are being asked to do something we are resistant to doing: to look deep inside our own souls and do an honest accounting of where we are, and where we are going. *Where am I needed? Have I strayed from the path of my life? Have I become self-satisfied? Have I stopped learning and growing and changing?*

Big questions. Heavy questions that require heavy lifting. And we're all tempted to look away. But if we just take selfies all the time we might miss out on all the blessings waiting for us. And certain blessings can only be uncovered by digging deep.

I realized I had arrived at my sermon: Our challenge in life is to learn how to take a "soulfie."

What's a soulfie? It is our daily attempt to meet our souls. It's our desire to cut through the surface distractions to get to know our own true essence. Taking a soulfie is the process that I believe Einstein was describing to Rabbi Marcus. He was saying that we have the capacity to move beyond the self and our sense of separateness to a higher realm where we can perceive the greater whole that we are part of, the whole that unites all of creation.

Taking a soulfie is a way to get to know your soul's contours, its yearnings and longings, its knowledge and its wisdom.

Of course you can't point a camera at yourself and snap a picture of your soul. So what does it mean to take a soulfie?

Taking a soulfie is the practice of greeting our souls.

What is the soul?

The rabbis tell us the soul is a mirror of God within us. The soul fills the body, just as God fills the world. The soul outlasts the body, just as God outlasts the world. The soul is one in the body, just as God is one in the world. The soul sees but is not seen, just as God sees but is not seen.

The soul is the god of the body. God is the Soul of the world.

The soul is calling you, just as God is calling, but listening is not always easy.

There is a beautiful parable that a mentor of mine, Rabbi Harold Schulweis, of blessed memory, liked to tell:

When God was creating the world, God shared a secret with the angels: human beings will be created in the image of God.

The angels were jealous and outraged. Why should humans be entrusted with such a precious gift when they are flawed mortals? Surely if humans find out their true power they will abuse it. If humans discover they are created in God's very image, they will learn to surpass us!

So the angels decided to steal God's image.

Now that the divine image was in the angels' hands, they needed to pick a place to hide it so that man would never find it.

They held a meeting and brainstormed. The angel Gabriel suggested that they hide God's image at the top of the highest mountain peak. The other angels objected, "One day humans will learn to climb and they will find it there."

The angel Michael said, "Let's hide it at the bottom of the sea."

"No," the other angels chimed in, "humans will find a way to dive to the bottom of the sea and they'll find it there."

One by one the angels suggested hiding places, but they were all rejected.

And then Uriel, the wisest angel of all, stepped forward and said, "I know a place where man will never look for it."

So the angels hid the precious holy image of God deep within the human soul. And to this day God's image lies hidden in the very place we are least likely to search for it. Lying there it is farther away from you than you can ever imagine. Lying there it is closer to you than you will ever know.

WE HAVE THE POWER to prove the angels wrong. We can learn to uncover and tap into God's very image. All we need to do is locate the treasure buried inside.

It's time to take a soulfie.

Here are four questions for you to meditate on that can help guide you in taking your own soulfie. Allow yourself time on a separate piece of paper to answer these questions—not once, but repeatedly as you make your way through the pages of this book:

1. What has my soul been trying to say to me that I've been ignoring?
2. What activities and experiences nourish my soul that I don't do enough of?
3. What does my soul want to repair that my ego is too stubborn or too fearful to repair?
4. What does my soul want me to reach for?

The answers to these questions will deepen and enrich our lives. The answer, in part, *is* our life—or at least the part that matters most.

If we can learn to take a soulfie, it may very well transform our lives.

By making a decision to access and follow our souls, we begin a journey.

It is a winding journey full of bumps and pits, stops and starts. Sometimes the road becomes flat and we can cover great distances. Sometimes we will get stuck in one place for what may seem like an eternity before we are ready to continue forward.

Yes, there are times when we will get lost, when we won't know what to do or which way to turn and it's frightening and frustrating and we wish it could all just be easier. With soul it *can* get easier.

Life's paths are anything but straight. And yet those winding paths, as frustrating as they may be, can lead us to a life of meaning and blessings.

I pray you will choose to follow your soul on its journey. May it lead you to paths of peace. Amen.

5

Encountering the Three Levels of the Soul

EVAN CAME TO SEE ME a week after his best friend, James, died of cancer at the age of twenty-eight. James and Evan were college roommates. Evan sat across from me and he was trembling, holding so much back. He wanted to ask me something, but the words just wouldn't come. He apologized, saying, "I'm sorry, Rabbi, I didn't want to cry here."

I said, "There's no need to apologize. Your tears mean you care."

Evan took a deep breath and began to talk. He said, "Rabbi, I want to believe that life matters. That James mattered here and that somehow, someway, he lives on." Evan described himself as a superficial person who was obsessed with sports and women and cars and getting rich. And now, all of a sudden none of those things mattered.

I saw the past and the present converge in Evan. He looked and dressed like someone from a Budweiser commercial, in a baseball cap, T-shirt, cargo shorts, and flip-flops, with big biceps and a thick neck, but there was a deep sadness in his eyes, a sadness that said, "My life has to mean something." He asked me, "Rabbi, can you tell me about the soul? I want to know, I need to know."

I said, "I'd like to share with you some of the wisdom that guides me and comforts me."

Evan pulled out a notebook from his pocket and began taking notes. I said, "The first thing traditional Jews do when they wake up in the morning is to recite a prayer thanking God for restoring our souls." I told Evan that sleep is considered a mini-death in Jewish thought.

Evan asked, "Does that make morning a sort of mini-resurrection?"

"Yes," I replied, "every time you open your eyes is a time when you can start fresh with gratitude for life restored." I went on to explain another prayer. I said, "The next prayer we recite in the morning is about how the soul is pure and how God breathed soul into you and me." I told Evan that the Hebrew word for soul, *Neshama*, comes from the same root as the Hebrew word for breath. The soul enters with the breath and departs with the breath.

Evan said, "I was there with James when he took his last breath." He began writing feverishly in his notebook.

Thinking of Evan at James's deathbed, I said, "The soul is not of this world, it is of God. It comes from the place of eternity and it returns to the place of eternity. The soul enters this world against its will, and the rabbis say it departs against its will too."

Evan asked, "What do you mean, against its will?"

I said, "The rabbis tell us the soul doesn't want to enter life below. God has to convince the soul to leave the world above. But the soul refuses and pleads to remain where she is. God tries to reassure her by promising her, 'The world you are about to enter is more beautiful than this one.'"

Evan's voice cracked. "How is this world more beautiful than heaven?"

I said, "I've always imagined it has to do with the difference between potential and fulfillment. In the world above, the soul lives in a state of pure potentiality. It's a messenger with no way to fulfill its mission. It's only when the soul descends to the human realm that it can actually live out its purpose. The difference between the soul in heaven and on earth is like the difference between fantasizing about love and actually falling in love and building a life with someone."

Evan said, "I still don't see how this messed-up world could be better than heaven."

I said, "The rabbis call the soul's journey 'a descent for the sake of ascent.'" I explained that the soul enters our broken world in order to raise it up, and perhaps that's what makes life here so beautiful, and so tragic too.

Evan wanted to know about the soul's longings. I said, "I believe that more than anything, the soul longs for connection." I told Evan about the World of Unity that the soul comes from and the World of Separation where the soul finds itself here. I said, "The soul wants to get closer, it longs for God, for eternal things like beauty in nature and music. Mostly it wants to connect with other souls."

Evan was silent for a while. He said, "Yes. I believe that too."

Evan told me he'd heard that the soul has different Hebrew names and different aspects. I said, "Evan, you're referring to a Jewish mystical teaching. The mystics actually envisioned the soul as a spiritual entity that has layers."

Evan said, "Layers?"

I said, "In the mystical understanding of things, acquiring your soul doesn't happen all at once when you're born. Soul comes in stages. The mystics believed we can learn to experience more and more of our soul's power. Some say the soul, like wisdom, is acquired through age and maturation. Others say the soul is only acquired through merit."

Evan was weeping. He told me he thought James had acquired a mighty high soul in his brief time on earth. He told me he thought his own soul was pretty shallow and superficial. Suddenly Evan popped up from the couch in my study and sat himself down on the floor cross-legged. He looked like a boy in kindergarten. From the floor he asked me to explain more about the layers of soul.

I said, "When I first studied the levels of the soul, I wasn't sure what that meant. I had trouble picturing a three-tiered soul, but over time the idea of the soul and its layers has come to mean a great deal to me. It means that you have to earn your soul, layer by layer."

I talked with Evan about the body's decay with age, and how the soul keeps growing, taking us higher and higher if we let it.

"I saw that with James," Evan said. "His body got so weak, but something inside of him kept getting stronger and more and more honest. Rabbi, he would look at me and cut straight through all my B.S."

It was then that I laid out the three layers of the soul. I told Evan that the Jewish mystical tradition compares the levels of the soul to the different gradations of color in a flame. I shared with him a verse from the Book of Proverbs: "God's candle is the human soul." I said, "Evan, we are carrying God's light within us. It burns like a pilot light always available to help us and guide us. It's our responsibility to honor and tend that light, to keep sharing it and spreading it."

I took a votive candle off my desk and I got down on the floor opposite Evan. I lit the candle on the wooden floor between us.

I said, "When you stare at this candle, do you see that the flame actually has different colors? Tell me what you see."

Evan said, "I see bluish on the bottom of the flame and then I see yellow above it. But I don't see a third color."

I explained, "The lowest level of soul is called Nefesh, the Life Force. The mystics taught that the lower soul is like the blue color at the bottom of a flame. The Life Force is closely aligned to the body and its needs. It is the soul we share with all living things."

Evan asked, "So would you call that bottom layer the will to live?"

I said, "Yes, but also, the will to act and grow, like grass pushing through the crack in the sidewalk."

"I think I get that," Evan said.

"With time the Life Force becomes a throne for Ruach, the Love Force, just like one color of the flame seems to give way to the next color. The mystics said Ruach is like the yellowish light that appears at the higher level of a flame. Ruach is the seat of emotion, it's the door to intimacy."

Evan asked me, "Is it the same as love?"

"Yes," I said, "but so much more. The Love Force gives us our depth and wisdom of the heart. It is the key to our calling."

Evan drew a candle with a flame in his notebook. He put the names of the soul into his drawing and said, "And what's the top layer called?"

"Neshama, the Eternal Force, is the light of a flame that's not visible to the human eye," I explained. "Neshama is the uppermost level of soul, the place within us that allows us to experience unity with all things in this world and beyond." I said, "The Eternal Force is the window to experiencing heaven here."

Evan said, "I thought you said this world was more beautiful than heaven."

"Yes, and we can only understand that when we see this world through Neshama's eyes," I said.

As we were talking I flashed on Einstein's letter to Rabbi Marcus. I realized that it's only when we access the Eternal Force that we can begin to understand Einstein's vision, we can begin to see the unity.

Evan said, "To me, the invisible part of the flame is the heat. You can't see it, but when you put your hand on top of a flame it's the hottest part."

I said, "Neshama is elusive and seriously hard to access, and most people live their entire lives and never reach it. But it's the Eternal Force that can save the world." I was thinking about Einstein, about seeing beyond the optical delusion of our separateness.

Evan and I began talking about the ways the three levels of soul operate in the world. I explained how the levels of soul take us higher but they also radiate outward like ripples in a pond. The Life Force is concerned mainly with the body and its needs. The Love Force is what makes us able to achieve intimacy, to love, to be a true friend. It spreads outward from family and friends to community. And it's only at the level of the Eternal Force when we can begin to see and take in the whole world and the world beyond this world too.

Evan pleaded with me, "Rabbi, I want to connect on a deep level. Where do I start?"

I said, "Let your soul be your guide. Be available. Listen carefully. Study. Pray for help."

Evan asked, "And how will I know if I'm getting anywhere?"

I said, "You will come to understand the power of time and the importance of timing." Evan looked confused, he wrote something in his notebook. I said, "One more thing. Treat your mistakes with kindness. See them as steps toward learning and growth."

Evan said, "And then?"

"And then . . . you will learn to see how two separate lights come together to create something brighter and more beautiful than either could ever be alone."

Evan said, "And?"

I said, "And then you may come to feel that the love you share or the work you do no longer seems to be coming from you, but through you. That is what the Eternal Force is all about—becoming one with God's infinite flow."

Evan didn't want to leave. He wanted to keep asking more and more questions. I said it was time to stop. I invited him to study Jewish texts and meditation with me.

As we both stood up from the floor I said to him, "Evan, the more you access soul the more you learn. The more you learn the more you grow. The more you grow the more you love. The more you love the more you give. The more you give the more you live . . . with meaning and with beauty."

"Rabbi," Evan said, "you've just described my friend James."

May you become fertile ground for the three levels of your soul to take root inside you. May you learn to grow and love and give and live a life of meaning and beauty. Amen.

TAPPING INTO THE LIFE FORCE: THE KEY TO VISION AND ACTION

Nefesh, the Life Force, the blue hue of the flame, is the foundational level of the soul. Nourish the soul and it will begin to feed us, and guide us. As the soul grows stronger it begins blessing us with wider vision. The greatest gift of the Life Force is the power to act, to rise above our own paralysis and to transform intention into achievement.

RAISING THE VOLUME OF THE SOUL'S VOICE: FEEDING AND AWAKENING THE SOUL

"Not to nourish the delusion but to try to overcome it . . ."
—from Einstein's letter to Rabbi Marcus

The delusion that we are separate beings alone in the world has grown fat indeed while the soul remains stranded, unfed and unheard, waiting for us to notice and to listen. Give the soul love and nourishment and it will feed you, whispering secrets of the One. It will teach you and guide you and sing to you and remind you that the blessings you seek are closer than you know.

6

Giving the Soul What It Wants

WHAT DOES THE SOUL WANT?

The Book of Ecclesiastes warns us, "All the labor of man is for his mouth, yet the soul is not filled." I love this verse. It perfectly captures that empty place inside us. It was as true in antiquity as it is today. We earn a living and feed our egos and surround ourselves with all sorts of stuff, but we remain hungry because we don't understand what our souls need.

The rabbis compare the body's relationship to the soul to a peasant who marries a princess. The poor peasant tries to impress his princess by bringing her beautiful things, but nothing he gives her matters to her, because she grew up in a palace surrounded by wealth. She didn't marry the peasant so that he could shower her with gifts, all she wants is his love. The same is true for the soul, the rabbis teach us: "If all the delights of the world are brought to her, they are to her as nothing, for she belongs to the world above."

The soul comes from the place of eternity and it longs for those things. It longs for God, for beauty, for nature, for learning, for love, for unity, for peace. But more than that, there's something your soul wants that only you can satisfy. Each soul is unique and has its own inclinations. There's a mission embedded in your very being that only you can fulfill.

Joel is in his late thirties with a scruffy hipster beard and kind eyes. He came to see me because he said he was feeling a constant state of anxiety that he couldn't put his finger on. He didn't know why he was feeling agitated and out of sorts. It was getting so bad that he was having trouble choking back tears at work for no reason at all.

I asked Joel to close his eyes and see if he could identify the moment he began to feel unsettled. I asked him to actually ask his soul for the answer. Joel thought for a while, and then tears began flowing down his scruffy cheeks. He told me that he became a high school teacher because he loved sparking teenagers' minds. He relished the amazing challenges that teens brought to every discussion. He welcomed every "Why" and "How."

Joel worked at a small private high school where he'd become an extremely popular and respected teacher. He was so beloved, in fact, that he was asked by the board to become school principal. Joel excitedly took the position. But in the fall as Joel settled into his new role he began spending his days doing administrative work, managing teachers, dealing with angry parents, and much of his time was devoted to fund-raising. Joel became more and more anxious during the endless meetings he had to attend each day.

On the outside Joel seemed to have everything. He said, "Rabbi, I don't get it. Life is good." But as he continued speaking about his work, Joel hit upon what his soul was missing: he had stopped doing what he loved.

Joel and I talked about how he might be able to remedy this situation. He didn't want to quit his job, but he knew he needed to carve out time for being in the classroom with students once again. Joel decided to begin teaching a seminar to the seniors. He loved developing the curriculum for this class, and it didn't take long for Joel's uncomfortable feeling to subside. He was once again doing what he was born to do.

We can feed our egos and nourish our desires but our souls will remain parched. Without proper sustenance, the soul inevitably loses its vitality. Starved and thirsty, the soul becomes sick, weakened.

The soul's infirmity affects us deeply. We can all recognize some of the symptoms of soul sickness: materialism, a sense of emptiness, excessive ambitiousness, jealousy, addiction, fear, anxiety, melancholy.

Ignoring the soul can lead to a life of confusion and unwise decisions. Without the soul's voice to guide us, we may begin making poor choices. We seek out false comforts, destructive habits. We can fool ourselves into believing all is well for a while. Lost in the dark without a map, we stagger aimlessly, we bump into things and cling to them even though they are not suited for us. The true extent of the problem may not become clear to us until we experience a full-blown crisis. These are moments when the soul's anguished voice pierces through our certainties. We drag our shaken selves to the therapist's office, where we begin to see that the choices we made did not save us, did not satisfy us, did not nourish us on the deepest levels of our being.

There is one mystical teaching about the marginalized soul that I find deeply unsettling, but it also offers a compelling description of what can happen when we fail to nurture our spiritual lives. If we do enough harm to our own souls, then at some point Neshama, the Eternal Force, the highest level of our soul, just decides to leave us during life. It simply detaches itself from us and returns to its source in the supernal realm, the world above.

The metaphor of the soul abandoning us gives us the language to explain our feelings of emptiness and hollowness. Like the Tin Man in *The Wizard of Oz*, who is without a heart, our spiritual self can become a void. The soul's departure also helps to explain that feeling we sometimes get when we meet a person who seems to be lacking a soul. Perhaps they are.

Is it possible to breathe life back into a withered soul? Is it possible to convince a runaway soul to come home?

The most famous Psalm of all, Psalm 23, "The Lord Is My Shepherd," reminds us that God restores our souls. How do we let God help us? How do we learn to shepherd our own souls back to life? How do we help revive the souls of others?

The power to heal our souls is much closer than we imagine.

Healing the soul has to do with *heeding* the soul. We can learn to hear the soul once more. We can learn to cooperate with it, to partner with it. We must begin feeding it and tending it. You heal the soul by giving it what it wants.

Some say that to heal the soul we must extinguish the ego that has taken over. But the ego is here for a reason. The ego gives us our drive and our character. It would be unwise to crush it. We do, however, need to tame the ego, to teach it to listen so that it can be more receptive to others, to the soul, and to God.

The soul never stops speaking to us. Even if the highest level of soul leaves us, the Life Force and the Love Force are here to stay. Our challenge is to learn how to listen.

When we begin to feed the soul the volume of its voice begins to increase. If we train our ears we can hear the soul prodding us to wake up and claim the Me within me, the truest version of ourselves.

I'd like to share six small chapters that offer ways to nourish and heal your soul. Some are spiritual practices: meditation, prayer, learning, and a Sabbath day of rest. Others are secular experiences that can awaken and revive the soul: music, nature, and food. They may not all resonate with you, but give them a try and you will come to see what awakens your soul. Of course, your soul may have its own inclinations toward art or exercise or theater or dance or gardening. This world is full of paths for restoring your soul. The most important element is what we often neglect—to simply set aside regular times for giving your soul what it needs. Once you begin nurturing and cultivating your soul, it will begin showing you more and more of what it's been long-ing to offer and teach you.

Feed the soul, and like a chick breaking through its shell may you begin to break through the barriers that have been limiting and confining you.

May you reach out toward the mission that is calling your name. Amen.

7

Meditating Is Medicine for the Soul

MEDITATION IS MEDICINE FOR THE body. It can lower blood pressure, reduce pain, calm our anxiety. It is beneficial to the mind too, it increases focus, clarity, and attention.

But meditation also has the power to transport us beyond the realms of mind and body. Meditation is medicine for the soul. It can connect us more deeply to our own souls, to the souls of others, and to the Soul of Souls. Through meditation we can learn to raise the volume of the soul's voice so that we can actually begin to hear what it is trying to tell us.

I've been teaching Jewish meditation for over twenty years. On the first night of my beginner's class, I explain to my students that they are about to meet their own souls. How?

Try sitting still silently, and you will quickly discover how noisy it can be inside your head. We are bombarded by so many thoughts: *I need to remember to buy more toothpaste. Is the meditation almost over yet? I have an itch, is it okay to scratch it? What am I supposed to be feeling? Is it bad that I'm thinking so many thoughts? I'm no good at meditating. How much time has passed?*

If you pay careful attention to your inner monologue, you will realize that there is a consciousness that is watching the mind spin out. There is a presence that is silently observing all those passing thoughts and, in contrast to the hyperactive mind, it is steady and anchored. This is your soul patiently waiting for the mind to quiet down.

When we give the mind permission to calm down, we make room for the soul to speak to us and to show us what it sees—a world full of beauty and blessings. Soon we may begin experiencing oneness, our connection to God and to all things.

Of course the soul doesn't take us to spiritual heights all at once. Meditation takes time and practice.

I've found that mantra meditation is an excellent way to begin quieting the mind. Mantra meditation is the practice of silently reciting a sound to ourselves over and over again. By repeating the sound we are giving our minds something to do other than spin out. In some Jewish meditative traditions a mantra is not a meaningless sound. Instead, we repeat a letter or word or phrase that is full of meaning, a word full of echoes and shades and wisdom, a word that teaches us and changes us.

Any word can become a mantra. Too often in our lives, we have been practicing unconscious negative mantra meditations. The exacting judge that lives within us plants words in our thoughts that haunt us, words we repeat to ourselves when things go wrong or sometimes even before they go wrong.

We live with so much self-loathing. I've listened to so much self-inflicted cruelty over my years as a rabbi: *I'm ugly, I'm fat, I'm not strong enough, I'm not smart enough, I don't work hard enough, I haven't accomplished enough, I'm a loser, I'm lazy, I'm out of shape, I'm undisciplined, I'm weak, I'm not a competitor, I'm a bad spouse, I'm a bad parent, I'm a bad child, I'm a bad friend, I'm a bad person, I'm unlovable, I'm a coward, I'm a disappointment, I'm too old, I'm too young, I*

hate my hair, I hate my nose, I hate my face, I hate my body, I hate myself,
I hate my life.

How can we expect to make any positive strides at all if every time
we take even the most tentative step forward, there's a voice barking at
us, yelling at us for trying?

I suppose the one upside of these repetitive accusations is that we
are already very experienced mantra meditators! If we can learn to
change the words that we repeat to ourselves daily, perhaps we can
find a path to kindness and greater participation in our lives. A simple
shift like learning a new language for your inner monologue may indeed change your outer reality.

I'd like to introduce you to a Hebrew word that appears repeatedly
in Jewish prayers: *husa*. Say it aloud: *husa*. It makes a sound like waves
crashing against the shore. There's a whoosh to the word, a feeling of
cleansing.

What is *husa*? What does it mean? It's not pity, not mercy, not just
compassion. *Husa* is the special kind of love that an artist has for his
or her own creation, even when it's imperfect. That's the key to *husa*.
It's a compassion for something that's flawed. *Husa* involves the absence of judgment. That's why Jews turn to God and ask for *husa* in
their prayers: "The soul is Yours, the body is Your creation, *husa*, have
compassion for Your work."

When I teach Jewish meditation and try to describe *husa* to my students, I ask them to picture the pot holder we all made in kindergarten on that loom with the colorful fabric loops. It was lopsided, too
tight on one end, too loose on the other, maybe there were pieces of
loop dangling here and there. But just the same, your mother proudly
hung it on the refrigerator because you made it. It was beautiful even
if it was misshapen. Its imperfection made it more beloved, because it
spoke of your soul trying to express itself.

Husa is the way God loves us, even though we're imperfect, even
though we've messed things up here and there. Even though we are

lopsided. We are loved in our imperfection. Our uniqueness makes us more beautiful.

Too often we live with visions of God as a punishing judge. It's time to let those thoughts go. God is the Soul of the world—believing in us, cheering for us, praying for us, strengthening us, teaching us.

And yet, many of us walk around holding on to resentment toward God: *Where were you when I needed you? Why did this happen?*

A *husa* meditation is a softening. Through a *husa* practice you may begin to see that God didn't do this to you. God is rooting for you. God is trying to tell you: "You are precious to me."

Husa not only realigns our relationship with God, the main power of *husa* is that it transforms how we treat ourselves and how we treat others. *Husa* silences our critical voice and raises the volume of the soul's voice of compassion and hope.

The critical voice often dominates our internal conversation. Even though the process of looking within is called soul-searching, much of the time we fail to meet our souls when we look inside. Instead of finding the soul, we bump into the judge.

How do you know whether you've encountered the soul or the judge? When you're evaluating yourself if you hear a voice that says, *I'm rotten, I'm hopeless*, that's the judge. That voice doesn't lead to change or growth, it just leads to a pit of paralysis and darkness.

Looking within is not about hating yourself, it's about healing yourself. That's where *husa* comes in. When you are still, allowing the word to enter you, you may begin to hear a voice telling you, *Have a little mercy.* That's your soul speaking.

Sometimes we mistakenly think that if we are kinder to ourselves we'll become lazy and we won't accomplish anything. But what if we're wrong? What if it's the judge's hateful voice inside our heads that's preventing us from flourishing and growing?

The voice of the soul is a voice of compassion that says: *Try again, it's okay, pick yourself up.*

So instead of the judge's hateful mantra, let *husa* be your mantra.

Husa doesn't mean blindness or denial. It means that with kinder eyes we give ourselves permission to look at ourselves without cringing and without hate, so that we can actually see what's there, what needs fixing. So you can face what you resist.

The soul's voice says, I not only need to take stock of my failings, I need to take stock of my strengths. I need to know what I've been blessed with so I can understand what I have to work with.

It's the judge's voice of hate that leads to denial and to blaming the world for our problems: *He made me do it. She did this to me.* If you hate yourself it's going to come out in the way you treat others. That anger bubbles over in all sorts of destructive ways.

Husa can teach us to soften the judgments we place on others—loved ones, colleagues, and absolute strangers too. There are accusations we hold against people who harmed us in the past. *Husa* can help us to be more forgiving. There are snap judgments we make about people we don't even know based on nothing but their appearance or a single bad encounter. We label people at work, people in our communities, and people in our families too. We place them in a box—immature, lazy, annoying, stupid, ugly. And we rarely take the time to reassess the sentences we've passed against them. The truth is that by judging others we are the ones in the box, isolating ourselves from partnership, friendship, and love.

How do you practice a *husa* meditation? It's deceptively simple.

Sit quietly for at least five minutes at first and simply let the word *husa* float inside you. Don't say the word aloud. Let it roll around inside your mind and throughout your limbs. You can imagine you swallowed the word *husa* like an Advil, and soon it is relieving pain wherever you hurt.

Just let the word do what it needs to do. Don't worry if you lose the word for a while. If you notice you've lost it, just return to repeating it in your mind. Take it lightly, don't try to push or to stress over *husa*. Let it dance inside you like a flickering flame, illuminating you from within, burning away the muck.

Try living with *husa* as a daily practice. Let five minutes become ten. Let it stretch to eighteen minutes. That's my ideal suggested time with *husa*. In Jewish tradition the number eighteen represents life. Day by day the word *husa* begins softening our judgments, melting barriers. It allows us to look upon others with a more forgiving eye. We may soon discover we are feeling less stressed and anxious. We may notice we are becoming more accepting and more fun to be around.

John is an attorney who is divorced with a teenage daughter named Nicole who definitely inherited her dad's talent for argumentation. When she was younger everyone would say that Nicole was a daddy's girl—she and John were so close. But once she entered high school Nicole developed an attitude. She had a way of getting under John's skin like no one else could, and he would overreact every time Nicole rolled her eyes or said something snide. Things got so heated at home that Nicole threatened to go live with her mom full-time. That's when John came to me for counsel. John told me he was looking for ways to avoid getting dragged into battles with Nicole. I said, "I'd like to teach you a meditation." John looked confused. He wasn't the meditating type, he told me. I said, "Just try it for a month and see if it helps." I taught John all about *husa* and its power to help him. He seemed tentative about the whole thing but agreed to give *husa* a try.

A few weeks later John showed up in my study full of bounce. He said, "I want to thank you for giving me this gift." He told me he understood now that Nicole was a healthy teenager doing what all teenagers do: driving their parents crazy. She was no longer pushing his buttons every time she talked back to him. John admitted that sometimes he still reacts to something snarky Nicole says, but he said that he catches himself now and he's better able to see what's happening before things spin out. John was amazed at how rapidly things had shifted in his life. He said, "I don't feel angry all the time anymore. The best part is, we're actually having fun and laughing again."

That's the power of *husa*.

You may notice that your mood is lighter. Colors seem brighter and more vivid. You begin to feel more alert and alive. Your senses are heightened. Your mind is fertile. An insight may come and rest inside you ready to take shape and grow.

With time, as we practice *husa* and allow it to inhabit us we can go deep, beyond fear, beyond numbness, beyond that wall that separates the mind from the heart, that wall that keeps others at a distance.

Husa gives us the courage to see ourselves and the conscience to see beyond ourselves.

With time, *husa* may enter your day not only when you are sitting in silent practice. *Husa* may wait with you when you are on line in the grocery store, calming you when you are in a rush. *Husa* can enter you when you are fed up with your kids. *Husa* can help you deal with stressful situations at work. Let *husa* accompany you into meetings and interviews. Let it emanate from you as you speak.

Of course there will be days when nothing happens, when you are restless. When you meditate on *husa* with great expectation, but emerge feeling as lost as ever. That too is *husa*'s process—the art of remaining on a path even when the road is inhospitable, even when it seems as if you've made no progress at all.

Alternately, *husa* may take you to such a heightened state that you may think you've actually attained enlightenment. Beware!

Husa does not mean you can stop working or striving for more. The idea of having arrived, or attaining enlightenment, or even peace of mind, is a false goal. Adin Steinsaltz, perhaps the greatest Talmudist of our time, taught that a person who feels complete, anyone who feels as if he's arrived, is someone who has lost his way.

If a voice inside you says, *I'm perfectly at peace*, it is not the soul speaking. It is an impostor. The soul teaches us to see the beauty of what is *and* it knows there is more to be done. The soul eternally prods us forward.

> *May* husa *help you listen to the hopeful voice of your soul. May you have compassion for the complicated, paradoxical, precious person you are. May you never arrive. May you keep growing and learning and flourishing, forever unfolding. Amen.*

8

Letting Music Lift Your Soul

WHEN I WAS IN ISRAEL two years ago I had the rare privilege of meeting with Avraham Ahuvia, who was one of the founding members of Kibbutz Buchenwald, that group of teens Rabbi Marcus brought to Israel. Avraham was quite old and frail and other kibbutz members discouraged me from speaking with him, explaining that Avraham was mostly incoherent and hard of hearing. But I said I was willing to be disappointed, that I still wanted to meet him in person. So I walked into Avraham's flat and his nurse handed me a special microphone to shout into that was connected to earbuds Avraham wore.

I wanted to ask if Avraham knew about the letter Rabbi Marcus wrote to Einstein.

Our communication was looking hopeless. I shouted questions and Avraham seemed lost and confused, humming to himself. I kept asking Avraham about Rabbi Marcus and he kept talking about someone named Sonja. I didn't understand. I tried to steer Avraham away from Sonja and back to Rabbi Marcus.

Finally Avraham interrupted me. He said in a thin, high-pitched voice, "I can't talk about Rabbi Marcus without Sonja. They're connected." And suddenly I realized Avraham was lucid and had been trying to tell me a story all along, but I'd been too impatient to hear him out.

Here is what Avraham needed to tell me.

He said, "One day Rabbi Marcus brought a young girl to us at Kibbutz Buchenwald. Her name was Sonja. She was about fourteen years old, a waif, without family or friends."

Avraham told me that Rabbi Marcus promised Sonja he would adopt her himself and bring her home with him to America as his own child if it turned out that she had no surviving relatives.

Avraham went on, "Sonja was given a room next door to my own room. I felt a very special connection with Sonja," he said. "Sonja would cry alone in bed. She made me promise to come to her room every single evening to say goodnight."

Where was this story heading? I began asking myself. I had flown all the way to Israel to hear stories about Rabbi Marcus, but Avraham only wanted to talk about Sonja.

Avraham told me, "When I went to her room she begged me to tuck her in, 'Just the way Mama used to do.' She pleaded with me to sit on her bed and say goodnight so that's what I did, but she said, 'No, not that way, Mama would always sing me this lullaby. Put me to bed like Mama did.'"

Avraham became emotional, his voice cracked. He said, "It took me several days to learn Sonja's mother's bedtime rituals. I learned to tuck her in, sit on the bed and sing the lullaby, and say goodnight and to kiss her on her forehead, just like Mama, and then she'd stop crying and she'd let me go."

As Avraham spoke it occurred to me that he hadn't been an adult comforting a child, he was just a kid, only a few years older than Sonja. His parents had also been slaughtered in the most unimaginable way. Singing that nightly lullaby to Sonja wasn't only soothing her, it was easing Avraham's loneliness too and filling his aching soul with sweet love.

Avraham turned to me and said, "Sonja disappeared. I thought she moved to America with Rabbi Marcus, but later I learned that Rabbi Marcus never adopted Sonja, and I lost her and I feel so very sad. I loved putting her to bed."

Avraham began nodding off, it was time for me to go. Before I left we hugged and I promised Avraham I would do my best to find out what became of Sonja.

As I walked out of Avraham's flat a Hasidic teaching I once learned years ago came to me: "There are ten levels of prayer and above them is Song."

MUSIC IS HOLY. It bypasses the mind and goes straight to the heart. It gives us permission to cry. Sing a mournful song and a heavy heart begins to soften and release its burdens. Sometimes the melody can lift you up, sometimes it can break your heart. I believe our lamentations break God's heart too. When words don't suffice there is a melody that can reach straight to heaven.

Can you remember a time in your life when a song comforted you? When a melody let you feel your feelings instead of running from them? You listened to a song and it gave you a space to bear the full impact of a heartbreak or a loss and suddenly you knew you weren't alone.

Music can do this. It lifts us and unites us. It allows people who speak different languages to connect and express common feelings that no words can capture anyway.

I helped create Nashuva, the spiritual community I lead, because I was searching for new ways to revive Jewish spirit and resurrect a sense of joy, meaning, and ecstasy in prayer. The Hebrew word *nashuva* means "we will return." We all have a need to return—to passion, to our dreams, to love, to our own souls, to our God. I hoped Nashuva would be a place where people could receive the spiritual infusion they were searching for and emerge transformed. Nashuva would be a time to pray, to sing, to be still and listen to the voice of your soul.

When I was dreaming about Nashuva, before it had even begun to exist, I was hearing music in my head. Before I knew what the community would be like, I knew what the music would be like. I began looking for musicians who understood how to touch people's souls. One musician led to another.

We were interfaith: Jewish and Christian, and multiracial: black, white, Asian, and Latino—and we were committed to spreading the power of oneness. Our service would be blending musical traditions from all over the world. I was beginning to feel like Dorothy in *The Wizard of Oz*: I was surrounded by all these remarkable people who all seemed oddly familiar, as if I had known them in some other life.

The Nashuva Band and I began setting ancient Hebrew words of prayer to folk songs, to African rhythms, to reggae, to gospel and country melodies too. The first prayer we ever played together was: "Come let us sing to God, Let us create harmonies for the One who saves us each day." I was overwhelmed by the way we were lifting each other higher and higher and channeling something holy and divine.

Then came the night of our first Nashuva service. We had no idea whether we'd reach anyone or if people would come once and never return. We began praying and more and more people kept coming through the door, they were standing in the aisles. Everyone in the room seemed to be rising up. As we sang I saw people praying and crying, beaming and weeping. So many tears, so much light.

We've been together for thirteen years now, and it is such an honor to behold the way our music gives life to the words of prayer and enters people's souls, illuminates their faces, and just makes them happy. People are returning by the thousands, in person and via live webcasts, seeking a way back to their own souls and to the Soul of Souls. Even when people don't understand Hebrew, they find themselves humming along. Even if they walk into a service feeling lost and alone, they are soon swaying in time with others.

Stand shoulder-to-shoulder singing a prayer with others, and suddenly your soul takes flight and your worries fall away. In a room full of strangers, all those different voices with all their distinctive yearnings blend together to become a single unit, One Soul.

If you are feeling cut off from your soul, if you are having trouble finding it, if you can't seem to get out of your head, my advice is: sing. It doesn't matter if you are in tune or not, in the shower, in the car, in a worship service. Wherever you are, let out a melody or listen to a song you love and sing along, and you may discover where your soul has been hiding. Music awakens the soul, soon it feels safe enough to come out to play.

Music is prayer. It is the heartbeat of every revolution and every struggle for freedom. Think of the freedom song "We Shall Overcome" and how it impacted the civil rights movement. The anthem stirred and encouraged protesters, it steadied fears, lifted spirits, and fortified resolve at sit-ins and marches.

Music is time travel. We've all listened to a tune that brought us back to a special moment in our lives—your childhood, a first love, those rebellious teen years, your wedding day.

My father wasn't a man of many words. But he loved to sing—our whole family, four children and two parents, would sing all the time in harmony. Music was the language we used at our Sabbath table and at our Passover Seder when we'd sing together until well past midnight.

My parents are both gone now, but the songs of my childhood have stuck with me like loyal companions through my life. They come to visit me when I'm feeling lonely. A melody will pop into my head and whisk me back to precious days of joy and laughter. And I am comforted.

Music is the way the soul expresses love—from romantic ballads to the lullaby your mother sang to you as you drifted off to sleep. Sonja's lullaby.

I had not forgotten my promise to Avraham.

I made many inquiries about Sonja and what became of her. At last I discovered she had moved to Manhattan to live with her aunt Lucie on the Upper West Side, and that she found work as a window dresser for a clothing store. I tried to reach Avraham to tell him what had become of Sonja, but sadly he died before I had the chance to let him know that Sonja had found her family and her future.

When I heard the news of Avraham's death, I pictured him before me humming a lullaby, staring off in reverie. Seventy years had passed, but Sonja remained tangled up in his soul. I imagine Avraham sitting beside Sonja as she was drifting off to sleep feeling secure beside him, a young man playing the role of mother, singing a melody that would live on and on.

Whenever I teach rabbinical students about tending to the dying, they always want to know how it's possible to come home after dealing with a tragedy and switch gears in order to play with your kids or be present to your spouse. They ask me, "What do you do? Do you pray? Do you meditate?"

It's not uncommon for me to spend the morning offering a blessing at the bedside of someone who is dying, and to then rejoice at a wedding or a baby naming that same afternoon. Just this week I officiated at the funeral of a remarkable man I've adored for twenty-seven years, and then I got home and changed into a wacky costume for a boisterous Jewish holiday called Purim. How do I accomplish this transition? Music. Music saves me all the time.

Music is what lifts me and revives me. I leave a cemetery after a funeral, drive in silence for a while, and then I start blasting the Beatles or Aretha Franklin or Bob Marley—and my soul is transported to a new state of being. From the depths of sadness, music returns me to life.

There are ten levels of prayer . . . above them is Song.

9

Eating to Satisfy Your Soul

WHEN MY NEPHEW JARED was about to have his bar mitzvah, my mother, of blessed memory, asked him what he'd like for a present. This thirteen-year-old boy, who could have asked his grandmother for anything in the world, said, "Bubby, I'd like you to make me a cookbook with all your recipes in it." My mother could not have been more touched.

She spent an entire year writing out all the family recipes by hand, and along with the recipes she shared her stories, about special occasions and about special people and what carrying on the traditions of her mother and grandmother meant to her. On the first page of "Bubby's Cookbook" my mother wrote:

> Dear Jared,
>   I feel greatly honored that you asked me to put this recipe book together for you. I don't know of any other grandchild that ever made such a request. In every way I thank you.
>   It brought back so many wonderful memories of dinners prepared for the various holidays . . . Of course with the many

meals and recipes I recorded here came the memories of so many people that gathered at my home, sat at my table and became forever inscribed in my heart and mind . . . Especially Friday nights—the lit candles, the pretty braided challah . . . the beautiful faces that surround it all . . . I feel totally inspired . . . all this becomes my creative expression of my love for all of you.

. . . My attitude toward food centers around bringing people together . . . feelings of warmth toward each other and in celebration of life. What better way to display nature's infinite bounty and beauty, for which I have enormous feelings of appreciation and gratitude.

Jared, I designed these recipes so that they will be easy to follow . . . I hope you find them useful, that you enjoy the creative aspect of cooking and baking, but most of all, that you provide others, as I'd like to think I did, with the opportunity to share it all.

I love you dearly,
Bubby

My mother is no longer with us, and I am so grateful to Jared for asking her to pass on her precious legacy to all of us, a piece of her soul.

Food connects souls in love and creates community. Recipes get passed down from one generation to another. The flavors and aromas you grew up with shape you and remind you of where you come from and who you belong to. Food can teach you that you are part of a collective soul, that you are a member of a culture, of a people, with a common history and a shared destiny.

Food can tear down that delusion of separation. Break bread with a stranger and you will create intimacy. Share a meal with your rival and you may find common ground. I was talking to a rabbinic colleague recently about ways to inspire and engage Jews, and we both agreed that the best way to bring Jews back to Judaism isn't by teaching ancient texts—that comes later. You get much further with a bowl of *cholent* (a savory Sabbath stew) than you do with a discussion of Maimonides.

In the Bible there is a curse that sticks with me always. It's one of the most disturbing curses: "And you will eat and you will never be full."

This curse is always hovering over us. A feeling that there is a hunger within us that cannot be satisfied. We eat from anxiety, we eat for comfort, we eat compulsively, we eat out of boredom, out of loneliness, we eat because the food is in front of us. We often eat so quickly or so much that we feel sick, but still we don't feel satisfied.

So how do we learn to experience that spiritual state called "fullness"? Eat with your soul and you will learn to slow down and taste what is going in. You will learn flavor and color and texture and aroma. Let food awaken your senses. Rouse yourself to experience deep pleasure.

There is a famous Yiddish idiom reserved for savoring amazing food: *It has the taste of the Garden of Eden.* Food can give us a hint of heaven.

Food teaches us gratitude. The rabbis insist that anyone who partakes of this world without first giving thanks has stolen from God. That's why in Jewish law there is a blessing to say before eating even the smallest morsel of food or before taking even a sip of water.

In the Jewish tradition there are also various blessings to say after you have eaten. One blessing that I love reciting gives thanks to God for creating "souls with needs." It's such a strange blessing. Why should we be grateful for being born incomplete? Here is how I understand these words: Can you imagine how boring life would be if you were created self-satisfied, if you had no desire? If none of this world's pleasures called out to you? Notice also that the blessing after partaking in food thanks God for creating "souls" with needs, not bodies. That means that eating is a spiritual activity we can engage in all the time that satisfies the soul.

Eating is a path to awakening the soul. That's why religions turn eating into ritual. Food becomes sacrament, uniting heaven and earth.

For Jews matzah on Passover teaches us about affliction. We don't simply read about the bitterness of slavery, we eat bitter herbs to enter that soul-state. On Rosh Hashanah, Jews eat apples dipped in honey to pray for a sweet year. I've thought a lot about honey and the longing for sweetness. In a culture that offers us so many cheap substitutes, how do we learn to seek out true sweetness? We want days of honey, not saccharin.

Let eating become a meditation, a time to be mindful, present to our senses, present to those around us. Treat a meal like a sacred ceremony. Remember that something as commonplace as food can connect us to the supernal realm and replenish our own souls.

Yes, food *is* love. A meal someone cooks for you is an offering of the heart and soul. Your table can become the soul of your home, a gravitational force drawing extended families to feast together and create memories that will last a lifetime.

Before partaking in food ask yourself, *What is my soul hungry for?* Take a moment to listen carefully for the answer. Satisfy your soul and you will know fullness and you will give thanks.

IT WAS MY HUSBAND, ROB, who taught me the soulfulness of savoring a meal. Rob wooed me with food. I was the rabbi of a synagogue teaching a small lunchtime class called Love and Torah. My students were all moms whose kids were in our preschool. We were studying the Song of Songs in my office, and soon there was a man bringing the rabbi treats to class. At first it was fresh ripe strawberries from the farmers' market that melted in my mouth and dripped down my chin. Then he began bringing the spices mentioned in the sacred erotic love poem we were reading aloud in class. One week it was frankincense. The next week he brought myrrh. I started to feel woozy when he entered my study each week. Did my other students sense this? The words of the love poem were getting mixed with the spices he brought and our souls were rising and getting intertwined and I knew I was falling.

The first time I invited Rob into my apartment we spent hours talking over tea. I got up to check on something in another room, and Rob used that break in our conversation to peek into my cupboards. Apparently he was starving. He found a can of tuna and a bag of potato chips. No mayo, no bread. When I returned I found him standing in my kitchen. He held up the can of tuna and asked, "Do you eat it out of the can like a cat?" "Yes!" I confessed. He laughed and laughed. The next time I saw him he brought a present, a kitty bowl with the word "meow" printed on it for my tuna meals.

Rob and I have been married for twenty-five years now, and he still woos me with food. Rob was a chef when I met him, he owned a catering company and had worked in several restaurant kitchens and also as a pastry chef. The first meal he ever made for me was homemade pasta with homemade tomato sauce and homemade bread drizzled with olive oil served with a bottle of red wine. I loved watching his hands playing with the dough. There was no anxiety in the way he cooked, only joy and love. Before we even sat down, Rob offered me a fork of the pasta I'd been salivating over. I tasted the Garden of Eden.

I still love watching Rob in the kitchen. He can cook a dinner for thirty without ever getting harried. With his hands in food he always looks to me like a kid playing in a sandbox. He's a journalist now, but at home every night he's my chef. Our home is a gathering place for people to come and eat and enjoy good company, good conversation, and good food. Our kids grew up knowing that both their parents would be sitting with them every night eating amazing food together.

Love, sensuality, soul, friendship, community, family, food. Eden. Thank You, God. I am full.

May you partake in meals that awaken and nourish your soul, meals that leave you full, meals that bind you to loved ones and to the One who nourishes all. Amen.

10

Praying and Learning as Keys to Understanding

JUST AS THÉ BODY needs food to survive, the soul needs prayer to thrive.

What was the first thing on your mind when you woke up this morning?

That is the question I asked my students in a class I was teaching about prayer several years ago. I asked them to call out the answers: "I was thinking about my baby crying." "I was rehearsing a presentation I had to give." "I was thinking about making breakfast for my kids and packing their lunches for school." "I was thinking about hitting snooze on the alarm." "I was thinking about my e-mails." "I was thinking about coffee."

I said, "What do you think it would feel like to wake up with a prayer on your lips? A prayer of gratitude for waking up, for the gift of a new day." My students were mostly secular people, they didn't pray except when they felt they were required to at temple.

I said, "I've come to believe that a simple thing like a single sentence of prayer can change how you deal with the crying baby, can transform the way you approach the presentation you are about to give, can shape how you offer the breakfast to your kids, can fill you with a new attitude toward your to-do list."

Their expressions were full of skepticism. I said, "Why not approach it as an experiment? Try waking up and reciting a morning prayer for two weeks and we'll discuss it then."

When class resumed, my students' responses were overwhelming: "I've been so much more patient with my kids in the morning." "There's more fun in the house, less whining." "I've been sleeping better." "I'm not hitting snooze anymore, I pop out of bed after offering a prayer and look forward to entering the day."

One student wrote to me two years after that class: "Dear Rabbi Levy, I am not sure you remember me, but I was in your prayer class. In fact I still do the prayer every morning since you first asked us to try it, and continue to encourage others to try it as well. I find myself appreciating the daily miracles of life in a much deeper way than I did before. That practice has helped me to live a more present and appreciative life, and is something for which I am particularly grateful. Thank you again for this gift."

Something as simple as a morning prayer can change the way you face your day.

"My soul thirsts for you," the Psalmist cries out. When we are empty, when we feel as if we have nothing left to give, prayer fills us up. It revives our souls. It calms, it reassures, it rekindles hope. Prayer in community connects disparate souls in a great oneness. Prayer on your own reminds you that you are not alone, that the Infinite One is close. Prayer helps you remember your dreams, your longings, all the hopes you've been ignoring or running from. Prayer helps you remember that you have a soul that is crying out within you. Prayer is the space we make for the soul within us to speak. It is an outpouring of our inner life.

There is a famous Yiddish saying, "From your mouth to God's ear." The phrase is full of hope, but it's full of audacity too. It speaks of our confidence that the God of the universe cares about you and me. Prayer is chutzpah! It refuses to be a monologue. With our words we draw God near, we weave God into the fabric of our daily lives. A God who listens, who is with us through life's celebrations and sorrows, and through the deadening gray days too.

"Pray for me, Rabbi," is probably the most common request people have made of me over my years in the rabbinate. I am always honored to be able to pray for people. But of course I worry when people ask me to pray for them. Are they asking because they don't think God will listen to them? Do they think prayer requires a correct formula and if they don't know the magical incantation that their cries won't be heard?

Once, about twenty years ago, I went to visit a man in the hospital. He said, "Pray for me, Rabbi. I don't know how to pray." I said, "Of course I will pray for you. But first, tell me, what is it that you want me to say to God?" He thought about it for a moment and then began trembling as he spoke: "God, I am Yours, I know that. But I belong here with my family. My heart is aching. I've never let myself love like this before. Give me time. I pray to You, God, give me time."

These words flowed from the soul of a man who felt he didn't know how to pray. When he was done he sighed deeply, and I could see the worry and tension depart from his face. A calm overtook him, a light, a grace. I witnessed with my own eyes how prayer heals.

From that day on, any time anyone asks me to pray for them I always ask the same question, "What do you want me to say to God?" And it never fails. People astound themselves with words they didn't know existed inside them. The soul speaks of its own accord.

When I was a child my father taught me a prayer. I loved the melody, but I didn't understand what the words meant: "I am my prayer to You, God, in this time of yearning. God, in Your infinite love, answer me, answer me, with Your true salvation."

It can take decades for words you learned as a child to find their rightful place in your soul. I can see myself as a child soaking up that prayer. I see her sitting on the living room couch, her feet too short to touch the ground. I see my father passing down a piece of his own soul, hoping his little girl will receive it and welcome it into her own soul. I see his eyes wet with tears behind his thick glasses, and my not knowing why the tears are there. I watch how this prayer lived on in me, the melody, the words I couldn't understand, biding its time.

I understand the words now. I've lived the agony of "Answer me, answer me," when prayer feels hopeless and the very idea of God seems like a practical joke your tradition has played on you. I've lived through times of yearning, longing to come close, a deep desire to stand in the presence of the God I love.

I've come to understand what "I am my prayer" means too—when there are no words, when the confines of language can't possibly capture what your soul is trying to express. "I am my prayer," all of me. Accept my very being, body and soul, as my prayer to You, God. I sing this prayer, my eyes wet with tears, I hear my father's harmony, our souls reaching out beyond the boundaries of time.

The most famous Jewish prayer is called "Shema Yisrael," or "Listen Israel." It begins: "Listen, Israel, the Lord our God, the Lord is One." Observant Jews utter these words morning and night, in bed before sleep, at the conclusion of Yom Kippur, and on the deathbed. Why this prayer? Why these words lifted from the Book of Deuteronomy?

To me, it expresses something beyond monotheism. It reminds us there is nothing but God. The soul within you knows this, it strives to teach you this: everything we are, everything we see, it's all a reflection of the One. The Shema speaks of the "whole" Einstein was pointing to. The Zohar, the Jewish book of mystical wisdom, describes the unity this way: "No place is devoid of God." All of creation is infused with the divine. There is God in everything you see and touch.

The Shema isn't our request, it doesn't ask anything of God. The Shema is God's request, God's prayer. It is God crying out to us, echoing through time: "Listen! Love! With all your heart, all your soul, and all your might." Listen.

Prayer isn't about receiving an outcome, and prayer doesn't always leave us feeling better. Prayer is your soul connecting to its Source, the Soul of Souls. Prayer allows us to see through the soul's eyes. It opens us up to our daily blessings, and helps us align the soul's highest intentions with the body's highest actions. Prayer ignites us to create the world we are yearning for.

What is the prayer lying deep inside your soul? Chances are you won't find it unless you give your soul the time and space it needs to express itself. Let your soul surprise you. Give it an opening to speak. Take the time to ask yourself: What is it that I've been wanting to say to God? Let the words come out of their own accord. Offer God your question, your hope, your protest, your longing, your gratitude. Pray for others, pray for yourself, pray for this world. Say whatever it is you need to say and listen carefully for a reply.

If you make room for this practice daily, you may notice things begin to shift within and without you. Soon you may find yourself longing not only to pray but to learn.

There is a practice that is prayer's twin. The flip side of prayer is learning. As the great scholar Rabbi Louis Finkelstein poignantly described it: "When I pray I speak to God; when I study God speaks to me."

WISDOM NEVER ARRIVES MAGICALLY. Your ego might fantasize about being given all the answers, but your soul longs to study, it yearns to expand and widen and grow in depth. Start learning, start with just one verse from a sacred text. Thirst for a richer understanding of the present, and what's available to you right here where you stand.

There is a Jewish tradition that every Hebrew name is connected to a biblical verse that begins and ends with the first and last letter of your name. When the soul passes from this world to the next it can get so overwhelmed by the world above that it will forget its life below completely. But the soul never forgets its verse, and that very verse will help your soul remember its name in the world below, and soon everything will come back to it.

The verse connected to my own Hebrew name is: "Guard your tongue from speaking evil, keep your lips from spreading slander." This verse has become my teacher, it hovers over me every day of my life, reminding me to watch my words and to always see people in the best light possible.

If you long to connect to the divine, begin studying, and you will receive timeless wisdom. Words will come alive inside your soul, verses will begin calling your name. Study the Bible. Study holy texts of other faith traditions. Read commentaries, mysticism, poetry, literature. Seek out great teachers, scholars, mentors who will guide you. Be open to new knowledge, to new ways of experiencing this magical world. Be social, study with a partner, let that person widen your perspective and challenge your thinking.

Honestly, I don't know what I would do without my study partner, Rabbi Toba August. Toba and I have been studying weekly for over fourteen years now. We recite a prayer before beginning our learning, hoping that our session will lift us up in some unexpected way. Our weekly date is also a time to catch up, to share longings, secrets, hurts, and hopes. Some days I walk into our study time distracted or tired or sad. But our learning never fails us. We open a text and soon we are swimming in a sea of meaning and comfort.

Pray and study. Speak to God and let God speak to you.
May you come to see that you are a blessing.
And may blessings surround you now and always. Amen.

Restoring the Soul in Nature

ONE OF MY FAVORITE Hasidic stories is about a little boy who keeps going into the forest every day. The boy's father notices that his son keeps escaping into the woods and asks him, "Why do you keep going into the woods each day?" The son replies, "I go there to find God."

The father tries to gently correct his son by saying, "My child, don't you know God is the same everywhere?"

The boy replies, "Yes, Papa, but *I'm* not the same everywhere."

We're not the same everywhere. In nature we begin to see that we are part of creation, part of something vast and holy and eternal.

Not long ago my husband and I decided on a whim to go camping in Sequoia National Park. As we got high up in the Sierras the oak trees and eucalyptus gave way to pines and redwoods. Soon we hit into a storm, there was lightning and thunder and it was dark and hailing and we got lost along muddy roads. It didn't take long before I started to regret our decision to go camping. The truth is, I'm from Brooklyn. I'm told a tree grows there somewhere, but to be honest, nature and I don't really have such a warm relationship.

Eventually we parked at an altitude of 8,700 feet and waited for the storm to pass. Then we got out and had to hike for a mile up another 300 feet in elevation to get to our campsite. As I was hiking up with my backpack, my asthma kicked in and I started panting so hard that I sounded like Darth Vader. *Maybe this wasn't a good idea*, I started telling myself, *I'm going to hate this.*

We reached our campsite just as the sun was setting into pinks and purples and reds. I stood at the overlook taking in the expanse of the sky and those majestic trees. Later it grew dark and I stood in awe before the sky all lit up with the moon and stars. My Brooklyn mind was beginning to melt.

The next day Rob and I hiked for eight miles to a lake and we both just jumped in. And then I came face-to-face with a massive sequoia. The tree was two thousand years old. I sensed its mighty soul and began weeping before it. I held on to it, whispering a prayer of gratitude, and for a moment "I" disappeared, that whirring thinking machine. All that remained was a being flowing effortlessly, hands outstretched. No thought, no weight, no ground, no body, no mind, no me. A quote of Einstein's washed over me, "The most beautiful thing we can experience is the mysterious."

Something happens to you, to your body, to your vision, to your pulse, to your breathing when you are out in nature. Your soul feels alive and fed. It sees God shepherding us. The words of the 23rd Psalm become personal: "You lay me down in green pastures, You lead me beside still waters, You restore my soul."

Our homes protect us from the heat and the cold, but they also protect us from awe and wonder. We live in a breathtaking world, but so often we miss it.

Our souls need us to make times to break out of our enclosed spaces and enter God's house illuminated by the moon and stars. Our souls are pleading with us to get away from our stuff—our possessions and our smartphones—and see God among the grasses and the trees.

Rabbi Nachman of Bratzlav, a great Hasidic master who lived in the late 1700s, advised his followers to talk to God daily outdoors. He believed nature was the place where the soul could be revived. He said, "When a person returns from such meditation, he can often see the world in an entirely new light. It will appear that the world is entirely new, and that it is not the same world that he knew before."

I offer you this moving prayer Rabbi Nachman composed:

Master of the Universe,
grant me the ability to be alone;
may it be my custom to go outdoors each day
among the trees and grass, among all growing things,
and there may I be alone, and enter into prayer,
to talk with the One that I belong to.
May I express there everything in my heart,
and may all the foliage of the field,
all grasses and trees, and plants
may they all awake at my coming,
to send the powers of their life into the words of my prayer
so that my prayer and speech are made whole
through the life and spirit of all growing things,
which are made as one by their transcendent Source.

12

Welcoming the Sabbath

REVIVING YOUR SOUL WITH
A DAY OF REST

I UNDERSTOOD FROM A VERY young age that my father didn't like his job. I would watch him in the mornings as he dragged himself off to work. I could see it in his expression, in his eyes, and in his body language.

As a young man my father dreamed of becoming a teacher, but World War II gripped at his heart and he enlisted in the army at the age of eighteen. During the war my father fell madly in love with my mother. When he came home he married my mom, and then his father encouraged him to take over his clothing manufacturing business. Why go back to college when he could already be making a living? Before he knew it, my father got trapped into doing work that didn't feed his soul. Not everyone gets to follow their passion and do what they love. Sometimes you end up doing what you must.

But on Friday nights in our home as the sun was setting, my mother would light the Sabbath candles, and it was like stepping into another reality. The aroma of roasting chicken, the table set beautifully, the whole family gathered together in conversation and blessings and love. Hopping out of bed the next day and seeing my father on a Sabbath morning was like waking up to a different man—his eagerness to get ready for synagogue, the buoyancy, the melodious quality to his voice. "Let's go," he'd call out to me as if he were singing the invitation.

To see my father at synagogue surrounded by his friends all robed in prayer shawls was to witness nobility. When these men would close their eyes and sing they were carried to another world. By day, they were ordinary men doing ordinary jobs, by Sabbath, they were Children of God, each one of them God's only child. And when my father was called up to the pulpit to chant from the Prophets, I could see that he had taken his rightful place in God's presence.

A glimpse of the world to come, that is how the rabbis of the Talmud describe the Sabbath. A hint of heaven here.

The Sabbath is a gift Jews gave to the world. We all have to step back in order to see, we all need to rest in order to keep climbing. Ahad Ha-am, a famous Jewish essayist, once explained, "More than the Jews have kept the Sabbath, the Sabbath has kept the Jews." Wherever they were, whatever situation they were in, the Sabbath was an oasis waiting for them up ahead where they could quench their weary souls.

Some think of the Sabbath as a day of prohibitions—you can't do this and you can't do that. But the Sabbath is actually a day of permission. A day when we give our souls permission to dream again. How long can we keep racing around, spreading ourselves so thin, contorted by stress and worry? There's so much within our grasp that we keep missing.

You've been offered a free trip to paradise and you don't have to travel anywhere to get there. All you have to do is rest.

How can something as simple as a day of rest take you into the supernal realm? The best way I know to answer that question is to repeat what your mother told you when you were a child reluctant to taste something new: "Try it and see."

"Try what?" Henry asked me. Henry founded an Internet startup company that was booming. He was making more money than he'd ever dreamed of. He was thirty-six, happily married with an adorable, energetic son. "But something's missing," Henry told me. "Rabbi, I've got no right to complain. I feel like I've won the jackpot—health, love, family, success . . . and I feel empty inside."

I asked Henry, "Can you describe this empty feeling?"

Henry said, "It's sort of a nagging feeling, like I've forgotten something, but I don't know what I've forgotten."

As we spoke further, Henry admitted to me that he was mostly distracted at home. Playing with his son meant texting on his phone while his son did whatever he was doing. Time with his wife was pretty much the same story. He said they'd both gotten into the habit of going to bed with their iPads, not a great aphrodisiac. Henry blushed and told me, "I don't think we've had sex in like six months."

I said to Henry, "Maybe the thing you've forgotten is your soul and your soul's connection to the people you love."

Henry said, "But, Rabbi, I'm living my dream."

"Henry," I said, "your soul may have other dreams." That's when I talked to Henry about trying to experience the Sabbath. I could see the hesitation on his face.

I said, "You've come here for my help, and here is my suggestion: try to experience a Sabbath day." Henry and I talked about turning off his work mind for a day. We talked about the whole family unplugging from technology and TV. We talked about lighting Sabbath candles as a way to welcome in a sacred time and a festive meal at home. We also talked about not using the day to go shopping or get errands done, but to be present to life, to friends and family and to nature. I said, "Start with Friday night. Just try it one Friday night. Don't worry about the whole Sabbath day."

Henry got up to leave, and I could tell he was weighing whether it was a mistake to have come to see me. He didn't expect to be given homework, he had plenty of work on his plate already. I didn't hear from Henry for some time. I wondered if he had given the Sabbath a try.

Several weeks later Henry came back to see me. There was something lighter about him, a peacefulness. He was laughing. "We tried it all right."

"How did it go?" I asked.

"The first Friday night I just kept reaching for my phone, so I finally turned it off. But, Rabbi, it felt like an amputated limb. I kept listening for it and looking for it."

"And?"

He said, "I don't know how to thank you. I feel like a real father for the first time. I think I was just faking it before. I love playing with Jake and reading him books and looking into his eyes." Henry got choked up. "He's so special and I wasn't letting him in." He went on, "And my wife and I, we've broken through our six-month dry spell. No more tech in bed, that's our new thing. I go to bed holding her in my arms."

"Wow," I said, "you're a quick study."

"The weird part is that taking Friday night as a Sabbath is actually affecting all the days of the week," Henry said. "The nagging feeling, it's gone. I feel rich."

"You *are* rich," I said.

You might think that making the decision to set aside your to-do list in order to peek at heaven would be an easy choice to make. But for most of us, the thought of parting with our smartphones for an hour sounds like a form of torture. Technology has such an all-consuming pull on us that it is slowly sucking away our soul's vitality—sucking away our happiness, our intimacy, our wonder, and our creativity too. How can we expect to feel passionately alive when our souls are depleted? In our own time, more than in any other era in human history, the soul needs us to live in the Sabbath.

I did not say your soul needs you to *keep* the Sabbath, I said your soul needs you to *live in* the Sabbath. If the Sabbath is a glimpse of heaven, then it is more than just a time, it's also a place we can go to receive what our souls are thirsting for. The Sabbath arrives and we are invited to enter its atmosphere.

What sort of place is the Sabbath? How do you describe it? I picture the Sabbath as a snowy day from my childhood. Waking up and peering outside into a new world blanketed in pure white. Everything familiar looked new, bathed in light. All the rhythms of life were transformed and everyone was free to frolic for the day. Picture the Sabbath as any place you've ever been that calmed you and helped you breathe more deeply, a place that filled you with awe.

No matter what your faith tradition is, imagine what it might be like to set one day aside each week for romance, for family, for community, for learning and prayer. A day of sensuality, physical pleasure, good food, nature, song. A day for welcoming the presence of God into our world. The Sabbath teaches us how to take back our lives, how to balance work and home, prose and poetry, ego and soul. On the Sabbath the present gives way to the eternal. Time releases its stranglehold over us. We're no longer ruled by the clock. We can stop rushing and stressing.

As Henry learned, the Sabbath's magic is that it spills over into all our days—those that come behind it and those that lie ahead: "My cup overflows." The Sabbath is the soul of the week. The days preceding it are days of expectation and eager anticipation, the days after the Sabbath are awash in its afterglow, like a sky in purples and reds after the sun has set.

Jewish mystics took the idea of the Sabbath one step further. To them the Sabbath was more than a day and more than a place. In mystical thought the Sabbath is alive. The mystics taught that on the Sabbath the spiritual presence of a holy queen called the Sabbath Bride descends from the Upper World to reside among us for one day each week. The Bride arrives to heal hearts and replenish weary souls.

Do you have a nagging feeling that you've forgotten something but you can't remember what you've forgotten?

The Sabbath is here for you, ready to reveal her secret wisdom, whispering your name. Your task is to learn how to greet her. To train your eyes to see her in her radiance, robed in white, like waking up to a fresh snow blanketing the whole world so that everything familiar looks new, bathed in light.

May all your days shine in that light.

MEDITATION, MUSIC, FOOD, PRAYER, LEARNING, nature, rest. Find the paths that your soul likes best, and practice them regularly until you begin to see how things are shifting within you and all around you. Take your time, let a path lead you to a deeper experience of calm, a sense of wonder, and a knowing. Soon you may begin seeing wider expanses with greater perspective and less fear blocking your way. This is your soul's vision. Welcome it.

And may you welcome the journey that is about to unfold.

ACCESSING THE SOUL'S EXPANSIVE VISION

"A kind of optical delusion of his consciousness."
—from Einstein's letter to Rabbi Marcus

Nourish and revive the soul and it will in turn begin reviving you. The first subtle shift you may notice as you begin tapping into the Life Force is in the realm of vision. What you can see with your eyes is only a piece of the truth. Daily our eyes deceive us and lead us astray. But the soul wants to offer us its expansive vision, a consciousness of the whole we have trouble seeing. Soon we may begin seeing a bigger picture, how random threads are all actually woven together in a single majestic tapestry.

13

Stepping Back to Gain a Wider Perspective

A FEW YEARS AGO, in the summer of 2012, I got a traffic ticket. I was rushing to a meeting when I looked behind me and saw the police officer flashing his lights at me. I pulled over and he walked up to my window in a chipper mood. He said, "Ma'am, you just performed a perfect California Roll." He added, "I've been watching the Olympics. If I had to judge the execution of that roll I'd give you a perfect ten. But instead of a medal I'm giving you a ticket."

I said, "Officer, I thought I did stop at that stop sign. Can you please describe the California Roll?"

"When you slow down at a stop sign but you never stop and you just keep on rolling, that's a California Roll."

"But I'm from Brooklyn," I said with a smile.

He said, "Then call it a Brooklyn Bagel."

I asked him, "Officer, in the future, how will I know if I've stopped long enough?"

He said, "Brake and count to three. Say to yourself, one, two, three, and you should feel yourself being pulled backwards. If there's no pull backwards, you haven't really stopped."

I thanked the officer for his driving tip, took my ticket, and drove on, counting one, two, three at every stop sign. After a couple of weeks I signed up for an online traffic school. I took all my quizzes, passed the final exam, and put the whole thing behind me.

Later that week a young woman named Maya came to see me. She was attractive, twenty-three, and confused. She said, "Rabbi, I don't know what I'm doing with my life. Help!"

Before I could open my mouth to ask some questions, she said, "Help me. Just tell me what to do."

Maya explained to me that she'd always had a master plan about moving to New York City to try to make it on Broadway. She said she was having trouble investing energy in her life in Los Angeles. When I asked Maya if she was acting in theater locally, she told me she wasn't. She said she was having trouble committing to her current life because she was fixated on that master plan of hers.

"I'm working in a clothing store right now," she said, "but I can't imagine doing that for the rest of my life, because I want to move to New York. And . . . I'm seeing a guy who's nice, but I can't imagine being with him for the rest of my life because he told me he has no intentions of moving with me to New York. And . . . I like LA but I can't imagine living here for the rest of my life because one day I'm moving to New York."

Suddenly a question from traffic school popped into my head. I blurted out, "Maya, when you're driving down the street, do you know how far ahead you're supposed to look? Half a block, two blocks, four blocks, or to the end of the road?"

She looked at me as if I were completely out of my mind. "Rabbi, is there a reason you're giving me a driving test?"

"The answer is two blocks," I told her. "Just two blocks! Maya, you don't need to worry about the rest of your life today. Instead, worry about the next two blocks.

"Are you happy with your job for the next two months? Are you happy with your boyfriend for the next two months? Are you happy in LA for the next two months? In the meantime, if you're serious about your acting career, why not begin auditioning for plays in LA?"

Maya started to tear up. She started taking long, deep breaths. Her whole body seemed to relax. "Two blocks," she said. "Yes, I can handle two blocks. I can do two blocks."

WHEN MAYA LEFT, I REALIZED how often we suffer because we can't see beyond our own windshield. We're so caught in confusion, doubt, and fear that we can't even see which way to turn or where to go. We can't even see the path before us when it's right here and all we need to do is to take the first step and start somewhere.

Sometimes we keep looking in the rearview mirror instead of at the road ahead. We keep glancing back, ruminating over events that can't be changed. Is it any wonder that we keep crashing into things?

And sometimes, like Maya, we get so fixed on the end of the road, on some plan the ego has for us, that we don't even take the time to ask ourselves if we still even want to go where we are heading. We entered a destination in the GPS a long time ago and now we've got tunnel vision, with our foot on the gas and no time to take in the scenery, and no thought of changing direction.

But the soul has an uncanny navigational system. It sees past, present, and future at once. As the ancient rabbis taught, the soul sees from one end of the world to the other. It lives on God's time. Within us there is a consciousness that is sensitive and open to the present even as it is alive to the past and the future. Our egos, however, can get so stuck on a plan that we lose sight of the magic all around us. We become blind to the openings that can change our lives if we let them in.

Every one of us has experienced a stubborn fixation on a goal. When you were so stuck on some plan you'd made that you couldn't veer from it, even when it was hurting you. Even when it was hurting the people you love.

I was recently counseling a man in his forties who said to me, "Rabbi, I don't just regret the past, I'm filled with regret about the future." I was trying to understand what he was telling me. How can you regret something that hasn't even happened yet? And then it hit me: you can see the way things are going, you can see the plans you've made, the momentum you've already set into motion. You can already see. You see the days and years ahead, how stuck you feel, how hopeless it all seems. The decisions you've made, the mistakes you've made that seem to stretch on into the distant, unwavering path ahead.

The greatest sin we can commit against our own future is to lose hope. We don't need to regret the future, because the future isn't fixed. We're not fated to be anywhere. We don't need to be slaves to the ego's plans. We can turn them around. You are free to rewrite the story of your life. You can repair what you have broken. You're not helpless or hopeless. You can start over. You can begin again.

Every day God keeps calling out to us, "There is hope for your future!" You may have fallen into a destructive pattern, but you're not destined to stay there. You have the power to change the course of your life.

What is the antidote to the ego's tunnel vision?

The answer is so ridiculously simple, but it's so difficult to live by. If we keep doing California Rolls, if we never really stop and look and respond to our surroundings, sooner or later we're going to crash. My police officer's advice to stop and count one, two, three and feel yourself being pulled back is exactly what Jews do when they pray the Amida prayer, the Silent Standing Meditation. There is a tradition to stop and take three steps backwards at the start of the prayer. Why? We imagine our souls leaving this space and entering a holy space. Suddenly we are standing in the very presence of God.

When you slow down, hold your plans lightly and stop long enough to give yourself some perspective, what emerges? Revelation.

As we all know, so much of what we call luck has to do with planning and openness. Planning, and then taking three steps back to relax and regroup and be aware. There are scores of discoveries and life-saving treatments that arose when plans changed, things got burned, and someone remained open and aware.

When we give ourselves time to step back we make room within us for answers we never imagined would come. It could be a walk in the woods or an afternoon at a museum or even a warm bubble bath. We all have our own ways of softening the mind's fixed focus, giving the soul the space it needs to express and reveal itself.

Last December I went to see the Grammy Museum in downtown Los Angeles. As I was walking around looking at rock 'n' roll memorabilia, I came upon a worn and wrinkled piece of paper framed on the wall. It had doodles on it and words scratched out. The handwritten note read, "L.D. feels like ice is slowly melting. L.D. feels like years since it's been clear."

Farther down the page it read: "H.C.T.S.—H.C.T.S. (and I say) it's alright." There was a simple line drawing of a sun with a smiley face on it. Just in case you haven't figured it out, it was the handwritten lyrics to the Beatles song "Here Comes the Sun."

I learned that day how that iconic song came into the world. George Harrison said that being in the Beatles had stopped being fun, everything was all business and "sign this" and "sign that." So one day in early spring after a long winter in England, George decided to play hooky from Apple Studios. He said it was such a relief to be away from those "dopey accountants." He went over to Eric Clapton's house and started walking alone in the garden with a guitar, and then he took out that scrap of paper and out came "HCTS."

Inspiration, revelation, it's all possible when we clear out the tunnel vision and make room for surprise.

Sometimes life smashes your plans and it forces you to rethink everything.

In his breathtaking memoir *Man's Search for Meaning*, Victor Frankl wrote that when he first arrived in Auschwitz he was hiding the pages of a scientific manuscript he'd written inside the pocket of his coat. In those early days in Auschwitz he saw people still thinking they could hold on to a precious ring, a loving memento. Of course, it was all so futile. He walked up to a man who had obviously been in Auschwitz for some time already and said, "Look, this is the manuscript of a scientific book. I know what you will say; that I should be grateful to escape with my life . . . But I cannot help myself. I must keep this manuscript at all costs; it contains my life's work."

The man just laughed at him, mocking him. He uttered just one word, "Shit!"

As if to say: It's all meaningless here, you think that bunch of paper matters? Of course the manuscript was destroyed, and Frankl went into deep mourning over it. He was crushed that nothing would survive him, no legacy would live on. Did his life have any meaning?

But soon an answer to the meaning of life was given to him. One day some months later in Auschwitz, Frankl was ordered to give up his clothing, and he received the tattered garments of a martyred man who'd been sent to the gas chamber. Frankl put the man's overcoat on and there in the pocket, just in the place where he had hidden his scientific manuscript, he saw that the dead man had hidden a single page.

He pulled it out. It was a page from a Jewish prayer book, the words of the Shema: "Listen, Israel, the Lord our God, the Lord is One." Frankl wrote: "How should I have interpreted such a 'coincidence' other than as a challenge to *live* my thoughts instead of merely putting them on paper?" Frankl came to realize that his life's work wasn't a manuscript, it was to learn to live each day with meaning in even the most inhumane conditions.

After liberation, Frankl managed to reconstruct his lost scientific work from memory. But as it turned out, it was not his masterpiece. His stunning and lasting success was the book he wrote about the human ability to find meaning and purpose even in hell.

When we learn to take three steps back, we may be surprised by a breakthrough. We have the power to make room for something real, for something honest and immediate. We have the power to make room for welcoming an unexpected blessing.

Hold fast to those moments when the soul breaks through your defenses and whispers in your ear, "Make space for new visions and new inspiration, because they're coming!"

Yes, I do believe great things are coming, sweet blessings. The gates to new openings are flung open before us daily. And our challenge is to see the opening, and seize the opening.

When we practice taking three steps back we may indeed find ourselves in a new place. We may see our souls standing before us full of strength and wisdom, ready to show us the way to a life of meaning and the fulfillment of our divine purpose.

And the question is, are you ready to remain true to your soul's journey?

If loosening your grip on your narrow plans frightens you, if you're scared to step back long enough to look around and widen your tunnel vision, if taking your soul's hand and allowing it to be your guide worries you, imagine that God is saying, in the words of George Harrison, "It's alright."

14

Moving Beyond Our Narrow Thoughts

IT WAS ONE WEEK BEFORE Beth and Eric's wedding. They sat down on the couch in my study facing me. They could barely look at each other. "What's the matter?" I asked. Silence.

I waited and then Beth began sobbing, "He wants to wear red Converse high-tops with his tuxedo. He's making a joke of our wedding."

Then Eric blurted out, "What about the tablecloths! Tablecloths, tablecloths. I'm sick of hearing about tablecloths. Beth wants pink, my mother wants blue, and I'm caught between two bickering hens."

Sitting opposite Beth and Eric, I smiled. This wasn't exactly the first time I'd seen a couple get stuck in the minutiae of planning a day instead of planning a life.

Someone might have looked at these two snapping at each other and thought it was time to call the wedding off before it was too late. But I wasn't worried at all. I looked at them sitting there all stiff and angry. I knew how to defuse this bomb. I would have to gently lead them out of their place of pettiness into a state of gratitude and generosity.

One of my favorite verses from Psalms is, "I called to God from my narrowness, and God answered me with a vast expanse." I love this verse, I sing it to myself all the time. I use it as a mantra when I meditate. To me it means we come to God with all the burdens of mind and body and ego, with all the ways life presses in on us. And the gift God gives us is the ability to experience the expansiveness of our own souls, the breath, the openness.

We all have the power to do this—to move from constriction to expansiveness.

Something can happen to you, a tragedy or a failure, or maybe someone was mean to you. And too often we forget that there is actually an expanse between that painful event and the way you respond to it. You can respond impulsively and get depressed, jealous, angry, hurt, or hopeless. You can say and do things you regret. Or you can enter an expansive place and come up with a more positive and measured response to that painful situation.

The soul is the force that dwells in that expanse, just as it is the presence that watches our minds spin out when we meditate. Its understanding of the events we experience is far more open and thoughtful than the knee-jerk response of the ego.

If we spend more time in our soul's expanse, we will see that we have more choices than we think about how we want to respond to life.

When you get good at entering the soul's expanse, you'll grow kinder to the people around you. You'll stop and breathe before saying something you'll regret. You'll choose another way to react to them—even when they are annoying you or arguing with you.

So what became of Beth and Eric, the bickering couple I was counseling just one week before their wedding? What did I say to them when it looked like they had forgotten how to love? I said, "Listen, we can talk about the sneakers in a little while. But first I need some information from you. Can you tell me how you first met?"

With that single question they were able to move from the narrow problem at hand and take in the breadth and depth of their connection.

At first there was only silence. Then Eric spoke. "I was at the Urth Caffé and my eyes landed on this beautiful creature just sitting there sipping coffee and reading a book. And I thought to myself, if I could just get up the nerve to talk to her and she smiles back at me, I'll be the luckiest guy in the world."

Beth laughed and said to me, "So he comes up to me and he smiles at me and there's a giant hunk of food caught between his two front teeth."

Now they both started laughing and suddenly Beth saw how red Converse high-tops actually kind of matched Eric's quirkiness, and that it wouldn't ruin the wedding if he wore them. It might actually give it warmth and flavor.

Next Eric said he was sorry he didn't back Beth up on the table-cloths, and he admitted that his mother has really bad taste. He said, "I know you want things to be beautiful. I so admire how you care about creating something special."

Before long their laughter mixed with tears and their hearts softened.

You know how Beth and Eric's story ends. It doesn't! Fifteen years have passed. They are happily married with two boys and a girl.

"I called to God from my narrowness, and God answered me with a vast expanse."

The truth is, most of our arguments are trivial stories. But we let them grow and take root and if we're not careful, they take over. Lean on the soul's expanse and you may very well begin to see people in their richness, to see what they mean to you, what their good qualities are.

The narrow mind sees only what's in front of it. The expansive view of the soul sees the answers to problems that have been plaguing us for a lifetime. The soul's expanse is revelation, it's prophecy, it's that "aha" moment when everything suddenly becomes clear and the path that eluded us suddenly opens up before us.

That's what happens to Hagar in the Bible. She and her son, Ishmael, are cast off and alone wandering through the desert and they run out of water. She is sure her son is going to die, so she puts him down by a bush because she can't bear to watch her baby perish. And then the Bible says, "God opened her eyes and she saw a well."

That was the miracle! Not the well, but the eyes to see what was right before her all along.

In the place of narrowness we assume we have no options. With the eyes of the soul, we realize we have so very many choices.

The same is true in our prayer lives. Sometimes in our narrowness we pray for crumbs: "God, if I could only have a little bit more of this." But imagine if we could capture a larger vision of what is possible. As Isaiah teaches, "Lift up your eyes and take a look around." See the world that needs you. See your blessings. See your potential to make a real impact. "Then you will see and you will shine." When you see with the eyes of your soul, you will begin to affect the world around you.

Does expansive vision mean that you can heal every relationship or fix every problem? No.

Actually, it is the expansive view of the soul that wakes you up to let you know there *is* a problem, or even that it's time to let go. That you've put up with too much for too long, and it's over. The job, the relationship. That you've settled for too long. That you've been denying and pretending for too long, and it's time to face the truth with open eyes and an open heart, ready to embrace new hope and new blessings.

It isn't easy to make the journey from narrowness to a vast expanse. But we all want to wake up from our sleepwalking. We all want to topple the barriers that are standing in the way of a full life.

There are steps you can take for widening your perspective and seeing with the eyes of the soul. Take one step toward the soul's expanse and it may cause a chain reaction.

It begins with the breath. Set aside time to be still. Focus on taking steady, slow, even breaths. Remember the soul is connected to the breath. Close your eyes. Begin silently repeating the verse: "I called to God from my narrowness, and God answered me with a vast expanse."

When you let more air into the system, when you make room for your soul's point of view, it may enter your emotions so that your reaction is no longer automatic. Perhaps your natural reflex is to get angry or defensive. But instead you may notice, *Huh, I'm not angry. I'm actually hurt.*

And as your emotions begin to open up so will your senses—you'll start seeing the world from your soul's perspective. It may travel to your eyes, and soon you'll be seeing things you've never noticed before. And then perhaps it will affect your ears, and you'll begin hearing things you've never heard before. And before long it will spread to your thoughts, and you'll start considering problems from new angles with new creativity and insight.

And then it may travel to your limbs—to your arms and legs. And you'll begin to open up and take people under your wing instead of competing with them. And you'll begin to influence people in new ways, understanding them in new ways.

I pray you will come to see that the soul's vast expanse is the path to true and lasting change. Maimonides, the great Jewish philosopher, taught in his Laws of Repentance that true change doesn't happen when you say you're sorry or ask for forgiveness from someone you've hurt. It doesn't happen even when you make up with someone. You don't earn trust by apologizing, you earn trust by changing. And change is only complete when you face the same condition that caused you to behave badly, but this time you choose differently. Same situation, but this time you think and reflect. This time you act differently. You sit there with your soul and you choose a new path.

Then you know you've changed. Then you know you're a different person.

We all have the power to claim the soulful, expansive version of ourselves. It's not a miracle, it's not a mystery. It's simply our willingness to see and act from our place of spaciousness.

"I called to God from my narrowness, and God answered me with a vast expanse." Yes.

> *May you break out of your narrow vision, your narrow arguments and resentments.*
> *May you enter the place where your soul dwells and respond with spaciousness to all that comes your way.*
> *May you forgive, repair, soften, see.*
> *May you open up. The gift of a great expanse is yours to have. It already resides within you.*
> *May God be with you.*
> *And may God work through you, now and always. Amen.*

15

Seeing Through the "Truths" We Tell Ourselves

ON THURSDAY NIGHT, JUNE 4, 2015, I was sitting beside my in-laws (we call them Grammy and Papa) looking on as my husband, Rob, delivered the commencement address to the graduating seniors of Daniel Pearl High School. Rob talked about a journalist's curiosity, about viewing all angles of a story and never taking anything at face value. We were so proud of him.

Afterwards the four of us went out to dinner, and then Rob and I drove home.

As we got close to our house I reminded Rob, "Honey, please don't park behind my car, because I have to leave early in the morning for Torah study, so don't block me in."

"No problem," he said. So we parked on the street and then we went to bed.

The next morning I was out the door at 7:15 a.m. for my Torah study. I looked . . . and my car wasn't in the driveway. I began wandering down my block asking myself, *Where's my car? Where did it go?* A car doesn't just vanish.

I called Rob on his cell and asked, "Did you move my car?"

"No," he said, "I didn't touch your car."

And then we both realized, "Oh my God, it's been stolen."

Rob told me, "You'd better call the police."

I was preparing for a Nashuva service that night, and all I wanted to do was have a day of study and peace and reflection, but I guess God had other plans for me. So I called the police to report my stolen car and the officer said, "Well what's the VIN number?"

I said, "I don't know, it's inside the car."

And right then I knew it was going to be a long day.

Later that afternoon, I did some serious meditating and I was able to find calm. I comforted myself that it was only a material possession. I was grateful that my family was healthy and safe. Thankfully, I had insurance, and I'd be able to get a loaner car until everything was all worked out.

That night as I was leading the Nashuva service I gave a sermon about my stolen car and feeling violated. I quoted the famous Yiddish proverb, "Man plans, God laughs."

The next day Rob informed all our neighbors to be on alert. I started to feel unsafe in our home. Rob called a security company to see how quickly we could install an alarm system. He went to Home Depot to buy motion sensor floodlights. I started looking into bids for building a six-foot fence around our property.

I began having visions about my car being full of heroin needles and crack vials. I imagined my car being totaled and stripped.

The next week I started thinking about what was inside the car. *What did I lose?*

I realized there were handwritten sermons in the car that would be lost forever because I'd never backed them up on a computer. And I had all the letters of my meditation students in the car. I always ask my students to write themselves a letter at the end of the course about what they've been learning from their meditations. I was just about to mail those letters.

The only meditation letter that was not in my car was the one I wrote to myself: "I really am learning to be more connected to my soul, to see and to hear and to be more present in the moment."

Three weeks passed. I still felt violated, I felt unsafe in my home. I mourned the things I would never see again that were inside my car. I imagined the crack vials and the heroin needles. And everywhere I went I found myself looking for my car. Every time I passed a blue Prius I stopped to look at the license plate to see if it was mine.

On Thursday, June 25, the insurance agent called to say everything had been processed and I was about to get covered for my loss.

Later that very day, I got a call from my niece Sari, who just moved into an apartment in a somewhat sketchy neighborhood in East LA near downtown.

She said, "Auntie Nomi, do you know what your license plate number for the Prius was? Was it 8CXC874?"

"Yes, that's my license. Sari, do you see my car?"

She shouted, "I found it."

"Where? In East LA?"

Sari said, "It's parked at Grammy and Papa's place in the guest parking lot."

I was totally confused. Did the thieves bring my car back?

And then it hit me—I must have left my car at Grammy and Papa's place and forgotten about it.

I started laughing so hard I was weeping and screaming in waves of laughter.

My son, Adi, heard me laughing and he came in to ask what was so funny, and I told him and he said, "Mom, from now on I've got a pass for life for doing dumb things. I may do irresponsible things every now and then, but you lost a twenty-thousand-dollar car?"

So Adi and I drove to my in-laws in my loaner car. We walked into their apartment and we were all laughing. I still couldn't remember when it was that I left my car there, but I knew one thing for sure:

it was no thief, it was me. I just left my car and forgot all about it. We started retracing the month, and then it hit me. I drove to Grammy and Papa's on the night when Rob spoke at the graduation. When he talked about curiosity and exploring all angles of a story! The three of us carpooled there.

Now I went to my car and looked inside. It was in perfect condition: no crack vials, no heroin needles, not a scratch on it. It hadn't been touched for three weeks. And then I found all my students' meditation letters. I suppose that meditation letter I wrote to myself wasn't exactly true. I wasn't very good at seeing and hearing and being present.

Now Rob came home. He pulled up behind my Prius, walked in the house, and said, "What happened?" He was completely confused.

I said, "It was in guest parking at your parents' place the whole time." Now there was a whole new wave of laughter and tears.

So obviously this was not a case of "Man plans and God laughs," this was a case of "Man forgets and God laughs and everyone laughs."

The strange part is, we both saw my car in our driveway on Thursday night, June 4. We both did.

There have been times when I've turned my house upside down because I lost a single earring. But I didn't even spend one second looking for my car or retracing my steps, because the narrative I had created was ironclad—Rob and I both saw my car in the driveway Thursday night.

So Rob called the police, because I couldn't be driving around town in a stolen vehicle. He dialed and said, "I'm calling to say that we've recovered our car, umm, it wasn't stolen, we just misplaced it."

The officer refused to take Rob's story at face value. They needed to come over and see what was going on.

So at around 11:00 p.m. two police officers showed up at our front door.

I was too embarrassed to speak to them, so Rob answered the door while I hid and listened in from our living room. Their conversation went like this:

The officer said, "What happened? How did you get your car back?"

Rob started telling the whole tale.

The officer said, "So who left the car at your parents'?"

Rob said, "My wife."

The officer said, "How did she forget?"

Suddenly I heard Rob call out to me: "Oh, NOMI."

"What?" I said sheepishly.

Rob said to the officer, "She's embarrassed."

Now I came out and met the two police officers. The officer said to me, "Help me get the facts. I've got to write this down. It's kind of hard to believe."

Rob said to him, "Has it ever happened that someone forgot their car?"

The officer said, "Nope, I've never heard a story like that before."

I said, "But, Officer, on that night we were so sure that we actually visually saw my car in the driveway."

The officer said, "Were you drunk that night?"

I said, "No. As sober as can be."

The officer was still in disbelief. He said, "So your car has been sitting at the parents' house for what? Three weeks? Since June fourth?"

I tried to explain. "Don't you see? It's all about the story you tell yourself."

Suddenly the officer's expression changed. His smile disappeared and he said, "Well, there have been times when, I mean, an officer sees something, he swears he saw a gun and he shoots and there was no gun."

Right then I began thinking about the power of the human mind to create facts that aren't true and to see things that don't even exist.

Forgetting my own car was a harmless mistake that led to laughter. But there are "truths" we tell ourselves that can cause great pain.

A NUMBER OF YEARS AGO, when I first became a rabbi, there was a man in his eighties named Izzy who used to come to synagogue every Sabbath. Izzy was a widower. He lived alone in a small apartment in Santa Monica. He was a quiet man who kept to himself, with a thick Yiddish accent that spoke of a world that is no more.

It was hard to get Izzy to chat or make small talk, but there was one subject that would light him up—his son, Howie. All I had to do was mention Howie, and Izzy's whole face would beam with pride.

Howie was an engineer living in Philadelphia, and I got the sense that he carried the unique burden of being the child of an immigrant.

And then one day Izzy died and Howie came in for the funeral. I sat with him in Izzy's small apartment comforting him and planning the service. Howie was holding Izzy's golden fountain pen. He told me the pen was precious to him and that he would be taking it with him.

He was quiet, just like his father.

And then Howie said to me, "Rabbi, my dad never loved me."

"What are you talking about?" I said. "You're the only thing Izzy ever spoke about."

Howie was trembling. He said, "Rabbi, I felt like I could never please him, like there was no way to live up to his expectations."

I thought about this for a moment. If Howie had come to me as a congregant and said to me, "Rabbi, my father never loved me," and I'd never met his father, maybe I would have validated Howie's reading of reality. Maybe I would have comforted him and said, "I'm so sorry you never got your father's love."

But I knew Howie's father and I knew I had a sacred responsibility, a holy charge to fill out this story. I wasn't there to deny Howie's experience. But I needed to testify to Howie about what I knew.

I told him, "Your dad may have been a flawed father, he may have been a difficult father, but there's one fact that I know, that's important for you to know. A fact that you must hear and accept: that man loved you with all his heart and soul."

Tears began streaming down Howie's cheeks. He was sobbing. I said to him, "Take it in. Take in Izzy's love. Your father is gone, but the love he had for you is undying. Take it with you together with that fountain pen, treasure it and trust in it."

Howie hugged me and said, "Thank you, thank you, I really needed to hear that."

There are truths we tell ourselves that just aren't true. You think you know something, somebody hurt you. Our minds play tricks on us. But we're here to see a bigger picture, the soul's wider perspective. We're here to ask ourselves, how else can I understand this person? How else can I read this situation?

We get so locked into what we think we know that we don't even give ourselves the chance to see what's really here.

And there are things we're sure we've lost that aren't really gone, they're just waiting there for us to reclaim them.

AARON WAS ONE OF RABBI Marcus's Buchenwald boys. He lived through hell and he lost everyone. After liberation he was placed in an orphanage in France. At first he hoped that a letter would arrive, a telegram, and he would find out that someone had survived, an aunt, an uncle, that someone was taking him home. But day after day when nothing arrived and no one came knocking, Aaron stopped hoping, stopped expecting and anticipating.

One day, after having lost all hope, Aaron got notice that his little brother Uri was alive and well in an orphanage in the Black Forest, Germany. He immediately packed a satchel and left in search of Uri.

After a week of travel, Aaron found Uri's orphanage. He was expecting a tearful reunion, the two brothers falling into each other's arms. But when Aaron ran toward Uri, Uri yelled at him, "You're not my brother. Go away. You're dead. Everybody's dead. You're not my brother."

Can you understand what was going on in the heart of this young boy? At the age of twelve, Uri had already made peace with the fact that he was alone in the world. And now here comes someone asking him to reopen his heart? Someone asking him to risk loss again? To risk getting abandoned again? He wasn't about to do that.

Does this sound like crazy behavior to you? I've seen many an adult incapable of intimacy because of this very same problem: *How do I let myself? How do I give anyone the power to hurt me again?* The pain of opening is real.

Well, Aaron wasn't about to leave Uri. When it was time for the children to go to bed, Aaron slept outside Uri's orphanage in a field under the stars. The next day, Aaron followed his little brother around silently like a duckling and Uri ignored him. At night Aaron once again slept outside in a field under the stars. He wasn't going away. He wasn't going anywhere.

This went on for an entire month. Uri going about his day, Aaron following him around silently.

And then one day as Aaron was following Uri around, Uri stopped and turned to him and said, "All right, you *are* my brother. I'm leaving soon for Israel. Come with me!"

A month later two orphan boys boarded a ship together for the Land of Israel.

THERE ARE THINGS WE'RE SURE we've lost that aren't gone. They're waiting for us to find them and reclaim them.

Is there something you're sure you've lost that might actually be waiting for you?

Perhaps it's a relationship you've given up on. Perhaps it's a dream you let go of. Perhaps it's your faith. Perhaps it's your true self that's gotten lost.

The soul within you is here to help you remember, to help you find what you've been missing.

Sometimes you may feel abandoned by God, lost and alone, but God hasn't forgotten about you. God has been following you around silently, watching over you morning and night.

There's a line in the Talmud that always haunts me. It says, "I am searching for something I have not lost." *Searching for something I have not lost.*

There's something you've given up on that you haven't lost. Maybe it's yourself. When we lose hope we believe the worst stories our minds can conjure up for us, but they're not necessarily true.

Your soul is here to light up your way and show you what you've misplaced in the darkness.

I keep thinking of my grandfather, who was always asking me, "Nechumaleh, where are my glasses? Help me find my glasses!" I'd say, "Zaydie, they're right on top of your head!" And we'd both laugh.

Searching for something I have not lost.

There's so much you've been given. So much goodness, so much strength. So much talent and vision and hope and faith. And perseverance. And sometimes we forget what we've been given.

You are here to reclaim what's yours.

And you don't need to file a police report to get it back, because nobody can steal it from you. Your blessings are here, aching to be noticed. Your gifts are here, hoping you will use them. Love is waiting for you. Abundance too and healing and joy. And God is with you, on your side.

May a time of sweetness open up to greet you, saying, Welcome home.

Glimpsing the Tapestry

DETECTING HIDDEN CONNECTIONS

ONE TUESDAY NIGHT IN October 2015 I was teaching the *husa* meditation to my beginner students. I offered them the metaphor of the lopsided pot holder and the mother who proudly hangs it on the fridge. We talked about what it means to love without judgment, to treasure something with all its imperfections. To see the beauty in the flaws, to stand in awe of the fragile, broken people we all are. That class was a night of deep compassion and opening.

But the truth is, I had been feeling frustrated for many weeks. Rabbi Marcus had been on my mind and appearing in my dreams. I had been imagining Rabbi Marcus's pain, his heartbreak, his crisis of faith, the depth of his loss. What was Einstein responding to when he wrote those words that spoke so deeply to me?

When I got back home that night I said to myself, "*Husa*, be patient, this will all come together." And then I placed an order from a catalog.

A few days later my husband, Rob, said, "Nomi, we got a strange package in the mail that must have been sent to us by accident. It's some kind of kindergarten art project."

I laughed. "No, it's mine." He looked puzzled.

I opened the package and began weaving the colorful loops together on the metal loom frame—over, under, over, under. I thought I'd be better at it as an adult than I was as a child, but I was mistaken. I made my very own lopsided pot holder, beautiful in all its imperfection.

I hung my beautiful colorful imperfect pot holder beside the copy of Einstein's letter on my study wall.

I thought about Rabbi Marcus's letter and *husa* and I whispered, "Somehow I will weave together all these loose threads into a single tapestry."

One week later I was reading the *New York Times* and I saw an article about a U.S. soldier during World War II named Alan Golub, who discovered Hungarian Jewish teenage girls dressed in nothing but rags after liberation in a German city called Eschwege. They'd been enslaved and starved in a German labor camp. Alan went to buy fabric for the girls, but the store owner refused so he raised his pistol and convinced the shopkeeper to cooperate.

The girls sewed lovely dresses from this fabric. It was the first clothing they'd worn in so very long. They were twenty-three girls all in the exact same dress made by their own hands, and someone snapped a photo of them, posing and smiling.

Seventy years later, the *New York Times* recounted the tale and reported on the day when three surviving girls from that photo were reunited with the man who secured the fabric to restore their dignity.

I looked at the photo published in the *Times* of the girls in their identical dresses, and who should be standing in the center of the photo, surrounded by all the girls? Rabbi Robert Marcus.

I couldn't believe my eyes. My heart was racing. I quickly called Eve Kahn, the reporter from the *Times*, to ask if any of the women remembered the man in the center of their group photo. Eve gave me some leads.

The next morning, Ibolya Markowitz answered the phone with a thick accent and a grandmotherly warmth. I said, "Ibolya, do you remember Rabbi Marcus, the man standing in the center of the photo with you and all the girls?"

Ibolya laughed. "That was a long time ago. I remember everything, Mamaleh. I felt so close to him."

I asked, "Ibolya, what do you remember?"

She said, "I see that day perfectly clearly. It's hard to talk about it, Mamaleh. I was so close to him. I didn't see his face in a long time."

I said, "Rabbi Marcus died in 1951, but you remember his kindness?"

"Things like that you can't forget," she said. "He was very special. He would check on us. If we had everything we needed. He came to see us. He would talk to us. We were loving him."

"Ibolya, do you perhaps know about a letter Rabbi Marcus wrote to Einstein?"

"No, Mamaleh."

Ibolya was tired. Her caretaker was helping her. She said, "Be well, Mamaleh, God be with you." And we hung up.

I tried to reach other women from the photo. Most of the women are deceased, and some of the living suffer from mental confusion or are too weak and infirm to speak. But Eve, the reporter from the *Times*, connected me to a woman named Laurie Goldsmith-Heitner. Laurie's father, Karl, was the U.S. soldier placed as military governor of Eschwege after liberation. Perhaps he might have known Rabbi Marcus.

I called Laurie to ask. Laurie said her father was deceased, but she would check his papers and see if there was any mention of Rabbi Marcus.

Then Laurie asked me, "Tell me, how did you become interested in this Rabbi Marcus?"

I said, "It's a strange story. Actually, it was an accident. I was inspired by a statement made by Albert Einstein about the universe, and it led me on a journey to Rabbi Marcus.

Laurie became animated. She said, "I've got shivers down my spine. There are tears in my eyes."

"Why?" I asked.

Laurie said, "Rabbi, I know you called to ask me about my father, but now that you've brought up Einstein I have to tell you that my mother lived in Einstein's house when she was a child."

"What?" I was stunned by the way all these pieces were intersecting.

Laurie explained, "Einstein built his dream home in a place called Caputh in Germany by the water in 1929."

I knew about the summer cottage in Caputh. Einstein loved to escape into his thoughts there, it was a place where he could daydream and contemplate the workings of the universe. He kept a boat there too that his friends had given him for his fiftieth birthday. Einstein would sail off alone, and let the boat take him where it wanted to go. He wrote eloquently about the perfect life he experienced in Caputh: "The sailboat, the sweeping view, the solitary walks, the relative quiet—it is paradise." In Caputh, Einstein ruminated over his famous Unified Field Theory, the theory he was never able to solve.

Perhaps it was the scenic beauty of the home by the lake that inspired Einstein to pen "What I Believe" in Caputh. It was an essay where he articulated the foundations of his faith:

> The most beautiful emotion we can experience is the mysterious. It is the fundamental emotion that stands at the cradle of all true art and science. He to whom this emotion is a stranger, who can no longer wonder and stand rapt in awe, is as good as dead, a snuffed out candle. To sense that behind anything that can be experienced there is something that our minds cannot grasp, whose beauty and

sublimity reaches us only indirectly: this is religiousness. In this sense, and in this sense only, I am a devoutly religious man.

By 1932 the climate in Germany grew ominous for all Jews. Einstein sensed the danger that lay ahead. On the eve of a three-month trip to the United States, where Einstein would be lecturing at Caltech, he surveyed the home he treasured and told his wife, Elsa, "Take a very good look at it. You will never see it again." His words proved to be prophetic. In early 1933 Hitler became chancellor of Germany and Einstein wrote to a friend, "Because of Hitler I don't dare step on German soil."

I asked Laurie, "How does your mother fit into all of this?"

Laurie told me that Einstein's home in Caputh was right next to a little boarding school for Jewish children. In the early 1930s Jewish parents were looking for places to send their children to be safe when Hitler rose to power. She said the boarding school became a haven for kids before they could get safe transport to England or Switzerland.

Laurie told me that before his departure from Caputh, Einstein told Gertrud Feiertag, the headmistress of the boarding school, "In my absence you can use the house for the students." Laurie said, "At ten years of age my mother, Marianne, was sent by her parents to Caputh to be safe. For six months she lived in the Einstein house."

Not long after his departure from Caputh, the Nazis raided Einstein's home and they seized his treasured sailboat as well. Many of the children would not make it to safety. In 1938, in the wake of Kristallnacht, the children were rounded up and sent to their deaths. Their headmistress, Gertrud Feiertag, was murdered in Auschwitz as well. Einstein's beloved home became a dormitory for the Hitler Youth.

Once again Einstein and Rabbi Marcus were mysteriously intersecting and getting intertwined in my soul. I looked at the pot holder on my wall: over, under, over, under.

Once again I realized I had pulled on a thread that bridged many worlds—the living and the dead, science and religion, the finite and the infinite, the mind and the soul.

So many threads. How would I weave them all together?

I would need to be patient. Like Einstein on his sailboat, I would let the unfolding story take me where it wanted to go.

Just then I cracked open a book on my desk and my eyes fell upon these words spoken by Einstein: "Life is a great tapestry. The individual is only an insignificant thread in an immense and miraculous pattern."

Yes.

May you begin to have glimpses of magical threads of connection. May those precious flashes of insight light up your way and all your days. Amen.

DISCOVERING THE POWER TO ACT

"The striving to free oneself from this delusion is the one issue of true religion."
—from Einstein's letter to Rabbi Marcus

Freedom isn't only a state of mind, it is a change in behavior. Our thoughts can keep us paralyzed, but even when we heal our thoughts we are not truly free until we begin to act. The Life Force, that blue light of the flame within the soul, can fire us up and get us moving. Remember, as much as the body needs the soul, the soul needs the body.

The great theologian and activist Rabbi Abraham Joshua Heschel explained the power of this sacred interdependence: "The body without the spirit is a corpse; the spirit without the body is a ghost." That's why when Heschel returned home after marching with Dr. Martin Luther King, Jr., in Selma, Alabama, he wrote, "Our legs uttered songs. Even without words, our march was worship. I felt my legs were praying."

Your dreams and prayers arise from the soul, but the soul needs the body to act in order to fulfill those very longings. Transformation comes when you unite intention with action.

Breaking Free of Old, Familiar Patterns

TWO YEARS AGO I WAS at one of those Hollywood parties where people mingle and look over your head as they're speaking to you, to see if there's someone more important they can meet. I found myself standing next to a psychologist, and I asked him about his work. Perhaps he'd had too much to drink, because he blurted out, "People don't really change. They might make some minor adjustments here or there, but trust me, people don't change." I don't think the psychologist expected to have a real conversation with me in the middle of this posh affair with champagne flowing and music playing.

I said, "But I've seen it with my own eyes." I told him I was a rabbi and I went on, "I've seen alcoholics who stopped drinking. I've seen people in midlife crises go back to school and change careers. I've seen people who have overcome destructive habits that plagued them. I've seen people find their way back to life from grief, from trauma, from abuse, from rape. I've seen people battle illness with a strength they never knew was inside them."

I started to feel sorry for this therapist who had grown so cynical. Of course, I felt worse for his patients.

The therapist broke the silence and said, "Rabbi, do you think you could counsel me?"

I gave him my e-mail address and told him I was happy to meet with him. I wish I could tell you that we met and had a series of deep conversations. But we met by chance at a superficial cocktail party and I never heard from him again.

Although I had made bold claims to the cynical therapist, there was a part of me that was shaken by his remarks. Are we really capable of change? Many of us continue to struggle with the same problems we've been struggling with for years. Or we make strides toward a new path but then fall back into our old, familiar patterns.

In the realm of change, I believe we live between two poles: SOS and SOS. The first SOS is the dire one, "Save Our Ship." We're going down. A true SOS is fertile ground for change. You get to a place where you can finally hear your soul cry, "You have to change or you will die." It can take a pretty big tailspin before we open our eyes to the truth.

A far more difficult place to change from is the second SOS: "Same Old Stuff."

What about those of us who never hit bottom? Those of us who have gotten used to squeaking by with our self-defeating ways. With patterns that bother us, but they're not killing us. Our temper, our disorganization, our procrastination, our envy, that weight we keep meaning to lose, our impatience, our laziness, our desire . . .

We can spend our entire lives deaf to our soul's voice calling out to us. And without that moment of truth, there's very little impetus for change.

How do we move from Same Old Stuff to a place of truth that will lead to real and lasting change?

Time and timing are crucial to our ascent.

One key to forward motion lies in our ability to see time through the eyes of our soul. The soul's understanding of time is quite different from the ego's. The eternal soul knows how brief its stay in the material world is. From the soul's perspective, every moment we spend repeating an old destructive pattern *is* a dire SOS. The soul sees the grains of sand slipping through life's hourglass. The soul is saying to us every day, "Can't you see how little time there is? If you could only see how your Same Old Stuff is killing you."

The soul wants us to feel the brevity of it all, the beauty. It wants us to behold each day, each minute, as a precious gift that we should not waste.

With the soul's help we can learn to raise the gravity of Same Old Stuff to the level of a true SOS.

ONE WAY TO TURN OUR Same Old Stuff into a path toward change is by raising the flame of urgency. But there is another way to break out of our predictable patterns. It has to do with our ability to recognize and seize openings when they present themselves to us.

There are openings available to us every day that can help us cut to the truth, openings that can help us break through our sleepwalking. Times when we can interrupt the desire cycle: "I want it, I want it." These times are your SOS if you can learn to see them and welcome them.

Sometimes something breaks through to you. It may be an unexpected feeling of ease or even holiness while you are simply enjoying a moment with a loved one. Or it may be the power of the words you read or a melody you hear, the power of being at one with nature, the power of praying in community, the power of a teaching, the advice someone gave you long ago. Suddenly the lesson you need to hear isn't just washing over you—it hits you deeply.

It's not a scary moment or a dire moment. It's a hopeful feeling, a time when you can sense new possibility. When you are quiet enough to really hear your soul showing you the way.

The rabbis describe these times as moments of grace. In Hebrew this opening is called *Et Ratzon*, a time of wanting and being wanted, when your longing is met by a divine longing. It is a spiritual time when doors that are normally locked are open. A time when we're given the vision to see our lives through a wider lens, to hold things in perspective. To see the truth we've been hiding from. It's a time when opposite poles fall into alignment. When the human desire to reach upward is met with the divine desire to reach out. When the soul's desire to repair the world is met with the body's desire to act. When the nagging pain of Same Old Stuff is released before our eyes.

With the soul's help we can learn how to preserve those openings.

A moment of grace can evaporate like mist or it can lead to lasting change. That depends on our willingness to stay with it and to honor it. Instead of letting a precious moment become a memory, we can learn to protect it, and to allow it to live on inside us.

In Hasidic thought a verse from Song of Songs becomes the key to retaining the wisdom gained by a momentary opening. The lover in Song of Songs says, "I held him close and would not let him go." That's how we can approach a moment of grace. Hold on to it for dear life and don't let it slip away. Notice it, welcome it, allow it to leave a lasting imprint on your life so that it becomes, in the words of Song of Songs, "a seal upon your heart."

Yes, I believe with all my heart that we are changeable! You may not be able to change your biography or your biology, but you can change your destiny.

Recently I had the honor of interviewing Dr. Kip Thorne, one of the most brilliant physicists alive today, in his office at Caltech. I was asking him to explain to me what Einstein meant when he spoke of "the whole" we're all part of. Kip said to me: "Rabbi, you may see yourself as a static, separate entity, but there isn't a single cell in your body that's the same as when you were born."

Everything is constantly being reborn, renewed, and replaced.

Of course, change does not happen overnight, but allow your long-ings to detect sacred openings to sit with you. Allow them to lie with you and to wake with you. Let a desire to see through your soul's eyes seep into your days and into your dreams as well.

May you notice not only more openings around you, but more room inside you. Room for magic.

May your Same Old Stuff give way to true and lasting trans-formation. Amen.

18

Pregnant Forever

FINDING THE COURAGE TO COMPLETE WHAT YOU'VE BEGUN

ON ROSH HASHANAH, the Jewish New Year, Jews recite a phrase in Hebrew over and over again: "*Hayóm harat olam.*" It's usually translated as "Today the world is born." It sounds like a very joyous phrase.

Not so fast. There is more to the story. The truth is, I never took the time to think about what those words meant. I recently learned from a teacher of mine, Dr. Tamar Frankiel, the true context and meaning of the phrase "Today the world is born."

It's actually a phrase that was spoken by the prophet Jeremiah in a moment of utter despair. Jeremiah spent his career offering the word of God to the Jewish people. Jeremiah pleaded with them to change their ways and stop the corruption, the sins, the materialism, the empty rituals and the shallow prayers. Did they listen to him? No.

Instead they scorned him and ignored him. Jeremiah became dejected. He was sick of being a prophet who never got heard. He wished he had never been born. "Cursed be the day I was born," he said. And then he added, "If only my mother had not given birth to me. If only her womb was pregnant forever."

If only my mother was pregnant forever.

These are the words Jews recite so joyously in their prayers. The true translation of the Hebrew phrase is not "Today the world is born," but "Today is pregnant forever." That is not a happy phrase. It feels more like a curse. What exactly does that mean, "Today is pregnant forever?"

When I learned the actual meaning of Jeremiah's words, *Today is pregnant forever*, I suddenly flashed on a memory of myself being nine months pregnant and holding my dear friend Helene's newborn baby in my lap. Let me explain.

Helene is from Brooklyn, I'm from Brooklyn. Helene went to Yeshiva of Flatbush high school, I went there too. She was very close to my older brother David when I was growing up, but then we lost touch.

Years later Helene and her husband, Rich, were visiting Israel, and she decided to look up her old friend David, who lives in Israel. They began catching up and David said, "Hey, by the way, you went to Cornell? Guess what? My little sister Nomi went to Cornell too." Later, when David learned that Helene had moved to LA, he laughed and said, "Guess what? My sister Nomi moved to LA too, and she's a rabbi there."

Helene was amazed at how closely our lives had paralleled each other—well, except for the minor detail that she went to medical school and I went to rabbinical school. But we're both in the healing professions.

The next thing I knew, Helene came to one of my prayer services and we reconnected. It was such a comfort to know someone in LA who shared so much history with me.

One day I called Helene and she said, "Nomi, how are you doing?"

I said, "To tell you the truth, I am really nauseous, but it's for a good reason—I'm pregnant!"

She laughed. "Guess what? I'm pregnant too!" We both started laughing.

Month after month we compared stories, and month after month we grew bigger together and shared dreams and prayers and anticipation.

Helene was due two weeks before me in July, and on July 2 she gave birth to a beautiful baby boy whom they named Michael. A couple of days later I went over to visit her. She looked so happy, so natural, like she was born to be a mother. I looked like a Butterball turkey. I was huge and I was ready to pop. All of a sudden Helene put her newborn son on my pregnant lap. And I freaked out! I know I was smiling on the outside, but there was just no way in the world to cover up my panic.

Here's what was going on inside of me: "Oh my God! What was I thinking? I don't want this. I don't want a baby. I'm not ready to be a mother. I don't even like babies! My life is fine as it is. Please make it stop right here, right now. If only I could just be . . . *Pregnant forever.*"

Trust me, pregnant forever is not a healthy state of mind. It is a state of a permanent un-living, of life being held back. I think Jews pray this phrase every New Year because it comes as a warning.

Every single one of us, somewhere in our lives, we are pregnant forever. There is something we've already conceived that is pleading with us, "Let me be born." Maybe it's a creative endeavor—a book, a painting, a poem, a song, a script, a story, a business idea. Maybe it's a career shift. You've been privately dreaming about it and exploring it, but doing nothing about it. Maybe it's the words "I'm sorry," or the words "I love you," or the words "I forgive you." They are fully formed inside your mouth, but you haven't gotten up the courage to actually speak them.

Pregnant forever is not a blessing, and so many of us suffer from this frustrating affliction.

Maybe it's a departure you're holding on to, a breakup. You know it's time to go. You know it's time to stop pretending everything is fine when nothing is fine.

Maybe you've already created something but you're just too scared to let it be seen.

Scott Tansey is a man who has been attending Nashuva, the spiritual community I founded, for several years. Soon after meeting me Scott offered to volunteer his time to take photographs of our events. At every Nashuva event Scott was there, snapping photo after photo.

Scott has been passionate about photography since he was a child, and he has always been particularly drawn to taking panoramas. He told me, "Rabbi, I like the wide view of things." Scott started to take his photography seriously when he was in his twenties. Even though Scott has a non-Parkinson's tremor in his right arm, he's always found a way to steady his hand just at the right moment. He's never let his tremor get in the way of his love.

For forty years Scott shot thousands of photos, breathtaking panoramas all over the world: glaciers, mountain peaks, seascapes, cityscapes, sunrises, clouds, sunsets, rainbows. For forty years Scott shot some twenty thousand photos. And he never printed a single one of them. Not one. What held him back? He told me he just didn't have confidence. He was full of anxiety and worried about the judgments of others. But there was also a deeper reason why Scott was full of anxiety.

When Scott was only six years old, his father was killed in a plane crash. This trauma left him feeling a generalized sense of fear that he's carried with him throughout his whole life. He said a feeling that something awful could happen at any moment got seared into his soul. He figured, if the thing you love most can suddenly get taken away, perhaps it was better to keep his photos to himself. So Scott kept taking more and more photos and never printing them.

"I just couldn't," he said. "I wasn't able to push myself out or show my talent."

In 2012 Scott gathered up the courage to take a printing workshop. There he learned all about the skill and the power of printing. Then a quote by the great photographer Ansel Adams got stuck in his mind: "The negative is comparable to the composer's score and the print to his performance." Scott realized he was holding on to his scores and never giving a performance.

That year, in 2012, Scott was sitting at services when I happened to give a sermon about overcoming our fear and reaching our potential. Something in that sermon broke through Scott's defenses and resonated deeply in his soul. That day Scott told himself, "No more excuses." I suppose you could say it was a moment of grace.

A few days later Scott told himself, "Okay, I've got to give Rabbi Levy a print. I want to give her a token of my appreciation." So Scott printed a photo he had shot several months earlier of my husband, Rob, and my two kids, Adi and Noa, and he handed it to me.

What a breathtaking photo! It was taken on the beach. It was so alive. Scott had captured a moment of pure happiness.

It was the very first photo Scott ever printed. Suddenly, a spell was broken. Scott realized it wasn't hard to bring his images into the light of day. Soon people started taking note. Scott's work was featured in two galleries in LA. Recently he had a show at the Leica Gallery, which I attended. I'm sure Ansel Adams would have been proud. Scott's landscapes stretched across every wall—it was a masterful performance indeed. I was considering purchasing one of his pieces, and then I saw that his panoramas were selling for ten thousand dollars apiece.

When I asked Scott what lessons he'd learned by sharing his private art form with others, he said, "Rabbi, I realize I have a gift, and all I need to do is just be me." Then he added, "God gives you gifts. Use them. Don't be ashamed. I'm sixty-one years old. It's okay if others don't like my work. My work's okay. I'm okay."

For forty years Scott captured such beauty, now he's giving it a life, a way to light up the world.

What is keeping you permanently pregnant? What is it that holds you back? For some of us it's a fear of judgment. For others it is a fear of the judge within, that familiar voice that says, "This is no good. I've got no talent." For some of us it's a fear of responsibility: "I'm not ready to take this on. I'm not ready to make this shift." For some of us it is the ego's hubris that keeps us permanently pregnant: "I've got all the time in the world to make this happen. I can do this tomorrow." For some of us it's the body's inertia, a lack of will.

Some of us are pregnant forever because we're comfortable being pregnant forever. We like the current routine, it's easier to live with the status quo than it is to make a change. And that's where Jeremiah comes in with his haunting phrase: today is pregnant forever. It echoes the soul's voice beckoning us to journey forward and rise up.

So many voices stop us up, but the soul's voice cheers us on. Why? Because the soul can't fulfill its mission alone. It needs us to act. The soul is intimately familiar with the world of potential. It descended to this realm so that it could know the meaning of the word "fulfillment."

Today is pregnant forever! And you are the one who gets to choose what will remain in a state of eternal potential and what will break forth into life.

You've been blessed with the potential to improve this world, but nothing will come of your remarkable gifts unless you first learn to turn your potential into action.

So take a moment right now, and hear your soul asking you, "What am I holding on to right now that I need to give life to?" Can you see it? Can you see what you are pregnant forever with?

We are not doomed to remain stuck forever. There are ways we can strengthen our resolve to act.

I'd like to offer you five tools that can help you move from potential to action:

Pray. Simply talk to God about your longings. Ask for the strength to break through, and listen for an answer.

Talk to others. Opening up to family and friends or a trusted mentor may release a burden from your soul and may be a terrific motivator to act. Tell the people you love what you've been sitting on and not hatching. Ask for their help. Ask for a pep talk.

Honesty is another critical factor. Look at your life and see the places you've left in suspended animation. Take the time to come face-to-face with your unfulfilled potential.

Listening and seeing are pivotal factors on your path. Be receptive to those moments of grace—to words that might resuscitate your momentum—an article in the newspaper, a book, a movie. Listen to the voice of your soul rooting for you to take even one step forward.

This final suggestion is perhaps the hardest of all: **feel the pain.** We must do something most of us spend our lives trying to resist—we must seek to feel discomfort. As we talked about earlier, we have the power to raise the flame of our urgency, to turn Same Old Stuff into a true SOS. Yes, sometimes it's your drive and your courage that get you going. But more often, things as they are have to get painful enough so that you can't live in a state of permanent pregnancy anymore. You just can't! We become aware of a deep aching within our souls, a knowledge that we are living well beneath our own potential. And once we allow ourselves to experience that pain, it gets to be too much to hold back the change that needs to come.

TWO WEEKS AFTER MY FRIEND Helene gave birth, I was so uncomfortable. I was so big, I was congested, I had heartburn, I couldn't find a comfortable place to sit or stand or sleep or eat. Suddenly, I couldn't wait to get that baby out of me and into the world. Ironically, the baby changed its mind. It decided it wasn't ready to come out. I was ten days overdue. So I jumped up and down, I jogged, I ran—nothing. I even went to a restaurant that had been written up in the *L.A. Times.* The article said that their balsamic vinaigrette salad had the power to cause pregnant women to go straight into labor. Well, after reading that article my husband, Rob, and I rushed over to the restaurant, and when we got there we saw that the entire restaurant was full of miserable overdue pregnant women. We sat down and the waiter came up to our table and said, "Let me guess, you'd like the balsamic salad?" I ate that salad—no baby.

Finally I had to be induced. And a beautiful blessed little baby boy entered this world. Our son, Adi, is twenty-three years old now. And not a single day goes by when I wish I could just have stayed pregnant forever.

May you come to see what is inside you waiting to be born. Today is pregnant forever. But you have the power to give it life. Break through, break free. Today is the day you get to decide what will live only in your dreams and what will be born and light up the world.

May you choose life. Amen.

LISTENING TO THE LOVE FORCE

The Key to Intimacy and Uncovering Your Calling

As we grow in Life Force and acquire wider vision, greater freedom, and the power to act, we prepare to welcome the Love Force, the second layer of soul called Ruach, the yellow light within a flame. Ruach's domain is wisdom of the heart, the realm of emotion and particularly love. Listen to the Love Force. It is the Love Force that helps us let down our defenses so that we can experience intimacy. It is also the aspect of soul that opens us to our calling. The Infinite One is knocking not only from the place of eternity, but from within us too. It is Ruach that helps you uncover the mission your soul has come here to fulfill.

LEARNING TO LOVE DEEPLY

"He experiences himself, his thoughts and feelings
as something separated from the rest . . ."
—from Einstein's letter to Rabbi Marcus

The Love Force plays a critical role in the realm of emotion. It teaches us how to melt a heart that a lifetime of hurt has turned to stone, and how to find the power to forgive those who have caused us pain. It is Ruach that enables us to be a true friend and a true partner in love. And it is this same Love Force that gives us the power to parent with soul, to offer a love that is pure and unconditional.

19

Turning a Heart of Stone into a Heart of Flesh

IT NEVER FAILS. EVERY YEAR, just as the Jewish High Holy Days approach, I have an anxiety dream. This year was no different. Here was my dream:

I find myself on vacation in a beautiful camp setting together with a large group of people. It's woodsy and peaceful. I must be on a retreat. At night we're all sitting around in a circle in a wooden cabin, and it instantly becomes clear to me that everyone around me is looking at me, expecting me to speak. I don't. Then somebody asks me, "So, Rabbi, what's Yom Kippur really all about? What's the true essence of the day?"

I look out at the people. I'm about to answer, but my mind goes blank. Completely blank! There's nothing in my head. It's as if I've never thought about this question before. As if I don't know a thing about Yom Kippur. I'm flustered. I have absolutely no idea what to say. And then I open my mouth and words start coming out all by themselves. The words don't really belong to me.

I hear myself say to the group gathered around me:

Yom Kippur comes down to just two themes: First: "And I will remove your heart of stone and I will give you a heart of flesh."

And second . . . I can see all the people leaning forward waiting expectantly for the second theme. I'm also curious to hear what will come out of my mouth next. I say, *And second: "And I will remove your heart of stone and I will give you a heart of flesh."*

And then I woke up.

Such a strange dream. I couldn't stop thinking about it. In my waking life I would never have answered the question that way. I would have talked about looking inward and making changes. I would not have just quoted a verse from the Book of Ezekiel, chapter 36, verse 26. Also I wondered why I said there were two themes, but all I did was quote the same exact verse twice.

This is what I came to understand about my dream. I realize that everything we hope and pray for in life really does boil down to turning a heart of stone into a heart of flesh. There's no possibility for intimacy, no hope for change, no chance for forgiveness if your heart is a stone.

But I still couldn't figure out why I said that Yom Kippur comes down to two themes when I only offered one. And then I realized: there really are two themes embedded in the words I spoke. First, you have to remove your heart of stone, which is a remarkably difficult and delicate undertaking. And then you have to acquire a heart of flesh, which is an art form all its own.

What is a heart of flesh? And what is a heart of stone? How does a heart of flesh turn to stone? And what does a day of fasting have to do with any of this?

According to Jewish mystics, the source of love is not the heart. The source of love is the second level of our souls, called Ruach, the Love Force. It is this higher level of soul that awakens the heart to give and receive love. Love happens when heart and soul work together in harmony. If the heart becomes frozen, the loving soul has no way of expressing itself or connecting to other souls or to God. Without the ability to take in and share love, the soul becomes weakened and parched.

What does the connection between heart and soul have to do with Yom Kippur?

On the eve of Yom Kippur, Jews recite a prayer called Kol Nidrei, which is a prayer that annuls vows. The prayer says, "May our vows not be vows. May our oaths not be oaths." Why would Judaism let people off the hook so easily? Is it possible that the prayer is actually saying, "It's no big deal. You don't have to keep your promises. Your word doesn't really matter"? I don't think so.

We all start life off with an open, curious, loving heart, and then inevitably we get hurt. Life can be cruel. Someone lets you down, someone shames you, betrays you, someone breaks your heart, someone abandons you, God does not answer your prayers. So we start making vows. We all know the vows: *I'll never get fooled like that again. I'll never talk to him again. I'll never forgive her for what she did to me. I'll never put myself on the line like that again.* And there are vows that we make about God too: *I'll never pray again.*

These vows we make, we take them to heart. We take them into our hearts and slowly, day by day, year by year, that open, curious heart of ours turns to stone. It makes sense, doesn't it? Who wants to get hurt like that again?

Of course, there is only one problem with our plan. The heart of stone isn't just armor that protects us from incoming attacks. It also makes us less receptive to incoming love and surprise and blessings. And the heart of stone prevents all the goodness inside our souls—all that love and forgiveness and joy and spontaneity and romance—from ever getting out.

We become cautious, controlling, judgmental, cynical, and rigid. We find ourselves living within a very carefully defined range of emotions: happy/sad, interested/bored. But your soul is capable, your soul is aching to experience its full range of emotions. And that's why I believe Jews recite the Kol Nidrei prayer each year. They come together to annul those vows we made that have caused our hearts to constrict. "May our vows not be vows. May our oaths not be oaths."

When I think about the scene in my dream and the words I spoke, I can't help but wonder: Why was that dream given to me? What was my soul trying to say to me? What is it that I need to learn? The truth is, I think I dreamed that dream with the verse from Ezekiel because I know about hearts of stone. I've lived it from the inside.

My father's murder was an earthquake that upended my life. Just a day before, I was a happy teenage girl, a curious, fun-loving kid, living in an amazing family. And then my world was shattered and I learned too soon what it was like to have a heart of stone. I was filled with anger.

I hated myself for being weak and vulnerable. I hated my mother for not being strong for me. I hated my father for abandoning me. I hated my friends for having trivial concerns about hairdos and parties. I hated the Sabbath and all the holidays for reminding me of beautiful days that were dead now. I hated the prayers with all their false promises about all the great things God does. *Really? Where was God?* I hated God for doing nothing.

This is the vow I made when I was fifteen: "I'm on my own now. I don't need anyone."

There was a storm raging inside of me. But outside my goal was to be normal. That's the dream of every high school kid: *I'm fine, I'm okay, I'm perfect. I'm a straight-A student. Just don't pity me. Just don't get too close. Just don't make me have to feel anything.*

Then one afternoon when I was in high school the loudspeaker came on in the middle of class. "Naomi Levy! Attention, Naomi Levy, please report to the school psychologist's office." I was so humiliated. Someone in my school decided for me that I needed to see the school psychologist against my will? And they blasted it through my entire high school? I could see my classmates' eyes on me. *That's the girl with the murdered father.*

I tried not to look around. I got up and made my way to the school psychologist's office. The sign on the door said her name was Mrs. Schwartz. When I walked in I saw that she was Hasidic—with long sleeves and a long skirt and a wig. *Great!* I thought.

I sat down and involuntarily I put my hand over my mouth. I was so angry and upset and there was no way in the world that I was going to talk to this woman. I was sure she was going to say, "Tell me about your father," or "How is it going at home with Mom?" or "How are you feeling?"

I knew I wasn't going to give an inch to this woman. But my eyes were welling up. They were betraying me. I was using every ounce of my being just to hold it together, and I could tell she saw the explosion I was holding back, the storm inside me that was taking every bit of my energy to contain.

She said, "It's okay. You don't have to say anything to me. You don't have to ever see me again." And then she said, "Hey, do you want me to teach you some tools to stop you from crying? I can teach you how not to cry."

Her response to me was so unexpected. She wasn't going to try to puncture my wall. She was saying, "I can help you hold up that wall." She was saying she was on my side. She was showing me I was seen and understood. And even though I had made a vow, *I'm on my own now,* she was telling me I wasn't on my own.

When I stood up to leave, she said to me, "One day when you're ready the tears will come. And trust me, you will welcome them."

A year later, on the first anniversary of my father's murder, I was sixteen and I was on my very first trip to Israel with all of my camp friends. We went to visit the Kotel, the Western Wall in Jerusalem. I walked up to the wall and at first I just touched the ancient stones. Then I got closer and closer and I smelled it.

I smelled the Kotel. And the Kotel smelled like my father. It didn't smell just a little like my dad, it smelled like my father's armpit!

There I stood, eyes closed, with both of my arms outstretched, leaning against the wall so hard that I couldn't tell anymore if I was standing up or lying down. Just lying there with my nose in my father's armpit. And I began sobbing. The wall melted.

And I knew in my heart I had a father who would never leave me. And I had a mother who had more wisdom and love in her heart than I would ever know. I had siblings who adored me and whom I adored. I had friends who had my back forever.

And I had God, who might be a little lame. *God, did you hear me? I said. You're a little bit lame, but I have come to love you again, even more. You are a lot less powerful than I once imagined, but more perfect than any of us can ever conceive.*

And I had me. I wasn't so weak after all. It was okay to be me. It was okay to be vulnerable. And all at once I annulled my vow. I didn't have to go it alone anymore. I wasn't on my own.

I never had been.

What melts the heart of stone? Sometimes it's a sense memory that cuts through all your defenses and brings you back to something precious. That's what happened to me at the Kotel. It's like that moment in the animated movie *Ratatouille* when the mean restaurant critic tastes the ratatouille and he's instantly transported back to his mother's table. "Mama!"

Now I understood why the famous Hebrew song about the Kotel says, "There are people with hearts of stone, but there are stones with hearts of flesh."

Cutting through the heart of stone and arriving at the heart of flesh isn't a one-time job. The stone heart isn't gone forever. At every loss, at every disappointment, at every new challenge, it's there ready to return, ready to take its familiar place inside you. And it takes so much courage to stay alive and soft and vulnerable.

To me today, it feels good to feel lost and hurt and to know that these feelings are essential to have, because it means you're alive with a heart of flesh that is also able to feel ecstasy and bliss and kookiness and abandon. So let down the *I'll never forgive him.* Let down your stubborn stance. Let down the *I'm not going to apologize first.* Let down the gripe you have been holding against God. Forgive. Forgive life. Forgive her. Forgive him. Forgive yourself. *May our vows not be vows.* Break down your defenses and get to the heart of flesh.

It takes a lot of energy to carry that boulder around. Put it down! Maybe there's a hurt you're holding on to, a resentment, a jealousy, a guilt, an anger. Put it down. Let its grip on your heart be released. Our souls are calling us back to ourselves. We long to return to our suppleness.

You have the power to strip away all that muck that's dimming the light of your true luminous soul. And God keeps whispering to us: *Open for me the eye of a needle, and I will make you an opening wide enough for chariots to pass through.*

So perhaps this is a good time to hear your soul asking you: "What are you running from? What are you afraid of?" And perhaps this is the right moment for each one of us to ask ourselves, *Whose heart is hardened against me? And whom is my heart hardened against?*

It's possible that with effort and intention, if you really put your soul, your body, and your stony heart into it, you may begin to experience surprising softenings. But even when you do experience a moment of softening, your work isn't over. It's just beginning.

Remember the verse from my dream: there are two steps. The first is removing the heart of stone. The second is gaining the heart of flesh. You gain a heart of flesh by remaining open when your impulse is to just shut down again and revert to old patterns.

But once you start doing the daily work, the work of daily softening, so many unexpected gifts may follow. These are the gifts that the Love Force showers upon us. This is how we gain a heart of flesh.

The first thing you may notice is that your breathing will change. Instead of your short, shallow breaths, there will be ease. The tightness in your chest will give way to a feeling of openness.

Your arguments with people may change. Instead of needing to win, your need will be to hear and to be heard.

Your parenting may change. You will be less rigid and you will make room for more fun.

Your approach to your work may change. Instead of needing to push things through or force things out, which sounds rather constipated, you will find yourself making room for inspiration, for new ideas, for collaboration instead of competition.

Perhaps your driving will change too. When someone wants to cut in front of you at the freeway entrance, instead of honking your horn and giving them the finger, which only makes you an angry person with high blood pressure, you will say to yourself, *It's only one extra second out of my day. Maybe this poor guy is late for work.* And you will motion to him, *Go right ahead.* And all day long you'll be thinking to yourself, *I'm the kind of person who helps people out.*

Your prayer life may change. Instead of saying, *Give me, give me,* you will feel gratitude: *Thank You, God.*

Your love life can change. When you're on a date, instead of thinking to yourself, *What's wrong with this loser?* You'll start thinking, *Huh, what's right about this person?*

Your marriage may change. Your predictable routine will give way to romance.

Even the way you read the news may change. Instead of learning about the suffering of innocent people and saying, *That's not my problem,* something will stir you and grip you and you will say to yourself, *What can I do about this? What can I do to help? I need to get involved.*

In your life in general there will be less whining, less worry, and more wonder and joy and a wider range of emotions.

And soon people will start gravitating toward you naturally because you will be radiating a light. Your soul's light. Soon people at work, and people at home, and lifelong friends will start asking you, "Hey, what's changed in you? You look great! What's your secret? Is it a new therapist? A new antidepressant? A new diet? A new workout?" And you will say to them, "Here's my secret: Ezekiel 36:26. I am turning my heart of stone into a heart of flesh."

Once again that perplexing line in the Talmud comes to me: "I am searching for something I have not lost." That's the paradox of our lives. We spend our days searching for what we've already been given. And God cries out to us, "If only you could see!" The relationships are here. All we have to do is repair them. The heart of flesh is here. All we have to do is access it. A world full of surprises and miracles is here. All we have to do is notice.

One of my favorite lines of all time comes from the movie *Moonstruck*, when Cher tells her mom she wants to marry Nicolas Cage.

Her mom says, "Loretta, do you love him?"

She answers, "Yeah, Mom, I love him awful."

And her mom says, "Oh, that's too bad!"

It takes courage to let down the heart of stone and replace it with a heart of flesh.

Is there a cause to fear? Yes.

Is it possible you might get hurt? Yes.

Can someone break your heart? Yes.

But is it still worth trying to melt your heart of stone? Yes.

Why? Because we don't want to be dead to life anymore. It takes courage to break down that wall, but oh, the payoff.

Remember you are precious. You are holy. You are loved. You are strong.

May we all find the power to fulfill the prophecy of Ezekiel: remove your heart of stone, and let your heart of flesh lead you back to the life you've been searching for. Amen.

20

Experiencing the Healing of Forgiveness

I'VE KNOWN MY FRIEND Rachel for sixteen years.

I want to give you a snapshot of Rachel on Tuesday, July 19, 2011.

She was forty-eight years old, happily married to her husband, Larry, for twenty years. She was a wonderful and devoted mother to her three kids, ages eighteen, fifteen, and seven. Rachel was always put-together—one of those women who could juggle being a mom, driving carpool, leading a professional life, and entertaining without losing a beat. She'd tell you she was a perfectionist, a multitasker.

Her husband was a successful man and they lived an exciting life—hosting parties, meeting senators, even presidents.

She told me, "I was blessed." There was an aura about her that said nothing would ever go wrong.

There was an edge to her too. If a mother was late picking up her kid from a playdate, Rachel would label her a flake. She told me, "I was judgmental and self-righteous, and I wasn't very forgiving of people who made mistakes."

Now I want to flip just one day on the calendar—to Wednesday, July 20, 2011. A typical LA super-mom day for Rachel. She woke up and exercised. She was going to do an errand with her seven-year-old, Joshie, to replace a keychain he lost, and then she was going to the Apple Store to pick up her older son, Jamie.

On that same day there was a Jewish man in his early eighties named Jack who owned a small retail business, a family business, where he worked with his wife, Hannah, and son Kevin. They were planning a father-son fishing trip together. In just a few minutes Jack would be on his way to the bank across the street from their store, checkbook in hand. It was a beautiful day. Life was good.

Rachel was crossing tasks off her mental to-do list as she was driving, and she was waiting for a mom to call about a playdate for Joshie. She was still in her morning workout clothes, with Joshie in the backseat. Her phone was on the center console—she wanted to make sure she didn't miss that playdate call. But the phone fell off the console onto the floor of the passenger seat. She began ferreting on the floor with her hand to find it.

In movies there's always a soundtrack to warn you, ominous notes that tell you how a happy scene on a summer's day is about to go horribly wrong. Rachel looked away from the road for only a second to get that phone, and when she looked up there was a man walking in the crosswalk. It was Jack, checkbook in hand.

She screamed, threw the phone, slammed on her brakes. She told me, "He saw me, his eyes widened in fear. I couldn't stop in time. I hit him."

It all happened very fast. Josh was asleep but he startled. "What was that?"

"Oh my God, oh my God I hit him," Rachel screamed. "Stay here," she told Josh. And then she ran out and knelt down next to Jack.

A woman behind her was screaming and cursing at her, "Didn't you see him?" Bystanders crowded around.

Rachel shouted, "Call 911!"

Kneeling beside Jack, Rachel said, "It's going to be okay, they're coming for you." Suddenly Jack's wife, Hannah, came out screaming, and then his son Kevin.

Time stood still. It seemed like the paramedics would never arrive.

Rachel looked at Jack's torn pants. He wasn't very bloody. She thought to herself, *He looks like he just broke his arm.* She was hoping it was less severe. *Let him be okay*, she prayed.

The police arrived and gave Rachel a sobriety test.

Joshie was out of the car now. He'd gone to the sidewalk, frightened and confused. By some miracle Rachel's uncle was sitting at a café nearby just at that very moment. He was her angel. He stood with Joshie and reassured him. He took Josh home.

Rachel was in a daze, in shock.

Later that day she learned how severe Jack's injuries were and how much was broken: he had a fractured skull, ribs, hip, spine, internal bleeding. The doctors didn't think he'd make it through the night.

Rachel told herself, *Life as I know it is over.* And she prayed, *Please, God, let him be okay.*

Jack survived that first night, he suffered in the hospital. Rachel was beside herself with worry, *He'll pull through, this is not his time yet. Please, please, please, let him be okay.*

Days passed. Rachel was lighting candles and praying. She knew she couldn't visit Jack in the hospital—she was the one who hit him. But her rabbi went as her proxy and stood outside Jack's door and prayed for him. That was a huge comfort to her.

Rachel's lawyer told her not to reach out. The police told her not to contact the family. She wrote them letters but didn't send them. She said to me, "I was hated. I was the evil person. I couldn't show my face to Jack's family."

Rachel stayed away as long as she could, but one day she couldn't take it anymore. She didn't care what the lawyers told her, she needed to apologize. She told the police officer who was her main contact,

"I know you advised me not to make contact, but I need to send these letters to Jack and his family."

Five minutes later the officer called her back saying, "I have some bad news, Jack just died."

Rachel's bottom fell out a second time. The worst had happened. She told me, "I felt like I was falling into this bottomless crevasse; you will never touch ground, falling, falling, falling, sinking in, falling into myself, falling into an abyss of horror and despair."

Now she was sitting in a criminal attorney's office, shaking. She never imagined herself a criminal. She had three children who needed her, a husband. How was she going to continue her life and live in that abyss?

Rachel said, "I so wanted to go to pay a condolence call to Jack's family, but I knew I couldn't." So she started saying Kaddish, the mourner's prayer, for Jack every day.

Rachel met with me in those early days after Jack's death. She wanted to know how to find forgiveness—from God, from Jack, from his family, from herself.

I remember telling her, "I want to offer you practical tools." I told her, "You can start reading the Psalms." I said, "The Book of Psalms is a reaching out to God from heartbreak and it is a healing." I also created a sacred amulet for Rachel to keep with her, called a *Kamea*. I said, "It's not magical, this amulet is here to remind you that God is with you. It's here to help you unite your deepest prayers with your outer reality."

I remember talking to Rachel about God's grace. I said, "Grace is love we don't deserve. God loves us not because we are worthy, but because we are wanting and broken."

I encouraged Rachel to buy a prayer book, I showed her what prayers she could say every morning when she woke up and what prayer she could say in bed at night before sleep.

Then Rachel said to me, "I want to ask forgiveness from Hannah and Kevin, but I can't speak to them and they don't want to hear from me. And I want to ask forgiveness from Jack, but I'll never be able to do that."

I told her, "You can pray to God for forgiveness, and you must find a path to forgive yourself, but you can't hang your hopes for forgiveness on Jack's family. You are going to have to let that go. One day there might be an opening, but then again, there might never be an opening."

And then I said, "Regarding Jack's forgiveness, I have a suggestion for you. I want to teach you something from Maimonides's Laws of Repentance. Maimonides taught that if you sinned against someone who is dead, you can go to his grave and plead for forgiveness from his soul."

Rachel said, "Really? I can do that? I can ask Jack for forgiveness?"

"Yes," I said. "It's an ancient Jewish practice." I could see Rachel's tired, grieving eyes light up a bit.

Rachel began reading the Psalms every day. She told me the words took her out of her head-spinning and helped calm her fears. She said it was comforting to read of someone else's anguish. I asked if she had a favorite Psalm. She said, "Yes, these words: *I am worn out with my sighing; every night I cause my bed to float; with my tears, I melt my couch.*"

Little by little Rachel began confessing to her friends. She said, "In telling them I can breathe a little easier."

She began praying the morning and night prayers. She told me, "I love that there are words I can say to guide me into the dream state— night is a scary time. And I love that there are words for waking when that harsh pain of returning to reality washes over you." She said the prayer book was getting her out of her panic.

And then came the day when Rachel was ready to follow Maimonides's advice. Driving to the cemetery was frightening, her heart was pounding. She stepped on the grass, and then she found Jack's grave with its temporary marker. Rachel began speaking to Jack—soul to soul. She began begging Jack for forgiveness. She prayed, she said Kaddish. She was sobbing in waves of tears. It was a hot, airless day. When she was done pouring out her soul, she suddenly felt a breeze brush over her. She wondered if it was a sign. She told me, "I felt like Jack heard me."

The High Holy Days were coming, and Rachel was absolutely panicked to face God in temple. She said, "I never felt like I'd sinned before. And here I was now, I felt like a murderer. I knew it was an accident, but I'd taken a man's life."

Rachel signed up for a Torah class called How to Prepare for Forgiveness. Every word the teacher spoke felt like an accusation. The word "sin" terrified her. She was sure no one else in the class was dealing with her kind of sin. And then, while explaining repentance, the teacher actually said these very words: "I'm not talking about murder, just the sin of gossiping about your mother-in-law."

Rachel began hyperventilating, she ran out at the end of class and could barely breathe. She suddenly realized she was around the corner from her childhood home, the place where she grew up and dreamed about a beautiful future stretching out before her.

Right there she cried out: "Oh my God, look what I did! I took a man's life."

And then she offered her own Psalm to God from the depths of her soul, a Psalm of bitter heartbreak:

Hear my moaning, O God
I am dizzy with despair
I tremble in the face of You
You are my witness.

Yom Kippur was a huge, horrible day standing before God and the heavenly court. Rachel was racked with guilt and pain and anguish. She recited the confessional prayers pounding on her chest. I remember Rachel saying to me, "All my life I don't think I was really pray-ing. I was singing along and reading words. Now I see every prayer was written for me."

Yom Kippur was a trial, but it was also the beginning of a healing. A day of mercy and forgiveness.

But then there was another court that Rachel had to face. She was charged with misdemeanor vehicular manslaughter.

An article about the accident appeared in the local newspaper. Rachel told me, "I felt naked and so exposed." She thought the pharma-cist and the grocer and everyone she knew were talking about her.

Rachel began working alongside fellow criminals in orange vests at the beach—she was with shoplifters and drug dealers. Rachel told me, "I trumped everybody." She was too ashamed to tell anyone her crime.

Day after day cleaning toilets and shoveling sand was helping Rachel to heal. She was sore and exhausted at the end of each day. She wanted to be sore, she wanted to hurt.

One day she finally told the driver of the orange vest crew what she'd done. And instead of judging her, he was sweet and compassion-ate. He said, "Oh God, man, that's rough." She realized no one was judging her.

Rachel told me she kept the *Kamea*, the amulet I made her, with her at all times. She said, "I would touch it like a worry stone. I'd feel the bamboo and remember the message inside of it."

A year passed. Rachel was in therapy, she was reciting prayers and Psalms. But she didn't know how to forgive herself. Rachel didn't feel very lovable or very deserving of love—she felt like a monster.

But she was beginning to feel God's forgiveness. Little by little she started to sense it. She began telling herself, *If God could love that woman who was so cocky, if my husband could still love me, if my kids can still love me and hug me, if my friends can love me, I must be able to find a way to love me. I deserve to have a second chance.*

Rachel started giving speeches to teens at synagogues and public

schools. She told me, "The speeches really, really helped." She was confessing publicly. Each time she confessed her wrongdoing to a new
audience she felt a little lighter. She prayed that with every speech she
was saving a life. She told kids: "In the time·it takes you to look away
from the road to read a text, you are driving the length of a football
field blind." She pleaded with them to take in the words of her Tech
Confessional Prayer: "For the sin we have committed before You
by texting and driving. For the sin we have committed before You by
reading an e-mail at a red light." She asked them to share it with their
parents and their relatives.

Two years passed. Three years.

Every year Rachel lit a memorial candle for Jack. She kept praying
that one day she'd be able to ask for forgiveness from his family, but
she understood that day might never come. Periodically she'd reach
out to Hannah and Kevin and ask if they'd agree to meet with her.
The answer was always no.

Three and a half years passed. Rachel reached out once again. This
time the answer was "Yes."

She told me, "This was the moment I had been waiting three and
a half years for."

Rachel wasn't expecting a "Kumbaya" moment. She was preparing
herself for the worst. She said, "All I wanted was the opportunity to
look them in the eye and tell them how sorry I was."

The meeting would take place at Jack's family's synagogue with
their rabbi and Rachel and her rabbi.

On the day of the meeting Rachel got there an hour early. She was
anxious and didn't know what to do with herself. Her heart was racing. Then as she walked in she could see the back of Hannah's head
through the glass of the rabbi's office. Rachel was pale and frightened.
This was the first time Rachel had seen Hannah or Kevin in three
and a half years since that awful day when they ran out on the street
to see Jack lying there.

Rachel walked in and said an anguished "Hello." Rachel told me, "I was prepared for them to leap at me, scream at me, wailing and pounding on me, scratching me." But Hannah looked so regal and beautiful, and Kevin was so dignified.

Rachel spoke first. She said, "I'm so thankful that you're allowing me to speak to you. I want you to know how sorry I am. I think about Jack every day, about what I did. I want you to know that I've changed. I'm so sorry, I'm so sorry I took Jack's life."

Hannah was holding several pages. She turned to Rachel and said, "I wrote down notes, but they're not very nice. I'm not going to read them." And she put them back in her purse.

Instead she said, "Let's just talk."

Words poured out, words that needed to be spoken and heard.

And then the rabbis suggested, "Can we say the blessing thanking God for bringing us to this day and to this moment?"

And they all took hands and prayed: "Blessed are You, O Lord our God, Ruler of the universe, who has given us life, sustained our lives, and enabled us to reach this joyous moment. Amen."

They were all crying.

And then Hannah turned to Rachel and asked, "How is your son doing?"

Rachel just melted, she dissolved into tears. She said to me, "They're the ones who had the loss, and she was worried about Joshie? That was so compassionate."

Then Kevin said, "Can I give you a hug?"

Rachel told me, "This man who I'd hurt so deeply wanted to hug me?"

Rachel said, "And then Hannah hugged me and I cried in her arms, repeating, 'I'm so sorry, I'm so sorry.'" Rachel felt Hannah holding her like a mother.

Hannah said to Rachel: "God bless you."

Never in her wildest prayers did Rachel believe she would ever live to experience this miracle—a meeting of souls.

The room fell silent.

And then Hannah broke the silence with these words: "I'm ready now to have the unveiling."

Hannah had not put up Jack's gravestone for three and a half years. She was finally ready. Forgiveness was the permission her soul needed to finally find some closure.

It was a big day, a holy healing for everyone.

IT'S BEEN FOUR YEARS NOW since Jack's death. Rachel knows she will never get over what she's been through and what she did. She says, "It's a part of me."

But Rachel also knows she has grown. She's learned that there's something inside every person that will help you get through even the worst nightmare. She's learned to be kind to herself and to not let shame crush her. She's learned to be forgiving of others. This ordeal has softened her. She's learned the hard way that we're all God's children and we all make mistakes. Some of us make terrible mistakes. Rachel doesn't judge people anymore—she's been blessed to know the healing power of forgiveness.

Rachel is a better listener. She doesn't multitask anymore. She knows she can't do two things at once. And she hopes people reading her story will understand this: just because you've had success multitasking up to now doesn't mean you always will. It's dangerous for your car to become your office space. You are putting yourself and others at risk when you text and drive, or check your e-mails or dial a number or look away from the road. A car is a weapon and it needs all our full faculties.

Rachel also told me, "I always felt God in my life, now I feel a connection to God that I didn't know before."

She said, "All I wanted was to return to the happy Rachel I'd been on the day before that tragic day. But I realize now that I can't ever go back to square one." She told me, "Naomi, I'm not at square one. I'm at square two now."

MAYBE YOU'VE BEEN PRAYING THAT things in your life will just get back to the way they once were, back to normal. I can promise you they won't. You won't. You can't. We're not here to return to normal. You've actually been given the power to *return* to someplace *new*. A higher plane. A greater wisdom. To cut through the numbness and get to someplace true. A deeper honesty.

Maybe you're holding on to a grudge, maybe you're holding back an apology. Maybe you're not talking to someone. Can you see how your avoidance is stunting you? Please know that the forgiveness you are delaying has the power to free you to move forward.

Forgiveness is a miracle. Such simple words:

"Please forgive me."—"I forgive you."

I pray you find the humility and the courage and the compassion to speak these blessed words. Do you want to spend your life withholding these words? Do you really want to wait until you have to follow Maimonides's prescription and recite a monologue of regret and heartbreak at someone's grave when you can have a healing here and now?

We are moving in the direction of softening. We are longing to experience days of grace, days of ascension. Where we can rise from square one to square two and higher and higher.

May you continue rising in grace, in love, in forgiveness, and in healing. Amen.

21

Praying for Holy Fear

LEARNING TO THINK BEFORE YOU ACT

"WHAT WAS I THINKING?" Rick's face was drawn, he was rocking back and forth in anguish. He repeated, "What was I thinking, Rabbi?" Rick told me about the affair and how he lost his wife, his home, his dog, and worst of all, how he lost his daughter's respect. She refused to speak to him.

I felt so sorry for Rick as he sat before me overcome by grief and regret. We've all done something we wish we could take back.

If only we could contemplate the repercussions before we acted. If only we could see the ripples our words and actions make that reverberate through time. People generally come to speak to me after the fact. After the affair, after the wrongdoing, after the temper tantrum. Only in the wake of the consequences of our actions do we begin asking: *What was I thinking?*

There are steps available to us that can shield us from making these same mistakes in the future.

The soul within you sounds an alarm when it sees you are about to stray from your own higher self. You've heard it.

The problem is, we have trouble feeling the soul's urgency. We are experts at ignoring and discounting the soul's cry.

In order to change, we must learn to listen to that higher voice, instead of the lower voice seducing us into believing it knows what is best for us. Understand that your life depends on listening to the soul. Your very happiness and all that you've come to love depend on your ability to hear.

When I counseled Rick and he said, "What was I thinking?" he pleaded with me to teach him techniques to do battle with his powerful desire.

I told him, "I'd like to educate you in the Positive Power of Negative Thinking."

He said, "What?"

"You can think of it as the Upside of Down," I said. Rick was hoping I'd encourage him with upbeat words about courage and optimism. So much of the spiritual wisdom offered in our society today, whether from the pulpit or from self-help books, emphasizes the light without ever giving weight to the importance of the darkness.

But the path I led Rick on was a path to boost the urgency of the soul's voice of caution. I began speaking to Rick about the supernal world that mirrors our world. I said, "Think of a Rorschach inkblot pattern or Mirror Lake in Yosemite National Park." Rick nodded, listening intently. I went on, "The spiritual world is near, mirroring you like your shadow." I saw Rick taking it in. I explained how in this same way, the Jewish mystical tradition envisions a tree of life containing God's divine attributes in the heavens above and a tree below that resides within us that mirrors those same attributes. I told him, "We are modeled after that supernal tree."

Then I asked Rick to look out the window. I said, "Take a moment and look at that tree." Rick gazed at an old mighty ficus. I said, "Look at the base of the tree and know that the root system beneath the ground is as elaborate as its branches and leaves. There is so much going

on beyond our awareness. The supernal tree of the kabbalah, the structure containing God's sacred qualities, is not growing the way trees
grow here on the earth below. Its roots are in heaven, that's where its
nourishment lies, and its branches and leaves are reaching down toward
us." Rick closed his eyes to try to imagine all this. I said, "Picture that
upside-down tree growing downward toward us."

It was then that I began explaining a holy balancing act that I'd
like to share with you:

There are two divine attributes that emanate from that tree toward
us: they are love and fear. Love and fear are always keeping each other
in check like yin and yang. Love is an outpouring that flows from the
soul, it pours and spreads like water. But love also poses a danger. Love
unchecked can smother, like a parent who can't let a child grow up.
Like a river with no levee, it overflows and floods everything in its
path. Love unchecked is a sea without a shore to give it a boundary.
Without a dam to contain it, love's waters can engulf us all.

Love unchecked is the challenge of the person who is blessed with
enormous talent and no discipline.

Love unchecked lies at the root of the cult of positivity that has so
captured American society. Nike tells us, "Just do it!" But the Bible
tells us, "Don't do it!" There's nothing wrong with building up our
courage, but ego unchecked can destroy us and unbridled desire
will lead us far from a holy path.

That's where the second divine attribute, fear, comes in. Fear is here
to counterbalance love. Not lower-level fear that cripples us and
prevents us from fulfilling our potential. But holy fear, holy fear is restraint, awe, trembling. The fear of losing it all. It is a force within that
says, *Stop!* Holy fear is a voice that says, think before you leap, weigh
the consequences before you act, take a moment to contemplate before
you hit "send." Recognize the beauty of what you have before you
trample all over it.

At Jewish weddings it is a tradition for the groom to stomp on a glass before the community cheers, "Mazel tov!" One of my favorite explanations of this unusual ritual comes from the Talmud, where a rabbi shatters a glass at a wedding, startles all the guests, and exclaims: "At every celebration there must be trembling."

A wedding is a joyous day, but it is also a sacred covenant, an awesome responsibility, and too often we give weight to the love and ignore the trembling. Your relationships require your devotion, and yes, even your fear. A wedding ceremony is holy ground, it is a foundation for a life—and yet we spend too much energy on the party and not enough on awe.

Holy fear is not panic. It is clarity of thought, calmness even: the moment you recognize your smallness in the face of God's vast majestic universe. It is the moment when the soul shakes you, and you recognize how deeply blessed you are.

The Jewish High Holy Days are not called days of love and peace. They are called Days of Awe. During the Holy Days Jews pray, "Please, God, fill us with fear." What kind of crazy person prays for fear? Who would ask for more fear?

But a wise person understands what it means to tap into the soul's alarm system. The prayer is a yearning for high-level fear—the fear of wasting your life, the fear of throwing your life away, the fear of not seeing the sacred mission God has placed in your hands. Praying for fear is an act of self-preservation. There is something the dark emotions are here to teach us.

I explained holy fear to Rick and he said, "Rabbi, at first I didn't get what you were saying. But now I understand what you mean by the positive power of negative thinking."

Your fear is a gift. Awe is a holy state. Your vulnerability is your strength.

Stop fearing fear, stop running from fear. Know that holy fear is a divine quality that is already inside you. It is a quality that can change your life and teach you to live on a new plane, a higher level of power and passion. You don't have to look far to uncover it. There is an inverted tree within you holding holy love and holy fear in a sacred balance.

I've always tried to imagine that balance, to envision the inverted tree within us. But it was not until I was diagnosed with asthma last January that I did come to see it. I was sitting in the pulmonologist's office and she was explaining asthma to me, and then she reached over and showed me a medical poster. I let out a gasp when I saw the diagram before me—there I was, face-to-face with the supernal tree I'd been meditating on for years. My doctor said, "Rabbi, the human lungs are like an inverted tree." And I sighed a sigh of deep knowing and said, "Yes, of course!"

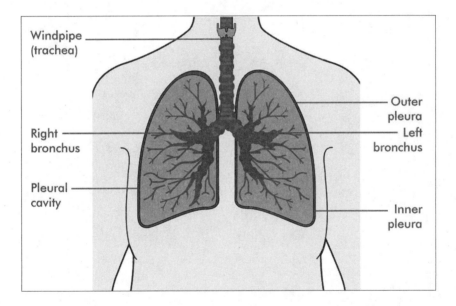

God's breath flows through us. Divine qualities are inside us, held in a powerful balance. Our roots *are* in heaven. Holy fear is your salvation, let it guide you and lift you above thoughts and feelings that are beneath you. Touch that place inside you. Listen to the voice that says, *Stop.* Think before you act. Take the time to really hear. Your life will thank you for it, your soul will thank you, your family and friends will thank you. You will suffer so much less and you will cause so much less harm to the people you love. Feel the urgency of the alarm, welcome the soul's warning. Find your awe.

The answer is closer than you ever imagined. It's here inside you. You no longer have to dwell in the regret of, "What was I thinking?" Instead, may you be granted the power to live in the realm of holy fear, saying, "How blessed am I for all I've been given." Amen.

22

Recognizing the Saving Power of True Friends

WHEN MY GRANDFATHER WAS SEVENTY-FOUR years old, he suddenly fell into a profound depression. No one could figure out why. He'd just sit in his chair all day and stare right through people. He wasn't living alone—he was married to the love of his life. He was surrounded by an extended family, our tribe, his three adult children with their spouses all lived nearby, together with nine grandchildren. We were all there. And the family retail business he started was still thriving, but he stopped going to work. He just wouldn't leave his chair.

One day my mother sat beside him and said, "Papa, what is it? What's the matter?"

He sat in silence for some time and then he said, "There's no one left." At first my mother had trouble understanding—my grandfather was blessed with health, a wife, children and grandchildren all around him. But then he added, "No one to kibbitz with." *Kibbitz* is a Yiddish word that encompasses all that amazing nothingness you do with your friends—hanging around, joking, gossiping, teasing, storytelling, unburdening, listening, laughing, and more . . .

Several weeks earlier, my grandfather had buried the last of his circle of close friends. The men from the old country who would sit around playing chess with their pants belted high around their chests, sipping tea out of glasses, smoking cigars. All gone.

Suddenly my mother understood the depth of her father's loss. To say to my grandfather, "What's the matter, Papa? Your family is here, you've got us," was to miss the point, to underestimate the power of his loss. Instead my mom said to him, "Yes, you do have cause to weep, Papa. I understand now."

CAN YOU REMEMBER A TIME in your life when you felt alone? Maybe you moved to a new city or transferred to a new school without knowing a soul, or started a new job. Think of a time when you didn't know who to sit with on the bus or who to eat with at lunch or who to play with at recess. The emptiness of that experience is palpable. Life without friendship is agony. The difference between having no friends and having just one friend is the difference between lost and found.

I remember that feeling when I was in college. Walking around forlorn and alone, wandering the campus like a ghost. Friendlessness really can feel like death. And then I met Rebecca. She said, "I work in the movie theater. Come! I'll give you free popcorn." She liked me! And I didn't even have to impress her. She was so easy to love. She accepted me without needing me to jump through any hoops. Someone saw me and picked me out of a crowd and I felt alive and known. I wasn't a ghost anymore.

Perhaps that's why there is a blessing Jews say when you are reunited with an old friend you haven't seen in years: "Blessed is the One who resurrects the dead." Friendship gives life to the soul. A lasting friendship means that you may be separated by distance and time and still when you come together it feels as if no time has passed at all.

In the Bible, the paradigm for true love is not a romantic bond, but the friendship between David and Jonathan. The connection between the prince and the upstart is immediate and deep, and it defies all logic. Jonathan has every reason to fear David, to feel threatened by him, but instead he can't help but adore him and trust in him. Jonathan's soul becomes intertwined with the soul of David. Jonathan loves David as he loves his own self. Because of that love, Jonathan is willing to give up his right to the throne for the sake of his friend. When Jonathan dies, David mourns him with these words: "I grieve for you, my brother Jonathan. You were most dear to me, more than the love of women." True friendship can transcend romance. It is a binding of souls.

The soul enters this world with a deep need to connect with other souls. The soul within you craves intimacy and honesty. Guess what? So does the soul within everyone around you. The soul longs for the love of family and the romantic love of a life partner, and yet the love of a true friend can be the soul's salvation.

You can be madly in love with your spouse and still you know that there are places inside you that your partner can never fill. I worry when I counsel couples who assume their mate has to complete them. There are empty places within us that only our friends know how to fill. Your friends will listen when your spouse tunes out, your friends will comfort you when your spouse freaks out. Beauty fades, romance wanes, but your friends don't need you to be good-looking or young or sexy.

Several years ago a young couple joined my community. Jeff and Denise had recently moved to LA to be closer to family because Denise was pregnant, and they both knew they'd need extra support and extra hands. What Jeff hadn't expected was the intrusion of Denise's girlfriends.

Jeff came to see me to complain. He told me he was feeling a bit threatened by Denise's two best friends, Margo and Allie. He wanted Denise all to himself. He wanted to be the primary figure in her life. He tolerated her friends, but deep down he wished they would both just disappear. I gently suggested to Jeff that these friends he was re-senting might in fact prove to be invaluable.

Six years passed.

Denise was thirty-eight when she was first diagnosed with breast cancer. Jeff was out of his depth. He didn't know what to say to her or how to be strong for her, or how to comfort her. He was so scared of losing her that all he could think about was himself: *What am I going to do without her? How will I raise the kids without her?*

Instantly, Denise's two best friends, Margo and Allie, swept in and took over—meals, carpools, playdates, doctor's appointments, hand-holding, praying, listening, cheerleading. And Jeff welcomed their help. He wasn't threatened anymore by these two powerhouse women and the bond they shared with his wife. He understood now how blessed he was to have them.

On the day of Denise's mastectomy surgery, Jeff uncovered an in-ner strength that he'd never tapped into before. He was there for her, he was solid, steady, loving, present. And later that evening when he returned home for a few minutes just to hug the kids and reassure them, he looked around. Margo was drying the dishes after the din-ner she'd cooked. Allie was getting the kids into their PJs after giving them their bath. And Jeff just broke down. He turned to them and said, "Where would I be without you?" He was grateful, so very grate-ful that God had sent Denise these two guardian angels.

A friend will see you through the abyss, and through the magic too. With your friends there is playfulness and laughter no matter what your age. Friendship is a sacred balance that doesn't deplete you, it replen-ishes you—the giving is the receiving, the receiving is the giving. A friend is someone you can talk to and trust with your secrets, some-one who keeps you honest, knows your tricks and calls you on them. With a friend you can let down whatever mask you wear out in the world and just get naked, reveal your soul. You say to that person, *See me! There is no part of me that's ugly to you because you know my soul.*

Over the years I've counseled scores of people who shared with me disappointments about family members not understanding them or not connecting with them: "I know I should love my sister because she's my sister, but I just don't like her." Family you're stuck with, but friends, you get to choose.

Choose wisely. Listen carefully to your soul. It already knows the difference between friends who will raise you up and those who will drag you down. Avoid the ones who are critical and judgmental toward others, be wary of anyone with a big mouth. You may have many acquaintances and all sorts of relationships that don't go very deep. Facebook may call those people your friends. I don't call them friends, I call them "friendlies." Ask yourself, is this person my friend? Or is he or she merely my friendly? You can have lots of friendlies. But true friends? Guardian angels.

So may it be for you.

23

Finding a Soulmate

IN THE TALMUD WE'RE told that once the work of creation came to an end, the Creator took on a new mission: matchmaking. And if you consider this a trivial matter for the Creator to dabble in, know that uniting souls is as difficult for God as parting the Red Sea. According to the rabbis, God's matchmaking began with Adam and Eve, and it continues to this day.

The Yiddish word for soulmate is *bashert*, which means predestined or preordained. It's a belief that the Soul of Souls has already chosen the one who is right for your soul.

In another Talmudic passage it says that forty days before a child is born, a heavenly voice proclaims who that child is destined to unite with when the time comes to marry. The Zohar, the book of mystical wisdom, asserts that the soul begins its existence as a compound being, and just before its descent into this world, God splits it in two and those half-souls enter two different bodies. The soul spends its days on earth searching for the one who will restore it to wholeness.

Has the Holy One already picked a mate for you? Is there just one possible match for each soul? Even Maimonides had trouble with the idea of *bashert* because it negates free will, and God created us to be free.

And yet there is no denying the mystery of souls uniting in love. I know I felt this way when I fell in love with my husband, Rob. It wasn't immediate, he knew before I knew. He said to his best friend, "I'm going to marry that woman," the first day he met me. I was a bit slower on the uptake.

We met in passing in the hallway of my synagogue. He was with a group of students who were taking a class with an Orthodox rabbi who rented a classroom in our building. The rabbi told his students, "Boys, let's go meet the lady rabbi."

Rob met me and was immediately sure I was the one for him, but I had no memory of meeting him. He began attending my prayer services on Friday evenings and Saturday mornings. He'd stay late after services for our Torah discussion and a nosh. Then there were those sensuous treats he began bringing to my Song of Songs class. He wasn't even a religious person, not a synagogue-goer. I didn't know that. I thought he was into God, little did I know he was into me. At our wedding, where there must have been about thirty rabbis in attendance, Rob's brother Mark offered this toast: "Rob, I didn't even know you were Jewish!"

I do believe the soul knows before the mind. Intellectually, I was treating Rob like one of the flock, but on a deep soul level, something else was unfolding. He felt familiar to me, as if I'd known him all my life.

One day after class Rob invited me out for tea. I said yes. We walked down the block to a café. Anyone looking at us would say we were mismatched. Perhaps I would have rejected his profile on an online dating site. He was in a T-shirt, ripped jeans, and flip-flops and I was dressed in a skirt suit. But the minute we sat down together my soul knew I had come home.

When people ask me, "How will I know if this is the right person for me? How will I recognize my soulmate?" I say, you may be nervous at first, it may take a while for one of you to catch up to the other. But sooner or later it will feel like home.

The Baal Shem Tov, the founder of Hasidism, famously taught: "From every human being there rises a light that reaches straight to heaven. And when two souls that are destined to be together find each other, their streams of light flow together, and a single brighter light goes forth from their united being." Those two lights both strong and complementary become One.

I don't believe there is only one possible mate for each soul. I believe the soul has the capacity to find love with more than just one person in the entire universe. That's what enables couples to remarry after divorce or after the death of a spouse. There is life after a broken heart and life after death as well.

What role does the soul play in finding and sustaining love? The soul is our teacher. It is forever reminding us that you can't rush love. You have to be patient and you also have to gather the courage to let down your guard and let another person in. Vulnerability is key in love. And the soul is here to remind us that the first rush of love and passion must be anchored in reality, in the day-to-day routines of life, or it will simply fly away like a helium balloon. Love may feel like a mighty force, but in truth, a relationship of love is a fragile thing that needs our attention, our protection, and our tending. Love can flourish only where there is honesty and loyalty, kindness and compromise and trust.

When a match works, two souls fit together so perfectly that they become one.

May you find the one you have been praying for. May your soulmate enter your heart, your home, your body, your soul. May your beloved enter your life, your days, your every thought and breath. Amen.

24

Entering Marriage with Five Holy Qualities

WHEN I STAND BEFORE a couple to unite them beneath the wedding canopy and recite the traditional Jewish marriage blessings, I remind them that the final blessing teaches us that there are five qualities that lead to a holy relationship—a relationship that can last, one that welcomes God's eternal presence. They are: joy, romance, friendship, camaraderie, and peace.

Joy. During my premarital counseling sessions with couples, I always ask the same question: "What is the one quality of your partner that you most treasure?" And I almost always hear the same reply: "Her sense of humor" or "The way he makes me laugh."

Yes, relationships require work and responsibility, but when souls find each other there is laughter, recognition, and a sense of abandon too. Life is hard enough, love should help lift your load.

The Jewish marriage ceremony doesn't just offer one word for joy. It speaks of joy in six forms: rejoicing, happiness, singing, dancing, celebration, and elation. If you are wondering whether your lover is a good fit for a life-mate, ask yourself: Does this person make me laugh?

Romance. What's a marriage without passion or chemistry? This holy quality is something you can't buy. It's given to you as a gift from above. Most couples are blessed with it from the start. It's our challenge and our responsibility to nurture and protect this sacred blessing. A great mistake couples make is to assume that romance will always be a given. Over time passion fades and romance must be fought for, revived and resurrected all the time.

Friendship is the ability for lovers to talk and share and have fun together. "This is my beloved and this is my friend," the Song of Songs reminds us. We must learn to be both. Unlike chemistry, friendship is not something you're given from on high. It's a quality you have to build with honesty, and earn with loyalty—a deep, true friendship. Marriage charges you to grow as friends in depth and wisdom and in blessing.

Camaraderie is akin to the love of siblings. It's not incest! It's blood. It runs deep, it's playful, it's a desire to call your lover: *my family.* That's what a wedding day magically completes. It transforms a lover and a friend into your nuclear family. On their wedding day, I always tell this to couples who have been living together for years: "After today everything will be the same and nothing will be the same. Same lover, same home, and everything will be new and remade in the Creator's light."

Peace. In Hebrew the word *shalom* means both "peace" and "wholeness." You enter a loving relationship with unique and separate attributes. And sometimes those differences can lead to antagonism, anger, and distance. But *shalom* means that your differences lead to a greater whole. That requires vision—to see that I am greater with you. And it requires humility—to see that I must compromise and make room for you and learn from you.

In Jewish mystical thought there is a concept called *Tzimtzum.* It means contraction. At the beginning of time the Creator filled every space. In order to bring the world into existence, the Creator had to willfully contract in order to make room for anything else. Creation was an act of love accomplished through the process of divine shrinking.

I believe the peace and wholeness we seek in marriage can only be accomplished through this sacred process of contraction.

Over my many years of counseling couples, I've noticed that the most common cause of suffering and pain between partners has to do with people stubbornly needing to get their way. When I speak to a couple dealing with issues of inflexibility, I say to each one of them: You can pick the restaurant you want to eat in every single night of the week. You can decorate your home any way you like. You can go to see any movie your heart desires. The only problem is: you'll have to do it alone.

If you want to make your life with someone else, you must find the inner resources to learn the sacred art of shrinking. You contract in order to grow. By letting someone else in, you become so much more than you were before. When you tune in to the right frequency, you can hear what your beloved is trying to tell you and you can get yourself out of the way. You contract because love means each person must be recognized, seen, and heard.

How do you accomplish this? Instead of leading with your ego, defer to your soul. Your soul is God's candle within you. It descended from the Upper World and contracted in order to enter you! It knows all about the art of compromise and listening and connecting to the soul of your beloved. Your soul doesn't only want to get along, it wants to dance and play and delight in all the sweetness available to you and the one you love. So instead of showing off your ego, reveal your soul, and your stubborn arguments will give way to understanding and to laughter and embraces.

A Blessing for Married Couples

May the Creator bless you with a lifetime of laughter. May your passion grow stronger with each passing year. May your friendship evolve in depth and in strength. May the bonds of your family grow deeper and tighter. And may God bless you with a sacred peace that reflects the wholeness of two souls becoming One. Amen.

25

Discovering the Secret to a Lasting Marriage

A FEW YEARS AGO I flew to Chicago for a lecture. I'd had to wake up at 5:00 a.m. to make my flight, the plane was packed and stuffy, and I was stuck in a middle seat. After we landed I got into a cab to take me to my hotel. My driver was a Russian man named Victor. I gave him the address, and just then I got a call from a dear friend who was seeking my input about a run-in she'd had with her boss. I was advising her, talking about how to best deal with the situation. We hung up, and I thought, *Finally, a moment of peace.* But suddenly I heard,

"Excuse me?" It was Victor, my cab driver.

"Yes," I said.

"Can I talk to you about my marriage?"

"What?"

Apparently the driver liked the way I'd been advising my friend.

He said, "My wife, she kicked me out. Should I try to get back together with her?"

I couldn't believe I was having this conversation with my taxi driver. I said, "Why did she kick you out?"

Victor began telling me his whole story. How he and his wife met and fell in love, and then came the marriage and the baby. "But you know, things got difficult . . . money, fighting, no more sex, I cheated on her . . . So what do you think? Should I try to get back together with her?" he said.

I said, "Um . . . can you back up a little with your list of what went wrong?" I felt like the priest taking confession in the movie *Moonstruck*.

"The money problems?" he said.

"No."

"The fighting?"

"No."

"Maybe I cheated?"

"Yeah, that one."

"But I apologized for that and it's not all my fault. And anyway," he said, "it takes two to tangle."

I said, "Victor, you can't ask for trust, you have to earn it. And maybe it takes two to tangle, I mean tango, but you have to take responsibility for your steps."

"So you think I should try to get back together with her?" he said.

"It's not what I think, it's what you want and what steps you're prepared to take to change and to earn trust."

"Steps!" he said. "Yes, I see now, steps."

He kept saying that: "Steps. Steps."

And then he smacked the steering wheel and laughed. "Thank you, Missus, I understand now, steps."

STEPS.

A holy relationship isn't about a grand gesture or a huge splash, and it's not about falling hard for someone. It's about the little daily details that make up a life. How you watch your words and curb your appetite. The daily shedding of old self-defeating and hurtful patterns.

Learning to release layer after layer of defensive armor. Learning to earn trust through action and learning to trust again so that you are ready to receive once more.

The art of receiving is no simple matter. How do you learn to trust? How do you find the courage to remain vulnerable and open not for one year or ten years, but for a lifetime?

The parting of the Red Sea may have been the Children of Israel's leap to freedom, but their forty-year trek in the wilderness was their Schlep. And that Schlep is every bit as important as the Exodus itself. The one can't exist without the other. It's true in every area of life—with the spouse you marry, the job you land, and the child you bring into this world. It's those steps, those simple sacred acts, they are the precious details that make up a life.

Love at first sight is a gift from heaven. Romance, chemistry, the rush of emotion, that high! But marriage is another thing altogether.

Yes, we may experience something grand and powerful in the realm of love, but what are we to do when the romance fades, when finances get tight, when life's pressures mount?

When someone is suffering, we say time heals, but when it comes to sexual desire, time dulls. Over time, passion gives way to familiarity and routine. How do you prevent monotony and stress from finding their way into your bed? The soul is key here. It can help us leave the pressures of the day behind and transform our predictable patterns into a magical encounter of intensity and wonder. The soul wants to teach you how to recapture the passion that once burned so brightly.

The body gets tired, the mind gets distracted, but the soul is always yearning to unite and show you the way to romance, to rapture, and to the blessing of oneness.

Isn't this the prayer of every person? To be unlocked, freed from the curse of separateness. To be known thoroughly, to be understood. A knowledge that transcends words, that transcends even flesh.

Building a lasting marriage requires us to see not just the

importance of endurance or even the payoff of endurance, but the sheer dignity and grace and beauty of what it means to stay on a path through the luminous times, and the gray times too.

The blessings a couple reaps from length of years are something young love can never match: a partnership, a bond, a soul-joining that runs deep like an ancient majestic tree that spreads its branches and its shade upon weary travelers.

I am not saying you should remain with a partner who constantly lies or betrays you. Endurance is not an ideal for its own sake. There are times when there is no love left in a marriage, or when a relationship is simply too broken or destructive to save, and endurance can actually be a mistake.

But bringing soul to marriage also means we must bring soul to our disagreements. There are healthy and unhealthy ways for couples to argue. You can see your spouse's faults, in fact, you must see them. But that's different from treating your partner as if there is a defect in his or her very essence. It's important to believe in the person you love, to believe in their power to rise up and to change. Your partner can make a mistake, but we have to have faith in them that they aren't essentially bad or stupid or cruel or defective. The soul within every person is pure, God's candle. We must learn to treasure our loved ones, to see them in their divinity in the face of all their flaws.

I was once reading a study about the longevity of couples, and the researchers found that they could predict whether a couple would remain together with surprising accuracy. The single greatest factor determining a couple's longevity comes down to one word: disdain. Couples may argue, fight, and disagree. They can have differences in backgrounds and even in taste and preferences. But the kiss of death for a couple is disdain. I've seen this. I'm sure we've all witnessed this— a husband or wife who treats his or her spouse not just with annoyance or anger, but with utter contempt. It's a heartless and crushing experience, and no soul can flourish in that environment.

Be careful of the way you react in moments of stress or anger. Your temper is a fire that can burn everything in its path. Watch your words, restrain your tongue, reel in the voice within you that seeks destruction and revenge.

Remember, it's all right to be upset, hurt, angry, even to get frustrated with your lover. But if you bring your soul to tense situations, you will begin to see what's right in her, what's holy in him, what's sacred and precious. When the soul gets involved, there can be no disdain.

May the bonds of your love grow deeper with each passing year. May you be blessed with health, with joy, with romance, and with peace. Amen.

26

Parenting with Soul

RYAN'S PARENTS, GREG AND SHARON, met and fell in love when they were both students at a prestigious Ivy League college. Throughout Ryan's childhood, Greg would reminisce about his fraternity days. He was a college football fanatic. Greg and Sharon were so excited when Ryan was admitted as a legacy to their alma mater. Greg was expecting to fly in for important games, and he was hoping Ryan would rush his fraternity too. He kept talking to Ryan about the coeds and the parties.

One day in late summer before his freshman year, Ryan came to see me. He was clearly distraught. It took some time for him to finally get out the words he was holding back, "Rabbi, I'm gay." He told me he wasn't interested in football or fraternities, he wanted to pursue a career in fashion design. I told Ryan how excited I was for him that he understood himself, and how honored I was that he felt safe enough to share his truth with me.

Ryan said, "Rabbi, I'm so scared to tell my parents. You don't know what it feels like to be a disappointment."

I felt so awful for Ryan. It's excruciating to believe that your very being is a disappointment to your parents, that "who I am" is a disappointment—not what I'm doing, but who I am.

One sure way to crush your children's souls is to expect or demand that they become someone they are not. How often have I counseled children who contorted and distorted themselves just to receive parental approval or attention or love.

I told Ryan that I believed his parents would come around, and I offered to speak with them. Not long after he came out to his parents, Greg and Sharon met with me. They were both clearly shaken up. Greg kept repeating, "It feels like a death in the family."

But after some conversation I gently asked, "Is there some recognition, some hint that you already knew Ryan was gay?"

Suddenly Sharon turned to Greg and said, "Honey, we always knew he was gay. We just didn't *want* to know." That was the beginning of a new beginning.

Often we have a knowing, but we are running from the knowing. Parenting is a holy undertaking. It requires that you tap into your own soul, because your soul has a knowing. And it requires you to let go and to understand that you've been entrusted with a precious soul. Yes, you've been blessed to raise and nurture a precious soul who is not an extension of you, not a replica of you, and not here to complete what you've left undone—whatever mission your soul failed to complete. As parents, our mission is to make space for the soul we've brought into this world to find its own way to grow and unfold and to shine and light up the world.

The Book of Exodus describes the famous revelation that took place when Moses stood on the top of Mount Sinai and God spoke the words of the Ten Commandments. It was at Sinai that they received the divine teaching from above. But at Sinai they also experienced something from below that they had never known before. What was that second revelation?

At Sinai when God entrusted the Children of Israel with the Ten

Commandments, they responded, "We will do it and we will listen and understand." When the people spoke those words, the rabbis explain that God was taken by surprise. In astonishment God asked, "Who revealed to my children the secret of the Upper World?"

I suppose you can compare God's reaction to the feeling every parent has when a child intuitively does something without you having to tell them or teach them first. You are in awe of this quantum leap forward and you say: "How did he learn to do that?" or "Who taught her that?"

So what secret of the Upper World did the people uncover that so surprised God? What is so amazing about saying, "We will do it and we will listen and understand?"

The rational mind has trouble with the order of those words. Normally, we want to first listen and understand, then, if it makes sense and seems valuable, we decide to do it. What is so holy about doing something before you even know why? How is that the secret of the Upper World?

We come into this life with built-in physical instincts. Last year I witnessed a goat just as it was born on a farm. Nobody had to teach the baby goat how to get up on its legs. No one had to show it how to suckle, it latched on to its mother and knew exactly what to do. No one has to teach us to eat when we're hungry or tell a baby to cry when it's uncomfortable.

Just as the body has its knowing, there are spiritual instincts that are woven into the very fabric of our souls. But for most of us, these instincts are so subtle that we don't know how to access them. That's why the rational mind says, "First explain it to me, then I'll decide whether to do it or not."

But in high holy matters there is a knowing that the soul possesses, and that knowing is so clear. When the soul knows, it immediately says, "Count me in." I'm not talking about impulsive or risky behavior. We take those dangerous leaps when we listen to the body's desires or the ego's ambitions without first consulting the soul. Here I am describing those sacred moments when the soul can sense what is right for you. It doesn't need to know more than that.

That is the second revelation the Children of Israel received at Sinai. It was a self-revelation, the Torah within. The secret of the Upper World is the voice planted already inside you that knows instinctively what is good, what is true, and what God wants from you.

There are parenting books to teach you how to raise courageous children, how to raise successful children, how to raise children with self-esteem. But I believe deep down we all want to know how to raise kind children who are soulful and true to themselves. And you don't need to read a parenting manual to teach you what your soul knows instinctively.

When I first gave birth to our son, Adi, I felt so lost as a mother. I didn't know how to nurse him or bathe him or diaper him, or how to swaddle him, or how to calm him when he was crying. When they discharged me from the hospital and sent Rob and me on our way I thought, *Are they nuts? This is child endangerment for sure.* I was petrified to take this fragile new life home with me.

But it didn't take very long for me to become an expert at my son's needs, to understand his sounds and to comfort him. Parenting can be terrifying indeed, but "a mother's intuition" is simply another way of describing the soul's knowing. If we allow it to guide us, we will raise children who know their own souls too.

To learn this truth, you simply need to listen to what's already planted in your soul and lead from there. See, trust, and know your own soul and then you will understand how to see, trust, and know your children's souls. Raise them to become who they already are. If you see your child, really see their soul, your child will learn to want to see others in their fullness as well, and that is the key to kindness.

My dear friend Elaine Hall adopted a beautiful child from Russia whom she named Neal. Soon it became clear that Neal was autistic.

There were doctors who told Elaine to place Neal in an institution, there were friends who advised her to return Neal to Russia. But Elaine always viewed Neal as a blessing, even in the most challenging, uncertain times. She didn't need any expert to tell her what her soul already knew—that she could and would find a way to tap into the voice of Neal's soul. Elaine has made the art of soul-knowing her life's work. She founded an organization called The Miracle Project where she and her colleagues use music and theater to draw out the talent and the passion of young adults with autism. Through drama, music, and art, Miracle Project students are learning to express their souls and to inspire people to listen and receive them as the holy blessings they are in this world.

Several years ago a young mother named Diana called me in tears. Her son Charlie had cerebral palsy and used a wheelchair to get around. On his ninth birthday as he was blowing out the candles Diana asked him, "Honey, what's your wish?" Charlie said, "I want to be able to walk this year."

Diana told me this story in tears. She didn't know what to say to her son. I remember asking her, "What are Charlie's gifts?"

Diana started listing them. "He's wise, he's kind, he's generous, he's joyful . . ." And then Diana stopped herself and she said with soul certainty, "Rabbi, God didn't give my child legs to walk, God gave him wings to fly and my job is to teach him to find his wings."

The soul has its answers for you in every situation of your life. As parents we all have our challenges and our fears, and we all have our frustrations. But your soul can see beyond every phase, every rebellion, and even every crisis into all the blessings that are here and all those that lie ahead.

Parents, I have one more suggestion for you: bless your children. On Friday nights as the Sabbath begins, it is a Jewish tradition for parents to place their hands on their children's heads and bless them. I've been doing this since the day each of my kids was born. My children are grown now and out of the house, but every Friday I hear from both of them—it doesn't matter if my daughter is at a party or if my son is in a bar. I get a call saying, "Mom, I'm ready for my blessing."

Bless your child and trust me, your hands will be on their heads forever blessing them no matter how far away you are, in this world and the next. It's never too late to begin blessing someone you love.

In the traditional Jewish Sabbath blessing, we pray that our children will grow to be like our patriarchs and matriarchs and we say the words of the Priestly Blessing: "May God bless you and protect you. May God's light shine on you and fill you with grace. May God's presence be with you and grant you peace."

Yes, it's wonderful to hope your child will become like one of the patriarchs or matriarchs, but I also think it's important to bless our children to become like their own unique souls.

I offer you this blessing I wrote for parents to say to their children:

May all the gifts hidden inside you find their way into the world.
May all the kindness of your thoughts be expressed in your deeds.
May all your learning lead to wisdom.
May all your efforts lead to success.
May all the love in your heart be returned to you.
May God bless your body with health and your soul with joy.
May God watch over you night and day and protect you from harm.
May all your prayers be answered. Amen.

And, reader, here is my blessing for you:

May your soul teach you how to fly and when you begin to soar may God laugh in surprise and say, "Who taught you the secret of the Upper World?" Amen.

UNCOVERING YOUR HOLY CALLING

". . . the way to reach the attainable measure
of peace of mind."
—from Einstein's letter to Rabbi Marcus

As the Love Force grows stronger within you, you may begin hearing and feeling something pulling you. Perhaps you are being called. The call is not restricted to your professional life. There are sacred calls tugging at you all the time, and you can learn to experience them and respond to them. Even your challenges can be keys to your calling.

You are needed daily. Every moment speaks your name, asking you to show up with all your gifts. But how do you uncover your calling? And how do you find the strength to answer the call when you'd prefer to ignore it or to run from it? You already know how to bring your body, your mind, and your ego to work each day. Imagine how your life might change if you could learn to bring your soul to work too.

I believe the soul within you is beckoning you to wake up and claim the life you were sent here to live. There is a prophecy echoing through time with only you in mind.

Heeding the Call of the Soul

I WAS SPEAKING IN NORTH CAROLINA several years ago and a driver was waiting for me outside my hotel, ready to take me to the airport. I got into the backseat of the car and he said, "When did you get the call?" I thought he was talking about the call from the car service company, but then I realized he meant the Call.

The Bible describes human encounters with the divine that send shivers down my spine. That's precisely what Dr. Berk was trying to tell me when I felt my father's soul beside me and I thought I was losing my mind in college. He said, "Naomi, you come from a tradition of the great prophets, of Abraham and Moses and Deborah and Samuel—they were all touched by a Presence." He reassured me, "Trust me, you're not losing your mind. You're meeting your soul . . . and your father's soul too."

It's not always easy to hear the call or to understand what's being asked of us. In the Bible, young Samuel hears a voice calling him, but he assumes it is his mentor Eli summoning him. It takes the young novice three trips to Eli to finally realize the call is not coming from his master.

The Prophet Jonah has another problem. He hears the call clearly, but instead of heeding the call, he runs from it. Sometimes you know what the universe wants from you, you understand your gift, but you suppress it. Some run from their call because it requires overwhelming effort. Others run from their call because they denigrate the very gifts they've been given. The soul is leading them in one direction, but the ego has other plans.

Our daughter, Noa, is hypothyroid and needs to get her blood drawn quite frequently. God bless her, she has the most uncooperative veins. We've been told she has "rolling veins"—veins that have a mind of their own and scare easily. The minute the nurse finds one, it runs away. Every blood draw involves many stabs in the first arm, and then inevitably the nurse ends up switching to the second arm, usually with no success. Then comes the heating pad and more stabs until somehow they can coax the blood out.

Last year we went in for a blood draw. The person drawing her blood was an African American man in his late forties who must have been close to seven feet tall. His hands were enormous and I wondered if they were delicate enough to detect Noa's invisible veins. He looked at Noa's left arm and rejected it immediately. He said to Noa, "Never offer your left arm." Then he looked at her right arm and in no time at all he found the vein and it was all over. I said, "Thank God."

He said, "Yes, thank God."

He let the words just hang in the air between us until I had to ask, "What do you mean by 'thank God'?"

That's when he opened up: "When I was younger I fought it, I didn't want to acknowledge this gift God gave me. I had bigger dreams so I kept running from it. But God gave me this gift and I'm good at it." He told me that for years he thought he was going to be a basketball star, and it never worked out. I said, "You don't know how talented you are. You have a gift, you are helping people. Use it with pride."

The renowned educator Parker Palmer once taught, "Our strongest gifts are usually the ones we're barely aware of possessing."

So often we yearn for something that actually runs against the grain of our souls. The ego has its own plans for us. Palmer taught that the word "vocation" is derived from the Latin word for "voice." He said vocation does not mean "a goal I pursue," it means "a calling that I hear." It doesn't come from willfulness. It comes from listening.

When he was in elementary school, our son, Adi, began running around in circles at home. He would do this for hours at a time. It was a bizarre behavior. Friends of mine suggested that I should try to distract him, to try to break this habit. I was a bit worried too. What was going on inside his head? Was he anxious? Upset? So I simply asked him, "Adi, what are you thinking about when you run your laps?"

He said, "I'm telling myself stories."

I said, "I'd love to hear them. Do you want to write them down?"

The next thing I knew, Adi began writing and writing. Stories about pirates and shipwrecks and cowboys with courageous heroes and dastardly villains. He was a remarkable storyteller. And he never stopped writing or running. He became captain of his high school's cross country team. And today he is a playwright living in New York.

Finding your way in life is not so much about choosing a direction. It's about uncovering the voice of the soul, the call that is already imprinted inside you, and then finding the courage to face down your fears and let your true voice be heard.

One of my favorite verses from the Song of Songs is when the lover calls out, "Let me hear your voice, for your voice is sweet." The ancient rabbis insisted it was God who was speaking those words to each one of us, "Let me hear your voice, for your voice is sweet."

It takes time and courage to find your voice. We spend so much time in life trying to imitate other people or trying to live up to the projections people put on us. Or the projections we put on ourselves.

Too often we heed the call of the ego and ignore the call of the soul.

I've watched high school kids contort themselves to get into a prestigious college, only to be miserable there because that school didn't suit their souls. People seek impressive positions that play to their vanity but numb their souls. Too often we make the same mistake in relationships. We confuse looks or wealth with love.

When you align yourself with the call of your soul it feels as if life has unexpectedly fallen into place and fears that have gripped at your heart begin to give way to a heightened sense of purpose.

When I was reading through the letters Rabbi Marcus wrote home during World War II, descriptions of the living hell Europe was at that time as he was tending to his soldiers, I came upon the powerful realization he shared with his wife, Fay:

> Sweetest,
> Returned to headquarters from a tough day in the field . . .
> What matters to me is the extent to which I can bring some
> hope into the hearts of my boys on the fields of battle; to get
> them to think intelligently about the better world we are
> striving for; comfort them when they are cut down by the
> enemy; and help them find inner spiritual peace in moments
> of trial and danger. Strange, darling, but doing these things
> has caused me to lose all sense of fear. It has made me
> extremely happy in an exhilarating sort of way.
> Love to you, my darlingest, as ever,
> Bob.

Doing the work you were created to do, even when it is harrowing work, will leave you feeling lifted up and fulfilled.

Your soul is beckoning you to uncover your calling. Listen. Let your soul lead you to true work, true love, to truth in all your ways. Amen.

Knowing You Are the Right Man for the Job

MY SEARCH FOR MORE INFORMATION about Rabbi Marcus and his letter exchange with Einstein led me to a remarkable woman who received an unexpected call.

On the day that Rabbi Marcus entered Buchenwald and discovered one thousand Jewish boys who had miraculously survived, he sent a cable to the OSE, a Jewish children's welfare organization in Geneva.

A young woman named Judith Feist who was working for the OSE in Geneva found herself on the receiving end of that astounding cable. Judith was only twenty-one years old and was studying social work. When the Nazis came to power in France, her father was rounded up and slaughtered in Auschwitz. Her family went into hiding, living in constant terror of being discovered. Somehow she, her mother, and her two younger siblings managed to sneak across the border to safety in Switzerland. But even in her freedom, Judith was tormented. She suffered from dreadful insomnia, she had trouble eating.

And there she was, reading about these boys who had miraculously survived. Reading their names.

It was April 1945, the war was over. Somehow, for some reason,

Judith felt an immediate connection to boys she'd never even met and began making plans to find them. "I think because my father was sent to Auschwitz, I felt very near to the boys," she told me.

As Judith searched for a way to meet the Buchenwald boys, Rabbi Marcus escorted 245 of them on a train to France, where they were placed in an orphanage called Ecouis in Normandy. When the boys arrived all hell broke loose.

The adults were expecting to receive pitiful, well-mannered children grateful for any drop of kindness. That's not at all what they got. The boys were exploding with rage. They were suspicious of everyone. They were petrified of doctors, who reminded them of Dr. Josef Mengele, the infamous sadist of Auschwitz. The boys hardly spoke at all. They were violent, and they obsessively stole and hoarded food.

Many of the boys couldn't even remember their names. Whenever an adult asked a child, "What's your name?" he'd answer by calling out his concentration camp number. The boys all looked alike, with their shaved heads, emaciated faces, and the black circles around their cold, apathetic eyes. They didn't know how to laugh or smile or play.

The experts who observed these boys proclaimed a harsh diagnosis: they were derelicts, damaged beyond repair.

One afternoon, the counselors at Ecouis brought the boys a special French treat: Camembert cheese. The Buchenwald boys smelled this stinky stuff and were immediately convinced they were being poisoned. All at once they started throwing the cheese at the adults in a wild rage. Outbursts and unruly behavior persisted day after day.

There was one day that stood out, though. A day that would remain etched forever in the boys' memories. On that day, Rabbi Marcus came back to visit them. They were so excited to see him and he was overjoyed to be reunited with them once more. They ran toward him and encircled him. They all sat together on the grass. The boys waited expectantly for Rabbi Marcus to say something.

Rabbi Marcus wanted to speak, he tried to talk, but when he opened his mouth, he just broke down. The children were watching him and they were overwhelmed by the depth of his feelings for them. They beheld the tenderness and vulnerability of the man who had been their savior. It had been a long time since they'd seen an adult cry, and their own tears had dried up long ago.

All at once a fortress of defenses came down and the boys began to weep with the rabbi who had led them to freedom. One of the boys described Rabbi Marcus's visit this way: "The Chaplain returned to us our souls. He reawakened the feelings we had buried within us." That reunion with Rabbi Marcus opened a floodgate of memories. Boys who had completely blocked their past began remembering their parents and siblings and sharing stories for the first time.

But as soon as Rabbi Marcus left, the boys returned to their incorrigible antics.

Several weeks later, one hundred boys from Ecouis were transferred to another orphanage in France, called Ambloy. Ambloy was an orphanage for boys who wanted to keep the Sabbath and remain kosher.

In Ambloy, the boys' appalling behavior continued—constant fighting and stealing food. The Hungarian boys and the Polish boys were forever beating each other up at night in their shared bedrooms.

When Judith learned that some of the Buchenwald boys from Rabbi Marcus's cable were living in an orphanage in Ambloy, she immediately made arrangements to go there. She felt called to go.

Judith first met these boys who had been described to her as derelicts when she arrived at Ambloy one Thursday afternoon. They seemed cold and indifferent and barely acknowledged her presence. But when the Sabbath arrived, Judith watched the boys as they sang the prayers they remembered from their own childhoods. They sang with such passion. Instantly, Judith understood these boys weren't cold or indifferent. They were frozen by indescribable experiences of horror and loss.

In Judith's first few days at Ambloy, the director of the orphanage quit. He said he'd had enough. He was appalled by the boys and their utter disrespect, unruliness, and violence. Like the other experts who'd passed judgment on them, the director concluded: "The boys were born psychopaths, cold and indifferent by nature." He reasoned that it was their callous personalities that had enabled these boys to survive the camps in the first place, when so many other children had died.

With no backup in sight, the OSE asked Judith to step in and take charge.

And so it was that a twenty-two-year-old insomniac refugee named Judith became the director of the Ambloy orphanage. She had one hundred boys in her charge who had survived Auschwitz, the death march, and Buchenwald. Boys who had been torn out of their mothers' loving arms, boys who had witnessed the deaths of their parents, siblings, and friends. Boys who had nothing, no family, no home, no future. The experts said they were irredeemable, damaged beyond repair. Their fate was sealed. One hundred incorrigible derelicts, sociopaths.

How was this twenty-two-year-old young woman going to manage these hardened delinquents? The challenge was mind-boggling. Judith had no training as an orphanage director. She wasn't a psychologist. She'd been studying social work, but she hadn't completed her training. She wasn't even a teacher.

Sometimes life forces you to rise up beyond your limitations.

I asked Judith, "Were you frightened when the OSE asked you to take charge of the orphanage?"

Judith replied, "I was very sure of myself. I didn't mind at all."

"Really?" I said. "Weren't you even a bit worried?"

Judith told me, "I was sure I was the right man in the right place. I was the right man for the job."

I love that answer. It captures so perfectly the certainty and the clarity that come when we allow the soul to fulfill its mission without muddying things up, without overthinking things.

That word "sure" kept coming up over and over again as Judith spoke to me about her days at Ambloy. A knowing deep inside that she was doing what she was created to do.

As she took charge of her one hundred derelicts, Judith began thinking, *How can I possibly restore these boys to hope, to laughter?* So with virtually no training at all, Judith became the Jewish Mary Poppins.

Judith knew that her first challenge was to earn the boys' trust. It was her top priority to learn every boy's name. She realized that to speak a boy's name was to restore him to his unique identity. She said she could detect a hint of a smile each time she would greet a boy by his name. She also began learning as much Yiddish as she could, because the boys were never going to warm up to her in her native German, and none of them spoke even a word of French.

Judith understood that it was her job to make openings for the boys to begin to speak about their parents and their brothers and sisters. She said, "They needed to speak and I was listening to them." Judith was assisted in this by a remarkable young woman named Niny Wolf. Many of the boys developed mad crushes on the beautiful, compassionate Niny. This too was a sign of hardened hearts melting. The boys were hopelessly smitten.

Next, Judith was determined to heal the way the boys approached food, the constant stealing and hoarding. Who could blame them? They had known starvation for so long. Judith trusted her instinct about how to solve this problem. She told the boys that from now on, the kitchen would be open twenty-four hours a day and they could come eat and take food as they pleased. Overnight the stealing and hoarding stopped. Soon the kitchen became the soul of the orphanage—yes, a home has a soul too. The kitchen became a place where the boys loved to congregate, especially around Niny.

There was one boy who didn't hang around the kitchen with the others. He sat and wrote and wrote in a journal. Was he antisocial? Withdrawn? Or was this writing too somehow the beginning of an opening?

Now that she'd solved the food theft problem, Judith faced another challenge. She needed to find a way to stop the fighting in the rooms between the Polish boys and the Hungarian boys. This was no small matter. Boys were getting beat up and injured. Judith contemplated the living situation in the orphanage and found an ingeniously simple solution. The previous director had grouped the boys in rooms according to their age. Judith set a new rule. She told the boys that she wanted them to group themselves in bedrooms according to their hometowns.

It was a stroke of genius.

Now boys were living with other boys from their own villages and shtetls. There were eight-year-olds living together with sixteen-year-olds, but there was comfort in familiarity. The older boys looked after the little ones, the little ones looked up to the older boys. They proudly wrote the names of their villages on their bedroom doors. And the fighting and the aggression stopped.

Judith was witnessing how a tiny modification could cause a huge shift in the boys.

Day by day, the boys were improving, but they were still plagued by flashbacks and horrible memories. Many of them weren't ready to believe that their parents and siblings weren't ever going to come back for them. They waited and they hoped in vain. And then Yom Kippur arrived and the hour of Yizkor, the memorial service for the departed, came.

An argument broke out among the boys. Judith overheard the debate. Some boys insisted it was wrong to say Kaddish, the prayer for the departed, for their parents and siblings. They might not be dead. "How awful and disgraceful to pray for them as if they were dead."

The others argued back, "But you have been in Auschwitz yourself! You have seen the gas chambers with your own eyes and the smoke and the corpses. You witnessed what happened to the women and the children. Why keep the illusion? We have to say the prayers for the dead."

Finally, one group of boys walked out of the synagogue in protest. Those who remained stood up and their tough, indifferent exteriors melted away. Imagine the sight of sixty boys mourning everything and everyone: mother, father, brothers, sisters, grandparents, aunts, uncles, cousins, entire villages. In one voice they began, "*Yisgadal, ve-yiskadash, shmey raba.*"

That Yizkor service at Ambloy marked a great shift in the lives of the boys who were able to recite the mourner's Kaddish. It was a letting go, a readiness to move forward and face a new day. Judith told me she saw a remarkable change in the faces of the boys who said Kaddish. "They were able to see that they lost somebody," she told me. "They looked different, they were less desperate. They were able to say goodbye."

Soon, Judith and the boys moved from Ambloy to a new orphanage in a town in France called Taverny and quickly settled into life there. Judith insisted that the boys take on chores, which they did reluctantly, but they all eagerly pitched in to prepare for the Sabbath because it reminded them of their childhood homes. A boy named Menashe looked forward to leading the services together with some of the older boys.

Every now and then a new orphan, lost and hungry, would come knocking on the door asking if he could live with them. Instead of making the decision herself, Judith would turn to her boys and ask them, "What would your parents have done? Would they have welcomed this boy?" She let them take control and invite the new boy to stay on.

What was Judith doing? She was restoring a sense of control to children who had been robbed of all control and freedom. They could make decisions now. And at the same time, she was also reminding them of the loving homes they came from. Reminding them that they were once loved and they would always be loved. And that they would love again.

By now the boys' hair had grown in and their faces had filled out, and Judith hit upon another inspiration. She took the boys on a train to the photographer so that they could have their pictures taken. These were boys who had lost all sense of identity. There were no mirrors in the concentration camps. The boys were mesmerized by their own faces. They couldn't get enough of looking at themselves in those photos. Judith told me, "I think they saw they were alive."

Soon smiles came and laughter.

One day Judith purchased tickets for the boys to see *The Magic Flute* at the Paris Opera House. She got front-row balcony seats. Judith told me, "This was a very, very sentimental evening." She took pleasure in seeing the dreamy expressions on the boys' faces on the train ride home. She was breathing new life into their hardened hearts, and day by day there was a softening.

Judith succeeded beyond her wildest imagination. She turned this band of incorrigible boys into a family, and the orphanage into a home. She indeed had given them back their souls. But before long, one by one, it was time for the boys to leave. Relatives learned of their existence and sent for them. Soon boys were departing for South America, Australia, Canada, Israel, and the United States. Judith told me, "Each time a boy left, it was very difficult for the others he left behind." And of course Judith knew it would be even more difficult for the ones who left.

How would these boys enter families and schools and a society that could never begin to understand the horrors they'd endured and the losses they had suffered?

The early letters from abroad were heartbreaking. One boy wrote to her from Bolivia, "My two brothers received me very well, but they don't understand me . . . My brothers show everyone the camp numbers tattooed on my arm. I'm an odd creature, a living museum

piece . . . I am going to find work, save enough money and then return to Taverny. Write to me quickly and tell me my place is not taken
and will always be reserved for me."

Judith had to sit on her hands and not respond to these early letters. She knew she needed to give the boys time to adjust. One by one
they departed until in 1947, after two years of devotion, there were
none left.

Judith was all of twenty-three years old and bereft of her remarkable nest, but she was very proud too. She would probably never see
her boys again, but she took comfort in knowing she had done her job
well, she had sent them off with hope in their hearts.

Judith told me, "By helping the boys, they helped me. I felt very,
very sure of myself. That's because of them. I felt very, very strong. And
very, very grateful that I could help them."

And there was a remarkable life awaiting her: love, marriage, three
wonderful children, seventeen grandchildren, and sixty-four great-
grandchildren! And a master's degree in social work, and a Ph.D. too.

What became of her derelicts? Those psychopaths who were beyond repair? They became successful, respected businessmen, an ac-
countant, an artist, a surgeon, an electrical engineer. Menashe, the
boy who enjoyed leading services, became a rabbi and scholar, Rabbi
Menashe Klein, who took his rightful place as the rabbinic leader of
a Hasidic dynasty in Brooklyn. He published twenty-five volumes of
commentary and became the head of a Talmudic academy. Naphtali
Lau-Lavie became a journalist for the Israeli newspaper *Ha'aretz* and
then became Moshe Dayan's right-hand man and spokesman for
Israel's Defense Ministry, and from there went on to became Israel's
consul general in New York. His little brother, Lulek, went on to
become Rabbi Yisrael Meir Lau, the chief Ashkenazi rabbi of Israel.
Kalman Kalikstein became a world-famous nuclear physicist and
professor at NYU.

And then there was that boy who was forever scribbling notes in his journal. His name was Elie Wiesel. He wrote the first draft of *Night* under Judith's care in the orphanage at Ambloy.

ONE DAY, TWENTY YEARS AFTER she first met the boys at Ambloy, Judith got an invitation to attend a celebration in New York to commemorate the twentieth anniversary of the liberation of Buchenwald. The letter came from her Buchenwald boys. She told me, "They organized it and they paid my journey to come to New York."

On her flight over to New York, Judith kept poring over a photo of the boys that had been taken in Ambloy. Twenty years was a long time. Would she even recognize their faces?

They met her at the airport with a bouquet of flowers. Judith told me, "It was a very emotional meeting."

Can you imagine that reunion? Many of the boys who flew in for the event hadn't seen one another in twenty years. Most of them were married with children, but they greeted each other as if no time had passed at all. They remembered all the old nicknames and kidded one another. They still called one boy "redhead," even though he had gone completely bald!

Then the night of the dinner arrived. Menashe, now a rabbi with a long gray beard, stood up and led the boys in the blessing for new beginnings: "Blessed are You, O Lord our God, Ruler of the universe, who has given us life, sustained our lives, and enabled us to reach this joyous moment."

And then Menashe said, "Tonight's gathering serves as a continuation of the Yom Kippur in Ambloy when some had refused to participate in the Yizkor service, refused because there was still hope. Today we know that our parents and our relatives will never return . . . Let us rise and think of them, let us say Kaddish."

Together in one voice with tears streaming down their cheeks, the Buchenwald boys began, *"Yisgadal, veyiskadash, shmey raba."*

After honoring the memories of the departed, it was time for honoring the woman who had done so much to give them back their lives. I asked Judith, "What did they say?"

She told me humbly, "They thanked me." And then she repeated, "It was a very emotional meeting."

Judith wrote a book called *The Children of Buchenwald* about her experiences with her derelict boys. The foreword is a heartfelt letter to Judith:

> Dear Judith,
>   . . . Did you know Judith, that we pitied you? We felt so sorry for you . . . You thought you could educate us . . . We observed you with amusement and distrust . . .
>   How did you succeed, Judith, to tame us? . . . It could not have been easy to educate a group of children like us, with our peculiarities and our obsessions. Nor did you have any guidelines.
>   We did not want your help, your understanding . . . The fact is that all the children could have chosen violence or nihilism but you succeeded to direct us toward confidence and reconciliation. You supported and encouraged us to choose a stake in the future and in community.
>   Judith, do you realize how much you meant to our very existence?
>   Elie Wiesel

I asked Judith, "Did you have any inkling that Elie Wiesel would become the voice of conscience to our world?"

She laughed. "I didn't know he was remarkable."

JUDITH RECENTLY CELEBRATED HER ninety-third birthday. I went to visit her in Jerusalem two summers ago. She lives in a retirement home with her husband, Claude. I was expecting to meet an old woman, but Judith is a powerhouse, full of energy and strength. She holds her accomplishments so very lightly.

When we sat down together I asked Judith if she wanted me to read her the letter that Einstein had written to Rabbi Marcus, the letter that had led me to her. "Yes, please read it," she said. So I did.

Judith asked me to read the letter three times. She seemed to be meditating deeply on it. Finally she said, "Yes, yes! This is a comfort . . . Yes! Peace of mind."

And then Judith said to me, "I'd love to talk for longer, dear, but you see, I have a piano lesson." And the next thing I knew, there was Judith sitting beside her piano teacher reviewing a classical piece that she was trying to perfect.

I'VE LEARNED SO VERY MUCH from Judith. She taught me what can happen when you follow the call of your soul. She taught me about the confidence that comes when you know you are "the right man in the right place."

We've all been hurt by life. Within us there is a voice that would prefer to walk out the door when painful memories arise, just like the Buchenwald boys who were not ready to say Kaddish. A voice that would prefer to ignore and deny our pain. But as Judith has taught me, somewhere in our past someone was blessing us. And those blessings, they never die. Time has no power to diminish them.

Twenty years can vanish in an instant. Suddenly you once again recall a hand stroking your head, the smell of your mother's kitchen, the laughter, the smiles, the love, the lessons. The blessings that keep blessing us. Sweet memories that will forever accompany us into every new sweet day.

And those blessings we received, they give us the strength and the desire to bless and heal others.

May you come to see you are the right man for the job. May you live to say the word "sure," to stand tall and strong in your convictions. May you be filled with a longing to restore the souls of others. And may you come to see that in saving others you are saving your own soul. Amen.

Feeling the Soul's Tug

EVERY YEAR, THE RABBIS in Los Angeles get together in late August for our annual High Holy Day sermon seminar. The anxiety in the room is palpable and it's contagious.

After the keynote lecture there are breakout sessions. Several classes run simultaneously. One year I found myself struggling to choose which session to attend. I thought to myself, *What if I pick this session, but it's boring? What if the one down the hall is where the great ideas are flowing?* When I finally chose my session, I was having trouble listening to the lecture because I kept imagining the wonderful discussion taking place on the other side of the wall.

At the end of the day I felt like I needed a Valium. As I was driving home, a rabbi friend of mine called and said, "So? Did you get any sermon ideas?"

"No," I said. "The whole time all I could think about was that I was in the wrong class. I went to session three, but I could hear everyone laughing in session four. I wish I knew what happened in session four."

My friend said to me, "Session four? I was there. Trust me, nothing happened in session four except a whole lot of talking!" He paused and then said, "So you went all day and no sermon ideas?"

And then it hit me. Wrong room. Wrong class. Wrong place. So much of our lives are consumed with a nagging feeling that we're not in the right place. Wherever we are, we're missing out. We're being pulled in a thousand directions and it's tearing us apart. And we are numb to the one pull we actually need to feel—the tug of our own souls.

There are so many forces pulling on us.

How many working parents have shared this frustration with me? "When I'm at home, I feel like I should be at work. When I'm at work, I feel like I should be at home." The end result is a person who can't enjoy work and who can't enjoy being at home either.

In the Bible when Cain kills his brother, Abel, his punishment isn't a death sentence. His punishment is: "You will be a fugitive and a wanderer upon the earth." His punishment is restlessness, an inability to find a home. Perhaps that's a punishment worse than death. Alas, we are all Cain's descendants. How many of us are having trouble settling down in our own skin?

A rabbinic commentary on the Book of Ecclesiastes says: "No man leaves this world with even half his desires fulfilled." Our problem of wanting everything isn't new, it's as old as humanity.

First, it involves a touch of envy—*I want what she's got. I want his life. That house, that car, that job, that spouse, that body, that vacation, that child.*

But it's not just envy. Our restlessness is part of the paradox of choice. *I want the freedom to choose, but I don't want to actually choose and give up my freedom.*

I recently read a book called *Willpower* by Roy Baumeister and I learned an interesting fact: the word "decide" has the same root as the word "homicide." To decide means we've got to kill off all the other possible choices out there. There's such a strong desire to keep all those alternative scenarios alive, to keep our options open.

Somewhere deep inside us we know it's not possible to juggle it all.

The challenge of our time is that technology gives us the false hope that we can be here and there at the same time, that we no longer need to choose. It's a hubris, a belief that nothing will suffer as a result of our multitasking.

Our thinking is suffering, our creativity is suffering, our relationships are suffering, our work is suffering, our bodies are suffering, our emotions are suffering, our driving is suffering, our sex lives are suffering. Our souls are suffering.

Not long ago I got a call from a rabbi whose teenage son had stopped speaking to him. My friend admitted to me that he'd often been distant and unavailable as a father.

He started sobbing, and he said, "I can see it now. I was the one who disappeared in plain sight and now I want to reach him and he won't look at me." He went on, "Naomi, I can remember him tugging at me, I can still feel him tugging at me, my little boy, 'Daddy, come see!' 'Not now,' I'd say. 'Stop it,' I'd say. And now I can't reach him."

Who's tugging at you? What are you ignoring? I believe that our souls are constantly tugging at us the way a child tugs at a parent.

All through your life your soul's been tugging at you: "Look!" The soul keeps trying to show you things of beauty: "Please, can you just stop to see that?" "Can you spend more time with this person?" "Can you study that wisdom?" "Can you slow down please?" But your ego has other plans, your body has better things to do. Your mind is muddled and distracted.

Parker Palmer wrote that the soul speaks to us only in quiet moments. He said meeting the soul is like encountering a deer in the woods. We've all been there, quietly beholding a breathtaking creature.

Imagine you're in the woods by a river. It's dusk, and you're sur-rounded by trees as far as you can see. And then you spot her, a doe.

Take it slow. How quiet you have to be. How still. The slightest noise will scare her away. You're patient. You stare into her eyes. You draw a tiny bit closer. Baby steps. You stop. You behold her.

And you give thanks for that precious meeting.

This is what it takes to meet your soul. She's got something to tell you. Something to give you. But how can we possibly arrive at a place of true meeting with our own souls, with others, or with the divine, if we're constantly scaring them away?

If only we could see what we're missing. If only we could see all the lost moments. A rabbinic commentary I once read cries out to us, "Yes, you can repent for a sin, but when your whole life is passing you by and you're asleep, repentance can't help you. You can't even see what needs to change."

In the Bible, God is preparing Moses for the moment of revelation on Mount Sinai. God says, "Climb up the mountain toward Me and be there." "Climb up," we can understand. But why does God have to add, "and be there"? Where else is Moses going to be? If Moses is already on top of the mountain, why does God have to say, "and be there"?

Here is my favorite interpretation of this verse: God adds "and be there" because it's possible to be standing before the very presence of God on the top of Mount Sinai and to still have your thoughts fixed on the ground below.

So if Moses had to battle distraction when he was all alone on a mountaintop standing before the very presence of God, how are we supposed to stay present to the divine when we're constantly being pulled away?

It's not just the soul tugging at us. God is tugging too. The Baal Shem Tov, the founder of Hasidism, taught that God never stops calling us. Every day God's voice echoes from the place of eternity. It ripples through time, tugging at us: "Come back, my children." But tragically we can't hear it.

No, our ears can't hear the call, but our souls can hear it, and the call gives rise to little tugs of return. Every day God is sending us little tugs calling us back from wherever we are straying. Little whispers: "Come back."

"I am asleep, but my heart is awake, the voice of my beloved is knocking." I love this verse from Song of Songs so much that my husband and I have it engraved inside our wedding rings.

I'm asleep, but there's a little part of me that's awake and it can hear the knocking. Love is knocking. The soul is knocking. God is knocking.

God's tug isn't just one more distraction in your day. It isn't a tweet, it's a life rope, a voice calling out to you, *Hold on and I will lift you up, hold on and I will show you how this world is more beautiful than heaven.*

What is a tug? It's not the pull of your "to do" list. It's not the tug of what I *ought* to do. It's the tug of what I was *born* to do. Too often we follow the voice of "What do I need?" But the tug isn't "What do I need?" It's "Where am I needed?"

How do we respond to those tugs? Like those precious moments of grace, most of the time we hear them and let them pass like a daydream. Or we say, "Not now." We say, "I can't." "I'm not strong enough, I'm not talented enough, I'm not good enough." "*I'm* not enough."

And what about the way you and I tug at others? You want someone's attention and you're not really getting it. You want to be understood. You want to be loved. You want to be appreciated. You want to be remembered. You want to matter and to make a difference in this broken, beautiful world.

Maybe you've forgotten how to tug. Maybe you're too scared to ask. Maybe you remember tugging long ago and being turned away. Maybe you're afraid of being rejected. Maybe you are afraid to want. Maybe you just don't have the words.

We tug at God too. Isn't that what prayer is?

In a breathtaking description of prayer, Rabbi Kalonymus Kalman Shapira, the grand rabbi of Piaseczno, Poland, who was slaughtered in the Holocaust, wrote these words to us:

> *It will also happen sometimes that you will not feel a need to speak words of prayer and you will not feel a need to ask for something from God, nevertheless you will feel something hard to describe, a kind of throwing yourself at God to endear yourself, like a child who in a sweet way is pestering his father—he doesn't want anything, but is just moaning and sighing, "Daddy, Daddy." His father asks him, "What do you want, my child?" He answers, "Nothing." But he continues calling, "Daddy, Daddy." . . . You too will sometimes feel . . . this kind of longing, without speech and without words and with nothing to ask of God. It is just your soul's unspoken chant, "Master of the Universe, Master of the Universe."*

The soul prays: *God, I just need to know You're there.* That alone is enough. No words, just a calling out and a longing to be heard.

All that restlessness that we suffer from—"I want this, I wish I was there"—it's just our egos messing with us. There's something real happening, and we're missing it because we're paying way too much attention to things that are unreal.

The tug is more than a promise you made to others. It's more than a promise you made to yourself. The soul's tug *is* your promise.

A few weeks ago a man who is going through a very tough time asked me, "Rabbi, do you believe in guardian angels?"

I thought about this for a while. I didn't want to dash his hopes, but I wanted to be honest too. I said, "I don't believe in force fields that repel all dangers. But I do believe in cheerleaders."

In a famous rabbinic commentary it says, "Every blade of grass has its angel that hovers over it and whispers, 'Grow, grow.'"

Think of the tug as the soul within you whispering to you, "Grow, grow."

So the next time you feel a tug, don't let it slip away from you. Ask yourself, *What was that?* Reach for it. Let it in. As we've learned to do with moments of grace, grab on, the way you grasp on to your lover. Concentrate on the verse from the Song of Songs: "I held him close and would not let him go."

Hold on to those sacred tugs for dear life. And may they lead you on a path to blessings. Amen.

Turning Your Weakness into Your Strength

HOW DO YOU FOLLOW YOUR soul on a mission? The rational mind tells you, *Play to your strengths*. Look at your gifts and your passions and they will show you the way. But your soul whispers, *Look to your shortcomings too!* Your very weakness may be the key to your life's work.

Dr. Alan Rabinowitz is one of the world's most respected zoologists, who has trekked the earth's last wild places to secure a home for animals at the brink of extinction. Alan is cofounder and CEO of Panthera, a nonprofit organization dedicated to saving wild cats. *Time* magazine described him as "The Indiana Jones of Wildlife Protection."

I first encountered Alan on the radio while I was driving. Listening to him tell his story, I was spellbound. I wanted to speak with him myself because I knew he would be able to share important soul lessons with me.

On the day of the interview we were both uncomfortable. Alan is used to being interviewed by *National Geographic*, why was he talking to a rabbi?

I could sense from his abrupt tone that Alan thought it was going to be a very short conversation. But he and I ended up speaking for several hours over two days. He told me our conversation was the single longest interview he's ever given. It turns out that a zoologist can teach a rabbi a whole lot of spiritual wisdom.

I'd like to share with you what Alan taught me.

I asked Alan, "How in the world did a Jewish kid born in Brooklyn in the 1950s end up spending his life in remote jungles communing with endangered tigers, leopards, and jaguars?"

Alan said, "Rabbi, as a kid I had a very, very strong stutter." He explained that at that time people didn't know how to deal with stutterers. "The New York City public school system put me in special classes, classes that all the other kids referred to as the 'retarded classes,' so we wouldn't be disruptive to the 'normal' school system." Alan said his stutter was so bad that he simply stopped talking to people.

As I was listening to Alan I pictured a vibrant child so utterly misunderstood.

Alan told me about his parents and how they tried to help him. He said, "My parents tried to fight the good fight. But they were simple middle-class Jews, they didn't know what to do." Still, they did what they could. He said, "They tried sending me to psychotherapy, hypnotherapy, to drug therapy, to psychiatrists. At one point I even had a dose of shock therapy, thinking maybe that would snap me back into normality." Nothing worked.

Alan described himself as a kid full of rage and hurt. He was mute all day long at school and didn't have any friends to play with or to talk to.

I asked Alan, "Didn't anyone understand?"

Alan laughed. "The only living beings I could express my feelings to were my pets." Remarkably, Alan said he could speak in full, fluent sentences to animals without stuttering. Like Superman, Alan led a double life. By day he was awkward and ostracized. And then, like Clark Kent transforming inside a phone booth, Alan would slip into his bedroom closet at night, and there his true identity would emerge.

"I would come home from school, where I was viewed as at best different and at worst retarded, and I would go into my dark little closet with my green turtle, a chameleon, a hamster, a snake—New York pets—and I would talk to them."

Alan believed that the animals understood him, and he had deep empathy for them as well. Alan said, "I realized that they had no voice either. Animals have feelings and thoughts, and yet people treat them as if they have none. So one day I swore that if I ever got my own voice back and learned to control my stuttering, I would use it for the animals."

Alan's father tried to help him deal with his anger by taking him to the one place he loved most: the old Great Cat House in the Bronx Zoo.

I'd been to that same Cat House as a child, and to me it was a depressing place with a stench that made me gag. So I asked Alan, "What did you love so much about the Cat House?"

He said, "There was just big cat after big cat in these very bare, ugly concrete jail cells. There were lions and tigers and there was one jaguar. The old Cat House would just emanate energy and power, but a locked-up power, which is what really drew me. It was energy that was begging to be released but was being held captive."

I said, "The stuttering boy could relate?"

Alan said, "I would just key right into that energy because it was the same energy I was feeling inside myself, just locked inside my own head, not able to get out." He continued, "I would always go over to one of the two cats and I would lean over the bar and I would put my face as close to the cage as possible, and I would whisper to the cats as I would talk to the animals in my closet at home. I would talk about how I was feeling. How I knew how they felt."

As he was about to leave the Cat House, Alan would whisper repeatedly, "I'm going to find a place for us. I'm going to find a place for us." Alan said to me, "I don't think I really knew what I meant as a child. I had no idea that I would someday be a wildlife biologist and save big cats like them in the wild. All I knew was they were like me and somehow I was going to find a place for us."

Eventually Alan went to a clinic in upstate New York where he received intensive therapy and learned how to control his speech.

Alan was nineteen when he finally learned to speak. Ironically, once Alan started speaking he realized he didn't really want to be among the world of people. He told me, "I was so excited to join normal society, but no one had much to say that was of interest to me." His work with animals was a welcome escape. He pursued studies in zoology and wildlife conservation.

Before long, Alan, that stuttering, lonely kid, talking to his pets in the closet, became a giant in wildlife conservation. He was determined to keep the two promises he'd made to animals as a child: "If I ever find my voice I will be your voice" and "I'm going to find a place for us."

Alan delivered on his promises. He established the world's first jaguar preserve in Belize and he secured the world's largest tiger reserve in Burma. Alan told me his greatest achievement was the creation of the Jaguar Corridor, a giant habitat where jaguars can move freely, stretching all the way from Mexico to Argentina.

I asked Alan, "Have you ever seen your work saving animals as a divine calling?"

Alan laughed. He said for years he was so angry with God. "I spent so many years tortured as a stutterer, thinking, *Why me? Why would God torture a child?*"

But Alan told me that over the years in the wildest jungles he found his way back to God. I asked him to describe his experience of God to me. He laughed and said, "Rabbi, I knew you were going to ask me this as soon as I mentioned it."

He said, "To me God is a presence, an all-encompassing energy. The more I understand about science, the more I see of this incredible world, the more I realize that we know so little . . . There is a realm which we will never grasp."

I told Alan that his story moved me because it reminded me of a mystical teaching I learned a long time ago. It says that if you're having trouble figuring out why God put you here, one place to look for an answer is the place of your greatest challenge, the area of your life where you are most blocked.

And I asked him, "Alan, looking back at that tortured kid, can you see your stuttering as the key to your calling?"

Alan got animated. He said, "Rabbi, I wouldn't wish stuttering on anybody. But I truly believe that it was a gift given to me that enabled me to get to where I am today. I never could have done this all-consuming work short of something as harsh as stuttering."

I started talking to Alan about Moses, who was the most famous Jewish stutterer. I asked if he'd ever thought about the obvious parallels between himself and Moses. I said, "Moses started off his life unable to speak, and that frightened stutterer ended up becoming the greatest prophet and orator. I see a lot of similarities between you and Moses. He freed the Jews, you freed the tigers."

Alan was astounded. He said, "It's no surprise to me that a stutterer became the greatest orator."

We ended our conversation there. And when we picked up our discussion the next day, Alan told me he'd spent the night thinking about our talk. He said, "Rabbi, much to my wife's delight, I told her how you compared me to Moses."

I said, "It's a good comparison."

"You've made me think quite a lot about it, actually. About things which I normally don't think about. Like whether there's a higher purpose for what I do." He said he'd always thought his life had a mission. But he'd never thought about it as a divine mission.

I laughed and said, "That's all I was thinking about when you were talking to me."

Alan described his stutter as a phenomenal gift that also taught him how to read people.

I asked him, "What do you see in people?"

"I can hear people loudest when they're not talking," he said. "I'm always listening between the words. I read them by their pauses, by their silence."

I was transfixed by Alan's words, and by his quiet too.

Alan added, "People think I stare too intently at them. I'm trying to see them. Words are almost irrelevant to me."

I told Alan, "What you're describing sounds like the soul to me."

Alan said, "Rabbi, language is a finite box you're working with. When you're speaking, it's not from your deepest self. How can you wrap a finite phrase around infinite emotions?"

And then Alan told me, "You don't need words to get to the soul of another person."

FOLLOWING THE SOUL IS LIKE tracking a majestic endangered creature. It's so easy to miss the soul's silent cry, so easy to ignore its tugs and calls. The soul is here to guide you, but you never know where or when you are needed. Your soul's mission might lead you very far from where you expect to go. If you're having trouble finding your direction, perhaps, like Alan, you must search in the very place you've been running from, the area that is your greatest source of pain.

Our weaknesses and the challenges we face can shatter us, or they can shape us if we let them. I wouldn't wish my sufferings on anyone. But I know that my sufferings have called me and inspired me to comfort people. For that, I am grateful.

Alan told me he used to ask, "Why me?" But now he asks, "Why not me?" He said, "What does a challenge mean? It means something good if I make it something good."

Perhaps the key to your future is hidden inside the challenge you are struggling with right now.

What is your greatest challenge? We've all got our struggles. Your obstacle may be the key to your soul's mission.

Life isn't fair. And it's natural to get angry. It's natural to say, "Why me?" It's natural. But we're not here to be natural! Why should we expect so little of ourselves?

Within you are powers that you haven't even begun to tap into. There's a purpose to your life. A high purpose. Turn your shame into pride. You can do that. You can lift yourself up. And as you lift yourself up, you will lift others up too.

May you live to turn your curses into blessings, your fear into strength, your greatest block into your greatest opening. Amen.

Bringing Your Soul to Work

I WAS FAST ASLEEP when my phone rang just after midnight. In a daze I heard a man's voice quivering, "Rabbi, Cate tried to kill herself." It was Cate's dad, Craig. He began sobbing.

Cate was a bright-eyed twelve-year-old girl who was studying with me for her bat mitzvah. She loved bombarding me with questions and showing me that she wasn't afraid to criticize God. I told her I welcomed her questions and reminded her that the name Israel means "The One Who Struggles with God." I threw on some clothes and raced to the hospital.

Cate was in a locked psychiatric unit. I met her parents in the hallway. They looked shattered, withered. Her mom, Lauren, kept repeating in a blur, "Why? Why?"

I asked if I could talk to Cate alone. They were both eager for me to go in and speak with her. In Cate's doorway there stood a tall, muscular man in a police uniform. He entered her hospital room alongside me. He spoke harshly to Cate, as if she were a criminal. He said, "Now don't you try anything stupid here. I'm your guard, and there's nothing in this room you can use to hurt yourself. So just settle in and don't try anything dumb. I'll be standing outside the whole time." Cate and I were both relieved when the barking guard left the room.

I walked up to Cate and hugged her. I said, "I'm here for you. It's okay."

Cate said, "I don't know why I did it. I really don't. I don't know what I was thinking. It just sort of happened." And then she got very quiet. I decided to allow the quiet and didn't try to interrupt it with words.

A few minutes went by and Cate said, "I'm scared." She took my hand. Her hands were freezing. I began rubbing them to warm her up. Before long there was a knock on the door. It was another guard—a new shift had begun. This man was even taller and more muscular than the first guard. I wondered what words of wisdom this hulking character was going to offer.

The guard came toward us. He sat on the edge of Cate's bed and spoke to her. "My name is Michael, and the good Lord has sent me to be your guardian angel. That's right. I'm here to watch over you and to make sure you're safe from harm. That's my job, watching over you and keeping you safe."

I could see a calm settle onto Cate's face. Her eyes were welling up with tears of gratitude. She didn't expect this stranger to be so compassionate, neither did I. Cate's hands were warming inside my hands. The guard got up and said, "I'm right outside your door. You call me if you need anything. Remember, I'm Michael, your angel."

That night took place some twenty years ago. Cate went home within a couple of days and began therapy. She grew strong and confident, and now she is in her thirties, married, with a baby girl of her own.

There are many things I remember about that night, but the Tale of the Two Guards has remained embedded in my heart. The first man was doing his job, but he was operating from a place of ego and dominance. Michael came from a place of empathy, love, and light. He saw his work as a divine calling, and he was flowing and connecting from a place of soul.

You have the power to choose how to approach any profession. You can focus on getting the job done, or you can understand that you are here to do God's work. You can demand respect, or you can earn admiration.

What do you bring to work? Ego or soul? What would it look like to wake up each morning and believe that you've been charged with a holy mission? In Hebrew the word for "angel" means "messenger," nothing more. An angel is not a creature with wings, but a soul that knows it's been placed here for a reason.

You can view your work as toil, you can keep people in line by intimidating them, or you can bring your soul to work and understand that the good Lord has sent you here to help and to heal some corner of this world. You can rule over people and get compliance, or you can lead from your inner source of strength and spark others to participate with you in service to a greater good.

The choice is yours. Do you want to just get the job done, or do you have a vision for the future and understand that you must plant seeds and be patient? Create a climate of collaboration that nurtures passion, perseverance, and creativity, and you will live to reap a mighty harvest indeed. The effort you make has the power to transform thousands of lives you will never meet.

Do you have trouble seeing your work as a sacred task?

Perhaps you once felt called, perhaps you once were fired up with passion, but now you have trouble remembering what that felt like.

Sometimes you wake up and you can remember your dream, you're sure you can remember it, but by the time you get out of bed it's gone, it just slips through your fingers. It's there somewhere, you know it's somewhere in your head, but you can't reach it anymore, it's vanished like vapor.

What if you and I, what if we're God's dream? What if God dreamed us, but we're slipping through God's fingers? What if God keeps reaching out: *Where is that person I dreamed of? Why hasn't he taken shape?*

Why is she wasting time? Why can't he see his gifts? Why can't she live out her soul's promise?

There is a life that wants to be lived through you. There is a light that wants to shine through you. There is a dream that wants to be realized in you. There is a suffering that wants to be lifted by you. There is a world waiting for you.

God's call from Eden keeps piercing through time: "Where are you?" It's not an empty call to an indifferent universe. It's personal.

And if you want to live out your soul's mission, your response needs to be, "Yes, I'm here." We must learn to say *Amen* to life's call. To be part of the flow. To be a channel for good. You are so much more than your smallness. You are so much more than your ego's needs for vanity and praise.

You are so much more than even what you pray for.

Remember, "God's candle is the human soul." We've been put here to light up the world.

I never saw Michael the guardian angel again, but I am sure wherever he is, in this world or beyond, he continues watching over us just the way the good Lord intended him to.

In his *Song of Zion*, the medieval poet Yehuda Halevi wrote, "I am the harp for all Your songs." That's what we're asking of God when we search for a life path. We are seeking to be played masterfully by the Hand that knows each string and each chord intimately.

That's the key.

Let me be Your instrument, God. Pluck me, I'll be Your harp. Dream me, Your dream is still alive and well in me. Use me, let me be Your instrument for good. Light me and I will shine.

Play me, God, I am ready to live up to the dream You had, the dream called me.

Amen.

Defeating the Soul's Adversary

ANDREA IS AN ASPIRING DOCUMENTARY filmmaker in her early thirties. She came to see me because she was upset with herself. She told me that she'd recently received a grant to create the project of her dreams. But instead of diving into her film, Andrea was wasting precious time. She said, "Rabbi, I keep hitting snooze on my alarm. I get up around noon and surf the Internet and before I know it the whole day is gone. It feels like there's this devil on my shoulder."

I told Andrea, "I think you've come up against your *Yetzer*."

"My what?" she said.

I spoke to Andrea about the eternal battle each one of us must wage.

As you get closer and closer to fulfilling the mission of your soul, to living out your calling, you will most likely awaken your soul's adversary, a voice that says, *This will never work, why bother?*

Whose voice is that?

First, take a moment and think about what it is that you want deeply. What have you been praying for and longing for? Try to visualize it. What does it look like? Can you feel it?

Now that you've named your soul's deepest yearning, here is a second question: Have you prepared an adequate container for receiving what you want? There is a Hasidic teaching I once studied that says the key to fulfilling your mission is striking a balance between fire and the container that allows the fire to stay burning. The fire is the passion, adrenaline, the blessings from above that spark you. The container is a lot less sexy than the fire itself. It's the vessel you must create and maintain to keep that fire burning.

So how solid is your container? What sort of space have you made for welcoming the fire and for keeping it alive? Have you prepared a foundation to contain the fire so that it won't spread uncontrolled?

This is a sacred balancing act—the fire and its container.

In the realm of love, is ego taking up too much space? Have you learned to retreat enough to make room for anyone to enter?

Regarding your mouth, what balance do you keep between your restraint and your words? Between breathing in and whatever you spew out?

The truth is, building a strong foundation for the fire is all about constancy, the daily care you take in love, in living out your calling, in all your ways. One thing is for certain: you can't cram and you can't pull an all-nighter to succeed at constancy. There is only one way to achieve constancy, and without that solid container, the Hasidic teaching goes, you end up walking around like someone with a hole in his pocket. Every day you receive sacred gifts, sparks of holiness, and they all just fall away because you haven't built an adequate vessel for containing your own blessings, the ones you've already been given.

Sometimes you *have* built a solid foundation, but you've welcomed in the wrong guest. You realize you've become a comfortable dwelling place for the *Yetzer*, a spiritual force the rabbis speak about that is always trying to subvert you from living up to your own gifts and your sacred mission in life.

What can I tell you about the *Yetzer*?

In the Talmud, there is a teaching that every person is born with a good impulse and an evil impulse. There's a world of good within us, but the evil impulse, which is known in Hebrew as *Yetzer Hara*, seeks to divert us from uniting our highest intentions with our actions.

The *Yetzer* is our tempter, our adversary, the voice always looking for ways to block us from improving and growing. Just as you get close to fulfilling your mission, the *Yetzer* kicks in and awakens. The *Yetzer* is the soul's nemesis, waiting for you, seeking to block you just as you enter the door that leads to your life path. The *Yetzer* is looking for you. It longs to cause you to stumble. It uses all sorts of sneaky tactics. It distracts us, demoralizes us, leads us astray. The *Yetzer* prevents us from seeing what needs to change. The *Yetzer* stretches us so thin that we become ineffectual. The *Yetzer* fuels our destructive tendencies. The *Yetzer* seduces us with unholy desire and longing for material possessions. The *Yetzer* induces despair: *There's no hope*, it whispers.

The *Yetzer* infuses us with the very quality Einstein described to Rabbi Marcus in his letter: the optical delusion that we are separate from the rest. The *Yetzer* deceives us into constricted vision, it feeds us false truths, causes us to plateau instead of grow. It deals in blindness and deafness.

Long before Freud taught us about the id, the rabbis defined our eternal battle with the *Yetzer*. The rabbis understood that like the id, the *Yetzer* is an engine that drives us. The Talmud offers us a dramatic story about a showdown between the rabbis and the *Yetzer*. In the tale the rabbis succeeded in trapping and jailing the *Yetzer*. They were elated. At last they could destroy the *Yetzer* once and for all and rid the world of evil. But during the *Yetzer*'s three days of imprisonment, the rabbis noticed that life was coming to a halt. Even the chickens stopped laying eggs. They suddenly understood that if you killed the *Yetzer*, the world would come undone. In the end the rabbis were forced to set the *Yetzer* free.

That's the paradox of the *Yetzer*. We need it in order to survive, but if we leave it unchecked it will destroy us, and everyone around us. The *Yetzer* is a foe, and we can't live without it.

The *Yetzer* isn't necessarily a demonic force. Much of the time it's just dimwitted and lazy, like Homer Simpson taking up residence inside you, making sure you accomplish nothing. So take a moment to ask yourself, *How have I given Homer a home within me?* As the rabbis taught, at first the *Yetzer* is a visitor, but then if we're not careful it becomes Master of the House.

We let the *Yetzer* get comfortable, he puts up his legs and spreads out. The *Yetzer* doesn't necessarily encourage you to cheat on your spouse or even to lie and steal, although it can lead you to those things too. Most of the time the *Yetzer* doesn't prod you to steal from anyone but yourself. The *Yetzer* says, *surf the Internet, check your e-mails, your Facebook, I need a new pair of pants.* It says, *I'm too tired, it's too sunny, it's too cloudy, it's too hot, it's too cold . . .*

Any step toward the fulfillment of our soul's calling will awaken the *Yetzer*. It is threatened by our ascent, and we must learn to see through whatever smokescreen the *Yetzer* sends our way. The *Yetzer* has many tools in its bag of tricks, all designed to trip us up—envy, pride, anger, indecision, despondency. The *Yetzer* tries to put us to sleep, to lull us into complacency.

We're all aware of the *Yetzer*'s excuses and how we allow it to have its way with us. Yes, you may have built a strong container, but it's become a receptacle for garbage. We consume junk, we listen to junk, we read junk. A twenty-four-hour news cycle of junk.

How do you stop being a hospitable home for the *Yetzer*? How do you learn to stay on your soul's path when the *Yetzer* is always blocking your way? In the Talmud the rabbis say: If you see the *Yetzer* is taking over your life, study Torah. If you manage to subdue it, well and good; if not, say the Shema prayer. If you manage to overcome the *Yetzer*, well and good; if not, consider the day of your death.

I love this teaching. How will thinking of the day of your death help you overtake the *Yetzer*? What does it mean? That in thinking of death you'll fear facing judgment from above? I don't think so.

Here is what I believe the teaching is saying: in thinking of death, you will look at your life and recognize all your soul was sent here to achieve and all the ways you've allowed the *Yetzer* to thwart you from following your soul on its holy mission. And for that you will truly have reason to kick Homer off the couch.

I didn't say kick Homer out! Destroying the *Yetzer* is not an option. The rabbis understood that nothing could happen without the *Yetzer*. They said, if it weren't for the *Yetzer* you would not build a house, or get married, or conceive a child, or even work. So why does the *Yetzer* become so agitated the closer you get to the truth of your life's calling? Perhaps it worries it will be left out once you no longer need its help.

Here is the only way I know to disarm the *Yetzer* and the roadblocks it seeks to send your way. Instead of demonizing it, welcome the *Yetzer* to join you on your path. Partner with it, but tame it. Let it know who is in charge. As the rabbis teach, the *Yetzer*'s desire is to rule over you, but you must learn to rule over it. Take charge with humility, love, and respect, and without judgment. Show the *Yetzer* that you recognize it. Say to it, "Come with me on this journey. I can't fulfill my mission without you."

The *Yetzer* will not acquiesce with ease. It will continue to tempt the body with desire and fill the mind with confusion and hopelessness. It will seek to steer you far away from your soul's calling by igniting your ego with vain ambition.

Be aware that the *Yetzer*'s most powerful weapon of all is one word: tomorrow. It seems like such a harmless word. It's hopeful even. But that one word causes more trouble than almost any other word. It's possibly the greatest obstacle to living up to our goodness. "Tomorrow" leads to so many missed opportunities. One day flows into another, and most of us haven't begun to prepare for the great gift of awakening that is ours to experience.

The *Yetzer* says, "I agree with you. You can fulfill your soul's calling. But start tomorrow."

The answer to the *Yetzer*'s "tomorrow" is so near. The answer is so simple yet so very difficult to achieve. The only antidote to "tomorrow" is "today." Today is the only day God ever gives us. You must say to your *Yetzer*: You won't have this day. Not today. I'm not going to let you have this day.

Every day you're given a chance to ask: Have I built an adequate container for my soul and all its blessings? Because ultimately the question we're asking is not: "What do I want to achieve?" It's: "What was I born to do, and how far have I strayed from the gifts I've been given?"

Every day is a time to consider the path of your life, what you have grown comfortable with—your failure to feel the holy in the daily, to see the holy in the daily, to live with the holy in the daily, and to walk with the Soul of Souls daily.

There's something your soul knows and wants to teach you, and it's not about the fire of passion. Creating a strong foundation is very unsexy. We would rather spend time and money on the magnificent architectural designs. No one cares about the foundation. But it's that sturdy foundation that saves us, the daily process of clearing out space with humility to make room for your soul to stretch out and make its home inside you. Building that foundation in what you read, what you study, in your silences, your listening, your constancy. Don't underestimate the smallest positive step, because even the smallest shift can have eternal ripples.

When I started writing my first book, a mentor took me under his wing and said, "Naomi, don't wait to be struck by lightning. Treat writing like you're a banker. Just get up in the morning and sit there and write. It's a job, just a job." When I was in high school a teacher of mine said to us, "If you want to learn, first you have to put your backside in the chair." That's the key to accomplishing any goal. A backside that's willing to stick to the chair.

Building the foundation is not very glamorous, but there is majesty in it, and magic too.

As the rabbi and founder of the Nashuva spiritual community, I know that there are many exalted moments in religious communal life. There are highs, intense connections, powerful prayer services, experiences that lift you up. But I also know that there wouldn't be a Nashuva without the foundation. Those are the people who give freely of their time and their talent and, yes, their funds, to keep our beautiful project alive, to give it wings and to keep its fire burning. There would be no community without all those little unsung, prosaic efforts.

It's our daily constancy, those small, simple practices that help us ascend beyond all the *Yetzer's* obstacles.

Every single day has its mission and its power.

May you live up to the holy power of today. Amen.

33

Know Who You Are

RECOGNIZING YOUR TRUE DIVINE POWER

IN APRIL 2016 I NOTICED a tiny dot on my nose, a dot as small as a pinprick. It seemed completely insignificant. I ignored it, assuming it would soon disappear, but it just wouldn't go away. On Friday morning, July 9, I went to the doctor to have that dot removed. It was supposed to be a totally routine procedure. But it turned out that the tiny spot was actually the tip of an iceberg, and beneath it there was an extensive infiltrative tumor. By the end of that day I was missing a lot of my nose. A lot.

It all happened so quickly. And the cancer wasn't on my arm or my leg: it was bull's-eye smack in the middle of my face. My nose was gone, and I'd need to get a new one really fast. The surgeon who removed the cancer told me I was going to need total nasal reconstruction. I didn't understand what that meant or who to go to for help.

The whole thing was so crazy, so unexpected.

And I always liked my nose!

I thought I had a good nose. Okay, it was a Jewish nose. But my name is Naomi Nechama Levy, for God's sake, and I'm a rabbi. Why shouldn't I have a Jewish nose? It fit me. And just like that, poof, it was gone.

And I missed it.

It's strange, a piece of my anatomy that I never spent five minutes thinking about and now I was mourning it. Suddenly I realized my nose was the sign of my clan. You're part of that tribe, the Levy nose, it looked like this. You could see the family resemblance. It was the seal of my family imprinted on my face.

In Hebrew the word for face is *panim*. In English, "face" means the surface of things, but in Hebrew *panim* means the interior of things. Your face reveals what's inside you, and now my face was disfigured, frightening, a freak show.

I kept contemplating that expression we say without thinking for a minute about its true meaning: "It's no skin off my nose."

It means, no big deal. I can handle this. Who cares? *No skin off my nose.* But suddenly I was realizing that having no skin on your nose was actually a really big deal. The situation was not life threatening, but it was full of life lessons.

The Jewish mystics have a concept called *Rishima.* It means the imprint a life experience leaves on you. If you endure something and then you just forget about it—if it doesn't change you in some way, if you don't learn anything from it—then it's as if the event never happened, as if your life is vanishing behind you. But if you go through something and it leaves its impact on you—if you grow from it, learn from it, change from it—then even a challenging time becomes a blessed teacher. Lessons are for sharing. So I'd like to share an important lesson I learned from my journey with skin cancer.

On that Friday afternoon after my skin cancer surgery, my dear friend Dr. Helene Rosenzweig, who is my dermatologist, began helping me find a surgeon who could perform my reconstruction surgery. Helene had a list of seven plastic surgeons she'd gotten from colleagues. I began Yelping the names on Helene's list. I decided if a doctor had more than three bad Yelps, that was it, I scratched that name off my list.

By Sunday afternoon I had two doctors on my list, and two appointments set for Monday. But later that evening I remembered a woman named Byrdie Lifson Pompan who's been to my Nashuva services. Byrdie, of course! I remembered Byrdie's story.

Byrdie was a top agent at Creative Artists Agency. She lived a fast-paced life making Hollywood movie deals. She had the perfect skill set for taking care of her clients and navigating her way through complicated negotiations. Of course she flew first class whenever she traveled. By night she'd lie in bed and read scripts. But suddenly Byrdie developed a facial paralysis, and an esteemed, renowned LA doctor misdiagnosed her with only a temporary paralysis when it turned out she had a brain tumor.

Byrdie's life was upended. Not only that, soon her father was told he only had two months to live. Byrdie found a doctor who promised she could give her father not two months but two more years of quality life to live. With her persistence, Byrdie was able to provide her dad with that blessed extra time with his loved ones until his death. And then Byrdie's brother was misdiagnosed with tension headaches. He died of brain cancer.

So many tragedies. I suppose Byrdie could have looked at all this suffering and loss and said, "I'm cursed" or "God must have it in for me." Or she could have become bitter or frightened.

But instead of crushing her, Byrdie's experiences awakened her and transformed her life. Suddenly Byrdie saw that she could take the exact same skills that made her a top Hollywood agent, the skills she excelled at, and use them to be an advocate for patients.

So Byrdie quit her job at CAA and set out on her new calling: to be an agent for patients, pairing every patient up with the best possible doctor for their particular illness. Using the same set of skills not to make movie deals, but to save lives.

Whenever I think of Byrdie I imagine the arc of her life from God's vantage point. All these years God's been waiting patiently and saying, "Yes, my Byrdie is making a good living and helping people. But when is she going to realize why I gave her these very powers?"

I imagine God saying, "I've given her all the right skills, but when is she going to wake up and use them for the right reason, for the purpose I planted them inside of her?"

These days, instead of reading scripts at night, Byrdie reads medical charts and journals and all the recent articles about clinical trials. And Byrdie no longer flies first class. Oh no, trust me, she flies way higher.

ON THAT SUNDAY NIGHT, as I was searching for the right doctor to perform my reconstruction surgery, I just knew Byrdie could help me and tell me what to do. So I reached out to Byrdie and told her what happened to me. In no time at all Byrdie gave me my answer: "Naomi, there's only one man in this whole city for you and his name is Dr. Babak Azizzadeh."

Thank God, Dr. Azizzadeh was actually one of the two names already on my list. I already had an appointment with him first thing the next morning.

But even if Byrdie recommended this Dr. Azizzadeh, I still wanted to get a second opinion. There was no way in the world I wasn't going to get a second opinion.

On Monday morning I was feeling frightened and anxious. Helene, my guardian angel, took off work from her medical practice just to be with me and help me decide. She picked me up and we drove to Dr. Azizzadeh's office in Beverly Hills. It was a beautiful office and everyone there looked so beautiful. The receptionist was beautiful, even the patients in the waiting room were beautiful. And there I was, all bandaged up with no nose.

Someone called my name and led me to the examination room. And then Dr. Azizzadeh entered. Right away I could feel his kindness.

He began peeling off my bandages to examine my missing nose. I started feeling sick. I told him, "I think I'm going to faint." He went and got me a little juice box, the kind I used to give my kids, with the straw attached.

I sipped and I told him, "Listen, I have to tell you I'm totally freaked out. And also I want to make sure I never see what my nose looks like right now. Please don't show me." He promised.

I could just sense his compassion. And then he explained the situation to me. I was bracing myself for what he was about to say. There was still a part of me hoping that he'd say my nose could simply heal up on its own with time.

Dr. Azizzadeh sat in front of me and said, "Listen, your skin cancer was very extensive, and you're going to need to have three separate surgeries over the next six weeks." My heart was racing. What? He told me about my tissue loss. He was gently trying to tell me there was very little there.

And then he explained what my first reconstructive surgery was going to entail. How he was going to have to take a chunk of my scalp and my forehead and he was going to be flipping it all over and stitching all that to my nose. And he'd also be taking cartilage from my ears to rebuild my nose.

He said, the first surgery where the cancer was removed was already behind me, and now I just had to gear up for three more to go.

My eyes were tearing up. Basically, for the next six weeks there would be an elephant trunk going from my forehead to my nose. It would be a horrifying sight.

But Dr. Azizzadeh promised me that in the end, in seven weeks, I would have a nose. That's nothing to sneeze at when you're sitting there with no nose.

Helene and I took in everything Dr. Azizzadeh said, and then we thanked him and left and drove to the second doctor on my list. Let's call him Dr. Smith.

He, too, came highly recommended. He had already agreed to do my surgery and had already cleared away his schedule to fit me in.

They called me in to see Dr. Smith. He too was extremely kind and extremely patient. He explained how he would do the surgery.

I was listening to everything Dr. Smith had to say, and then suddenly he asked me, "Have you consulted with any other doctors?"

I said, "Yes, I just came from Dr. Azizzadeh."

And Dr. Smith, who is very highly respected, looked at me and he took a deep breath and was quiet for a moment and then he said, "I want you to go to him. I want you to go to Dr. Azizzadeh. He's better than me."

I was stunned. What doctor says that?

Later that night Dr. Smith called me at home. He said, "Don't get me wrong, I'm really good at what I do. I just want the best for you and I don't want you to ever look back and regret that you could have gotten a better outcome. Dr. Azizzadeh is the best and that's what I want for you."

And then he said, "Rabbi Levy, in your words you told me you were freaked out, but that's not the person I saw. I just want you to know that."

I was so moved. I said, "I can't thank you enough for your care and for your humility."

He was quiet for a minute and then he said, "Does Dr. Azizzadeh know who you are?"

I didn't understand what he meant, and he said it again: "You need to make sure. He needs to know who you are."

"Okay, I promise," I said.

But when I hung up I asked myself: *Who am I?*

Soon an answer to that question would come to me . . .

SO ALL ROADS LED TO ONE MAN, Dr. Babak Azizzadeh. I'd have to put my nose in his hands.

It was Monday night and my first surgery was going to be that Wednesday. On Tuesday Dr. Azizzadeh called me to talk about the surgery. He said it was going to be around a four-hour surgery under general anesthesia. And then I remember I asked him, "Can't you just give me my old nose back?" He said, "No, I can't, that's impossible, I can't give you back what God gave you, but I promise I will give you the best nose I can give you."

I said, "But can I send you photos of my old nose?"

He said, "Sure."

When we hung up I went on my laptop looking for close-ups of my old nose. Some were seriously unattractive. But who cares? I wasn't submitting headshots to a modeling agency. I wanted him to see the nose I was born with.

I imagine many of his patients want him to make changes to their noses, but all I was hoping was to get mine back. I started attaching photo after photo and I e-mailed them all to Dr. Azizzadeh. I felt so helpless. Sending the photos was the only act of control I had.

I couldn't sleep Tuesday night. I was terrified and my surgery wasn't until 5:00 p.m. Wednesday. No food or drink all day long. It was like a dress rehearsal for Yom Kippur.

Wednesday morning I was a bundle of nerves and tears, and the fear seemed to get worse with every passing hour. My mind was going to dark places. The shock of losing my nose had lifted and been replaced by a recognition of what I was about to undergo.

What can I tell you? I'm not a stoic warrior, I'm a Brooklyn worrier.

I was pacing back and forth trying to pass the time. I was spinning out.

At last it was time to head off to surgery. I grabbed my prayer book and a copy of a book of prayers I wrote in 2001 called *Talking to God*, and Rob and I drove off.

In the car I was starting to have a sinking feeling. I couldn't seem to find my center. I've been a rabbi for twenty-six years and I know the gift God has given me to help other people, to pray for others, to comfort others. But as the day wore on I wasn't sure that those same prayers could help me or that I could help myself.

I was starting to feel like an impostor. Like one of those commercials

I grew up watching on TV when I was a kid. An actor would come on and say, "I'm not a doctor but I play one on TV."

When the chips were down I was worthless to help myself. I was a frightened child, helpless, tearful. I was failing myself. I felt like I didn't have the resources, I worried I might not have the resources.

I'm not a rabbi, I thought, *I just play one.*

When we got to the surgical center Rob was with me, and my friends Helene and Carol. Helene's known me since I was eleven years old, Carol since I was fourteen. I was so touched that they wanted to be there with me.

They were sitting in the waiting room and I knew I needed to go pray, so I went outside in the courtyard with my prayer book and started to pray the traditional words, "I place my soul in Your hand."

And then they called me. It was time to go to pre-op. I was still a wreck.

Now I was in my hospital gown, a nurse put the IV needle in my hand. My heart was racing.

Rob, Carol, and Helene were with me, and though their presence and love and support were certainly a comfort, I needed something more from them. I reached for *Talking to God* and I opened it to the chapter of healing prayers. Of course when I wrote those healing prayers back in 2001 I didn't write them for myself. Of course not! I wrote them thinking of all the sick people I've prayed for and tried to help, never thinking I'd ever need them myself. The person who wrote those words didn't imagine praying them.

And then right there in the pre-op room I opened the book and started to pray. Rob, Helene, and Carol encircled me, and I began reciting the healing prayers I'd written fifteen years ago out loud. As I prayed I didn't recognize my own hand in those prayers. It was as if the me from the past had somehow channeled the exact words I needed to hear right now. It was me talking to me. I just took the prayers in like somebody had given me a gift.

I cried. Things started shifting, the air in the room even.

And then I said to Rob, Helene, and Carol, "Now I'd like you all to put your hands on my head and say this blessing over me." I closed my eyes and I could feel their hands on me as they recited the blessing from my book.

Then I said, "Please don't take your hands away, I need to meditate now."

Outside my tiny pre-op room I could hear all sorts of noises going on. It's a surgical center—people talking, footsteps, doors opening and closing. But you could hear a pin drop inside our tiny room. They all stood over me, surrounding me, perfectly still, with their hands on me, and I began to meditate.

There was sort of an electric feeling among us, the vibration of it, an energy was circulating around and around. All of us were fused as a single prayer, tight, intimate, so powerful. Nobody broke that intense energy of prayer. No one moved.

Soon we weren't even in that room anymore. No more sounds coming from anywhere. The whole room just levitated. We were flying to a higher place, it was beautiful and bright. Floating, rising. I had no idea of time, time just melted.

Just then a nurse opened the door and she said, "Whoa!" She could immediately feel what we were feeling. She said, "Something really powerful is happening here," and she backed away and closed the door behind her.

My heart was still beating hard in my chest. With my eyes closed I repeated in my mind over and over again the Hebrew verse that is my mantra:

I called to God from my narrowness, and God answered me with a vast expanse.

I called to God from my constriction, and God answered me with wide-open spaces.

I called to God in my need, and God answered me with grace.

I kept repeating this verse over and over and over again in my mind.

And all of sudden I crossed a river. From drowning in waves that were engulfing me to the purest, stillest water I have ever seen. It wasn't something I did, it just happened. Grace.

All that turbulence was gone, and all I felt was absolute stillness. The stillness was so real, so palpable, so pure, so crystal clear. *You lead me beside still waters, You restore my soul.*

And then . . . I heard a voice.

Before I go on I want you to know three things:

1. I'm not psychotic . . . at least I don't think I am.
2. There were no drugs going into my IV at that point.
3. I'm not saying this figuratively or metaphorically.

I'm telling you I heard a voice. I heard it loud and still. It echoed through me. The voice said: "Know who you are."

Know who you are. And I understood immediately what that meant. I'm not an impostor. I don't play a rabbi on TV. I'm not a frightened child, I'm a child of God. Whole and sustained and loved and strong, and with resources that I didn't even know I had.

I could be a rabbi to myself. Suddenly I saw that in my soul I'm built that way. There was no seam between who I am and who I am, and I don't think I understood that until that very moment.

Suddenly I flashed on what Dr. Smith had said to me on the phone about what I needed to make sure Dr. Azizzadeh knew. Dr. Smith had said to me, "He needs to know who you are!"

And it wasn't only that I had somehow moved beyond fear. I now saw from my place of stillness that I not only had the power to bless myself, I understood that I had the power and a sudden desire to bless others at that very moment.

When I opened my eyes I knew that was the necessary next step— to bless the people around me from my place of blessing.

Right then my nurse came in. I said, "I'd like to bless you." I could tell she was sort of taken aback, not something she hears every day, but she wanted my blessing and I blessed her.

And then my anesthesiologist came in and I said a prayer over her, and I could see she was taking it in, in the most open, beautiful way.

Then Dr. Azizzadeh walked through the door. I told him, "I just said a prayer over you." And then I blessed him. I remember looking at him in the eyes and saying: "I know who you are. I know you're not only a doctor, you're an artist, and I know you will give me the best outcome possible. I believe in you. I place myself in God's hands, and I place myself in your hands. I place my faith in you, completely, and God bless you for the holy work you do. God bless you and thank you for taking care of me." I had total trust in this remarkable man.

He took my hand and said, "Rabbi, it's my honor to be able to do this for you."

Right then I could feel it in the very depths of me, "I'm ready now."

I was in the place of still water. Calm, trust, faith, beauty, God, connected to my soul, blessed.

The surgery took nearly four hours. When I opened my eyes in recovery I could tell I must look like hell. Staples in my scalp, an elephant trunk connecting my forehead to my nose, a hole in my forehead that was so deep you could see my skull. I had a van Gogh thing going on with my ear.

If you saw me right then you would probably say, here's a person who must be so miserable, feeling so hopeless. But when I opened my eyes all I felt was gratitude, euphoria, ecstasy even.

Through a haze I saw Dr. Azizzadeh standing over me, and I know I was seriously out of it and rambling nonsense, but I clearly remember saying, "Thank you. God bless you."

And then his fellow, a woman named Dr. Irvine, walked in with a bright, warm smile. She said to me, "Dr. Azizzadeh was so meticulous during your surgery, and did you know he had a photo of you hanging up during the whole surgery?"

I must have bombarded poor Dr. Azizzadeh with maybe fifteen photos of me the night before. I wondered what photo was hanging up during my surgery. She said, "It was quite a sight, a photo of you in a prayer shawl with your eyes closed, and your hands were on your son's head, blessing him."

Know who you are, I whispered to myself, still in a haze.

I crossed a river that night, and the strange thing is, I've never gone back. It's a place I don't ever want to leave. A knowing I was given. Like an inheritance. But instead of it coming as a ring from your mother that belonged to your grandmother, it came from heaven and I don't want to lose it.

And at this moment all I want to do is to share the inheritance I received with you, to bestow it upon you.

Are you ready to receive it? Here it is:

Know who you are!

Know there are internal resources planted inside you to do things you can't even imagine you're capable of. That's my prayer for you. A big, eye-opening change.

Know who you are. Let these four words become your mantra. Don't set your sights too low. Understand what you're capable of. You are a child of God. You are strong, you are loved, you are not alone.

What are you praying for? What do you want? What's your big ask from the Soul of Souls? God has great hopes for you. You've been given the power to go to a very sacred place. So for God's sake, listen. Listen for a voice. A voice that will tell you something about who you are that you didn't know before. Listen for it.

Know who you are. Not the title that's printed on your stationery. It's not written on your diploma. It's not listed on your resume. It's imprinted on your soul with vision, clarity, expansiveness.

Your soul's voice is God's call to you. Daily, God is saying about you what I imagine God was saying about Byrdie: "Look at the gifts I've given you. When are you going to use them for the purpose I planted them inside of you?"

Many of us experience that nagging feeling that we have somehow missed our lives. That we've slept through them. That our life has happened without us. That we've never fought for it. That nagging feeling is your soul talking to you, trying to wake you up.

When we take the time to look back on our lives, we usually find ourselves regretting two types of sins. The first are sins we committed, the actions you regret: I lied, I hurt someone. Actions you still have the power to repair.

The second type of sins are much tougher to deal with. These are all the things that you *haven't* done. All the things you could have done, all the things you were born to do, but didn't do. How do you repair that?

I'm not talking about some bucket list of all the adventures you meant to have. I'm talking about the apology you never made, the forgiveness you didn't offer, the words you never spoke, all the goodness you intended to do. The person you hoped to become. The mission your soul was sent here to accomplish.

These sins are the most painful of all to face.

An unlived life. How do you repair that?

What's the dream or the prayer you've been too frozen or afraid to speak about? What yearning have you been too frightened to fight for? What has your soul been longing for? What do you want? And can you capture a vision of how to achieve it?

I'd like to help you with the vision.

Most of us wear or drive or carry things with designer labels on them. We are walking billboards for the companies that make our clothing, our shoes, our purses, our cars. As if they say something about who we are.

I want you to know that there's a designer label on you right now. And trust me, it doesn't say Prada or Porsche.

It's written across your forehead and across your heart in big capital letters: GOD.

The Creator's seal is on you. Let it inform your actions, your thoughts. God's seal is on you, in your essence. You were created to be a walking advertisement for the One who designed you.

You are unique, one of a kind, there has never been anyone like you. Know who you are.

This is the lesson I learned from my first reconstruction surgery. This is the inheritance I received and I am so honored to share this teaching with you: **there can be a very big distance between who you think you are and who God knows you are.**

Yes, there was still a seven-week journey ahead of me, and two more surgeries and many more lessons to learn and to share, but the incredible Dr. Azizzadeh restored me and blessed me with the ability to re-enter the world with pride. For that, I will be forever grateful.

The seal of the Creator is on you. God is waiting for you to finally use the gifts that are already planted inside of you. A new time of blessings is waiting for you.

Know who you are! Amen.

WELCOMING THE ETERNAL FORCE

The Key to Your Higher Knowing

As we nourish and awaken the soul, the Love Force transforms into a throne for Neshama, the Eternal Force, the third layer of soul, the invisible light of a flame.

Experiencing Neshama is not a onetime event. Few people learn to live fully in the realm of the Eternal Force, it is elusive indeed, and rarely alights on that throne. But when Neshama is in play within you, it's hard to miss it. You become aware of your soul's divine sense of unity, akin to Einstein's description of the "whole" we are usually blind to.

The Eternal Force opens our eyes to glimpses of heaven here. Time melts and gives way to eternity. Death becomes less frightening and less final. We may begin to realize that our deceased loved ones are never far from us, or perhaps that they have never left us.

EXPERIENCING UNITY AND A TASTE OF ETERNITY

"A human being is part of the whole, called by us 'Universe . . .'"
—from Einstein's letter to Rabbi Marcus

When the soul's voice grows stronger and stronger, slowly, a new perception begins to emerge from deep within. It is a knowing that verges on prophecy, a revelation that we are all connected, we see beyond the optical delusion that Einstein asked us to rise above. This is the Eternal Force stirring within you. Welcome it. Soon the world may begin to glisten in the Creator's light, and you may come to understand the way every soul is part of the Great Oneness.

34

Bridging Distances and Returning Home

WHEN I WAS A KID my father drove a succession of old, beat-up jalopies. They were stinky, the vinyl seats were cracked, and yellowed stuffing stuck out. The carpet was worn and matted. There was no air-conditioning, and you had to roll the windows up by hand.

My father manufactured women's sportswear, and he had a small, struggling factory in a poor, crime-infested neighborhood in Brooklyn called Bushwick, which has now become very cool and hip. But back when I was a kid, you didn't even want to stop at a stop sign in Bushwick.

My father felt that if he had an old, ugly car no one would bother breaking into it. A nice car would just be a target.

Then one year, my father sold his old, beat-up car and bought a used Buick LeSabre. It wasn't exactly a dreamboat, but it was a step up, it looked passable. My dad said the car handled well, and he was happy with it, happier than I'd ever seen him be with a car.

One day, when I was around twelve years old, I was coming home from choir practice after school. It was 5:30 p.m. on a cold and dark December night.

I was walking home from the bus stop, and I could see a couple of blocks away a man was trying to put out a fire inside the dashboard of his car. *Poor guy,* I thought to myself. The situation seemed so futile. The man was trying to smother the fire with rags, and it was clearly a losing battle.

I kept walking, looking inside lit-up houses and store windows. As I got closer, I could see the fire was growing and the man was now standing outside the car just looking on. *That's terrible,* I thought. I walked closer and I saw—it was our car, the LeSabre, and the man was my father. Instantly my thought went from *poor guy* to *not me.* This can't be happening to me, to my father, to us.

I grabbed my father's hand, my heart was racing. Scores of people were watching now as the flames climbed so high they were hitting the glass of the streetlight above. People stepped back in fear. The fire trucks arrived and smashed in the windows of the car to extinguish the blaze.

After all the excitement died down, my father and I walked home hand in hand. I don't remember my father's words to me as we walked home together, but I'm sure he reassured me that everything would be fine and reminded me to be grateful that no one had been hurt.

But the part of the story I find most upsetting was something I never shared with my dad that night: the moment I realized the man I'd been pitying turned out to be my own father.

Until I got close enough to recognize him, I'd been looking upon my own father with the onlooker's refrain of relief: "Thank God it's him, not me."

I understand now that I'd fallen into the very trap that Einstein described to Rabbi Marcus, that optical delusion of our consciousness that makes us see ourselves as separated from the rest, when in fact we are all bound together. Our delusion of separateness often leads us to an unfounded sense of superiority and invulnerability that makes us indifferent to human suffering.

How many times have I said the words, "Thank God it's not me." How many times have I counseled people who told me—in the face of a professional setback, a harsh diagnosis, or a devastating loss: "This can't be happening to me. Not me." Things like this happen to other people, to those unlucky, unfortunate souls.

We delude ourselves that we are separate from others because we don't want to feel vulnerable and small. But our denial makes us small. It is the source of pain, distance, and callousness too. We have the power to respond to suffering with soul. We have the power to step forward into our lives and into the lives of others with heart and compassion. If you find yourself feeling pity for someone who is suffering, know that you are not responding to them from your soul. Pity is the ego's way of protecting itself from admitting to vulnerability. But the soul doesn't need protection, it craves connection.

We are capable of so much more than "It's not me." Your soul wants to mentor you in the ways of conscience, kindness, and caring. It wants you to see beyond the cognitive barriers you've built that keep others at a distance. It wants you to understand that you are part of a collective soul that encompasses all of creation. So bring soul to the parts of yourself that stand in the way of your full participation in life. Lean on your soul and let it show you how you are tethered to people you don't even know. Let your soul lead you to acts of selflessness. Let it lead you to speak out, to get involved, to fight for justice. Put soul into the causes you are moved to get engaged in.

Counting ourselves in, saying, "It's me," means I recognize that I am human, mortal, and tied indelibly to the whole of humanity. Embracing our fragility is the key to our wisdom. Or, put another way, our awareness of our smallness is what makes us great.

Every day we have the power to welcome deep soul connections in this world and beyond.

I recently learned that the word "hobo" is an abbreviation for "homeward bound." We're all hobos looking for a way back to our goodness, to our holy essence, to our Creator, to our own hearts and souls.

And the Soul of Souls keeps calling out to us, "Return, my children." Can you hear it? It's a call your soul knows intimately.

So instead of saying, "It's not me," say, "I'm in. Count me in." The good news is, the homecoming you seek is already within you, within your very soul. You are hardwired for love. You are hardwired for generosity and humility, hardwired for giving and receiving comfort. Hardwired to help. Hardwired to connect.

You can bridge distances. You can repair the brokenness.

Lean on Neshama, the Eternal Force, the highest level of your soul, and soon you may enter a time of grace, when things are in alignment and truths become more apparent. Your vision becomes clearer and your mind becomes more astute. And your heart, with all the layers of muck and defenses, gets stripped away and becomes more supple. And your ego gets peeled back layer by layer until you get to the place where everything you thought was solid comes down. You will enter a time of knowing, when you can see through the dark like the light of day. You will see that great distances can be bridged. It's not too late! You can still set things right with the people you love, and even with those you've judged. All that bitterness can be sweetened. Distances can be bridged between strangers, and enemies too, it's not hopeless.

Self-defeating thought patterns like "It's not me," patterns that have tripped you up for a lifetime, can get washed away like that. And all that was unclear will begin to take shape inside of you, and all that was asleep will become awake, ready to hear and to respond.

You will come to see that people you've been labeling as "other" are actually your brothers and your sisters.

The Eternal Force is here to teach you, it longs to show you a bigger picture of the world around you and your place in it. There is a mission you are here to fulfill every day. The situation of our world demands that from you. Claim and own the true depth of your own humanity, because by claiming your empathy you are also claiming your destiny. And by doing that you will live to bless people you've never even met.

Say, "It's me!" Reveal yourself in all your imperfection and in all your awesome strength.

Distances can be bridged between how you're shut down and all that you are capable of. Distances between the mind and the heart, between your soul and the Soul of Souls.

You don't need to travel far to return, but you will need to travel deep. This precious world is expecting great things from you.

May you begin to see your own soul in the eyes of another. Your life is waiting for you to inhabit it. Our world is waiting for you to repair it. May you enter it in blessings and in joy. Amen.

Perceiving the Forty-Two Journeys of Your Soul

LAST SUMMER MY HUSBAND, ROB, and I took a vacation in Bali. It was so beautiful and peaceful. While we were there, we met with a holy man who began asking me all sorts of questions about my life. As we came to the end of our conversation he said, "I see something. I see that a problem from the past is still a problem."

"Thanks a lot!" I said.

He said, "But it's not as big of a problem."

I thought about that. About how a problem from the past never really does go away. But what once appeared to you as a mountain, an obstruction right in your face, blocking your path, can become a mountain that's very far away, that you can gaze upon from a distance as a vista. Something that you can see, but is no longer preventing you from moving forward. That's what it means to be on a journey.

In the Bible, at the end of the Book of Numbers, there is a listing of all the places the Children of Israel journeyed to during their forty-year trek through the desert. It's a scintillating list, let me give you a taste of it:

"They journeyed from the Red Sea and camped in the desert of Sin.

They journeyed from the desert of Sin and camped in Dophkah. They journeyed from Dophkah and camped in Alush. They journeyed from Alush and camped in Rephidim . . ."

It's like reading from the white pages, as inspiring as watching paint dry. The text goes on to list forty-two stops. Why the list? What's its meaning for me and for you?

Maybe this recounting of every stage of the journey mattered to the generation of the Exodus because they remembered what happened in each place. But how does a list of places that no longer exist on a map speak to us today? Who cares where they went? And why should we care where they stopped and camped? What spiritual lessons are we supposed to learn from this list?

Rabbi Sholom Noach Berezovsky wrote one of my favorite Hasidic commentaries, called *Paths of Peace.* In his analysis of the dry biblical list, Rabbi Berezovsky offers an interpretation that opened my mind and my heart. First he cites the Baal Shem Tov, the founder of Hasidism, who taught that this very list contains hidden high secrets pertaining not only to that generation, but to every generation. He said the forty-two journeys enumerated in the text teach us that every single soul must pass through forty-two journeys, from birth until that final journey home to the world above. He said the list of where the Children of Israel journeyed and camped is a blueprint for our lives, it teaches us how to follow our souls from journey to journey.

Here is what I think the Baal Shem Tov was getting at: Have you ever felt that your life was on hold? Or that you took a left turn somewhere? Or that some phase of your life was a total waste of time? A mistake?

Perhaps you're wrong.

Yes, life can sometimes feel disjointed, but every place you've been, every hardship, even your worst curses have been subtly raising your soul up rung by rung and leading you forward.

The biblical list isn't only about those people way back then, it's eternal and it's personal. It's our road map, our way. There's a story called your life—where you've been, where you got knocked down, where you rebelled, feared, where you got faith, where you got tempted by desire, where your heart got broken, where you triumphed, who you were with, and how you gave and received love.

There's a mission waiting for your soul to fulfill in every stage of your life. One way to grow is to learn by studying. Another way to grow is by experiencing life and learning from every encounter. The *Paths of Peace* commentary calls these life lessons "your personal Torah." You learn your personal Torah by understanding that your soul has work to do in every place you go and in everything that happens to you.

The journeys aren't easy. Some will test you to your core.

Sometimes your soul's job is to teach you about willpower, what to avoid. And sometimes its job is to teach you about drawing near, to show you how big your heart is and how much pain you can endure. Sometimes your soul teaches you how to receive. And sometimes your soul's job is to teach you to just give and give with no thought of getting anything back in return.

Another theory presented in *Paths of Peace* about the forty-two places on the biblical list comes from Rashi, the great medieval biblical commentator. Rashi taught that the places the Children of Israel stopped and camped are also called "journeys." Your setbacks, your stops are journeys that can lift your soul higher if you let them. So there's no need to beat yourself up for times of paralysis—love and learn, that's the key.

Have you ever felt led? That you've gone someplace or met some person or created something, but it didn't seem to come from you—it came through you?

Can you feel where you are on your soul's journey? Take some time to try to track the steps of your life so far. Take a sheet of paper, sit quietly, and begin to write a list of your life's journeys—the great moments and the challenges. By putting pen to paper you may begin to see a pattern, a direction, a bigger picture. Nothing is wasted. Everything has led you to where you are right at this very moment.

Why are you here right now? Is there something you're meant to give? Someone you're meant to meet? Something you're here to receive? Don't let this sacred day pass without gleaning the hidden secret that's waiting for you this very moment.

Whenever I must write a eulogy, I ask grieving family members to share stories about their loved one with me. Sometimes they tell me disjointed things, little bits and pieces. Sometimes all they can see are little bits and pieces. But I'm always looking for the story, the arc, the forty-two journeys of the soul from birth to that final journey.

A remarkable woman I've known and loved for twenty-seven years passed away recently. Her name was Dina Sneh. Dina grew up in a small town near the Polish-Lithuanian border called Grodno. When the Nazis invaded Poland, Grodno fell into Soviet hands. The Soviets deported Dina, her siblings, her mother, and her grandmother to Siberia. Siberia. It seemed like the worst possible curse—freezing temperatures, brutal stark conditions, no money, and no food for nourishment. But when the war was over Dina learned that every single Jewish family from her town had been murdered in the Holocaust. She survived *because* of Siberia.

When we look back on life, some of our harshest trials turn out to be sources of wisdom. A challenge can teach you about your strength. A setback can save your life. Every life experience is an opportunity to unlock the good that is waiting for you there. Every step of your journey is waiting for you, waiting for your unique presence to lift it up. Know that everything you do, every act of kindness, every step forward, and even every step back has cosmic ripples.

One of the most painful fallacies we live with is a nagging sense that the life we are living has no meaning, isn't interesting enough or powerful enough to be a "real" life. No one wants to live a pointless existence. The truth we fail to see is that no life is a chaotic mess devoid of meaning or structure or a message. Every day has its story. Through the lens of your soul you can begin to see your life as a meaningful story that is shared by all people.

Storytelling is the soul's domain. It is a sacred form of communication. The soul delights in stories, fables, myths, legends. The mind sees in snapshots, but the soul can sense the unfolding of a grand drama. Perhaps that's why children long to hear the same tale repeated over and over again. Perhaps that's why the Bible is not a law book. The Great Narrator knows the secret of a good story to spark the soul.

So where are you on your forty-two-step journey? Let Neshama, the Eternal Force, help you see the true arc of your life. Your soul can help you see the sacred story that you've been missing. Let it teach you to see why you are here right now.

I pray you will learn to view your life as a meaningful story. I pray you will learn to see how even your setbacks are leading you forward.

May you step up to your soul's mission in every place and may you be blessed to fulfill it. Amen.

Recognizing How Setbacks Can Lift You Higher

THE SEVEN WEEKS OF MY nasal reconstruction were definitely a signpost on my forty-two-step journey.

My first surgery was behind me, but there would be two more surgeries during those seven weeks. I understood that for many weeks I would be trapped inside my house with a gruesome elephant trunk hanging on my face. Because how do you go outside looking like the elephant man?

Seven weeks. When I first realized I was going to be a shut-in, it felt like a prison sentence to me. I thought I was going to go out of my mind. I imagined I would just be counting down the days.

But what started out as a time of imprisonment gave way to something new and unexpected. Soon I stopped counting. I stopped even being aware of time. At the beginning I thought, *How am I going to get through the day?* And then, I don't quite know how to put this into words, but the day was somehow moving through me in the most sacred way. Days filled with spaciousness and possibility and love.

I was taking in the love of my family and the love of my friends, and I was taking in the love of my Nashuva spiritual community and their prayers and blessings. I was taking it all deep inside me.

I would wake up in the morning and I would pray and meditate. It was like I was on a seven-week silent retreat in an altered reality, such a gentle place. Normally when I meditate it takes some time for my thoughts to settle down. But those meditations, during those seven weeks, I would drop down so quickly and so deep, it was like nothing I have ever experienced before.

I was more and more at peace with myself and my situation every day, an acceptance. Weirdly, I was happier and calmer than I'd been in a long time.

A new guest came to hang out with me inside my own head. I didn't even recognize her voice. She was so sweet. She was saying, "It's okay, you don't have to do anything you don't want to do. Take a nap, eat something, do nothing, take another nap. Just give your body a chance to do what it needs to do to heal and don't worry about anything. Be kinder to yourself."

It was the voice of my soul, I'm sure of it, and because of her a time of imprisonment became a place of liberation. A time became a space.

As the days and weeks went on, I expected cabin fever would kick in. I mean, you can only be a good sport for so long. But instead of the solitude wearing on me, there was this surprising grace lifting me.

It wasn't an imprisonment anymore. It was a gift.

I was having trouble finding a comfortable position for sleep, so I'd be awake at odd hours of the night. I didn't even mind it. I'd study the Zohar, the Jewish book of mystical wisdom, and remember that's how the mystics would study, in the middle of the night when the world and all its noises dies down and the magic begins.

During those seven weeks, I was beginning to understand that something you dread can actually become something you treasure. It can become your teacher. And then, as the days and weeks passed, and another surgery was behind me, and my final surgery was soon ap-proaching, what really surprised me was that I didn't want it to end, my days cocooned alone at home. It's so odd. You would have thought

I couldn't wait till the moment of freedom. Of course I wanted my ordeal to be over. But I had experienced this beautiful place, so divine, so sacred, and I wanted to ride it as long as I could. I didn't want to leave.

I wasn't becoming agoraphobic. I just felt there was this shift happening inside me, and I was scared that I'd lose it. That by returning to traffic and errands and the routines of life I'd lose the gift of the higher plane I'd been living in.

For the first time, I understood the impulse of the person who drops out of daily life and becomes a monk on a mountaintop. Because it can be so hard to live here in the real world.

I kept thinking of the great Rabbi Shimon Bar Yochai.

Legend has it that he spent not seven weeks, but twelve years in a cave, receiving divine mysteries and secrets of the Zohar from the very mouth of God. He comes out of the cave after twelve years and sees a man plowing a field, and he has nothing but disdain for the poor farmer:

"How can a person be doing something so mundane and low when you could be pondering secrets of the divine?"

Right then God says to him, "Go back in the cave, because you've learned nothing!"

He didn't get it!

To me the story of Rabbi Shimon Bar Yochai is about understanding that the secrets of heaven *are* in plowing the field. The secrets of heaven are what you do when your kids are whining and you get stuck in traffic and the demands of work are weighing on you. That's where you've got to be to experience what's holy.

It's so much harder to stay holy when you're in the dirt plowing the field.

Experiencing the place of still water is something I will never ever forget. But life is about living in muddy waters. You can't live your life on Mount Sinai. You can't. But can you hold on to what you learned at Sinai?

I kept worrying: What if I come back to my life and nothing has actually changed? If I just dropped back into my mindless life again, then everything I experienced and learned would all just be wasted time, like it didn't even happen.

The challenge of life is not that you *can* change. The challenge is, can you *remain* changed?

How do you make a lasting change in your life when the world tempts you and tests you every single day?

I am praying that something sacred will happen to you. Something unexpected. A turning. An awakening. A softening of the heart. A sweetening of the voice in your head. I'm hoping you will find a new place, a place you didn't expect to find.

Open yourself up to that possibility. That there's a power available to you that can actually affect you. Like lightning striking at your core and changing you. I am praying that you will experience something powerful and full of holiness and awe. And I am blessing you that you will find the way to hold on to that holiness, that it will remain with you and take up residence inside you.

Yes, it's possible to have a sacred experience so powerful that you just can't reintegrate it into your normal life. Maybe it changes you permanently on such a deep level that what you were doing before is no longer possible. Or maybe you learn to bring what you witnessed into your life and you're never the same because of it.

And maybe enduring change, lasting change, isn't about hanging on to your sacred experience anyway. Maybe it's not about hanging on to anything. You don't have to control it. Instead, just make room for something to possess you more and more and allow that new guest to settle inside you.

ON AUGUST 24, 2016, I had my final reconstruction surgery. When I woke up in recovery, my face was still in bandages.

One week later I went to see Dr. Azizzadeh and he gently started peeling the bandages off my face. Immediately I flashed on the first day that I came to see him and the way he gently peeled off my bandages to reveal my missing nose, and I pleaded with him, "Don't show me," because I was sure I looked like a monster. He promised me I'd never have to see that.

But now it was seven weeks later and he was peeling off my bandages and he was smiling and he was so happy and this time he handed me a mirror. I looked at my face. I had a nose!

I was so grateful. It was a new day. I was overwhelmed. My heart was overflowing. My eyes were tearing up. I just kept saying to him, "Thank you, thank you, thank you!" I texted him after I left, "God bless you, I have no words to thank you! Just my gratitude from the depths of my soul. I will be forever grateful, eternally grateful."

A week passed. Dr. Azizzadeh said I was now healed enough to be able to put makeup on to hide all my scars—but I know very little about makeup.

So I went to a department store, and a guy named Gabriel was working at the makeup counter. He was so sweet. He said to me, "Honey, what happened to you?"

I started to get all emotional with the guy at the makeup counter, telling Gabriel my whole story. He started tearing up too.

I pointed to my nose and said to him, "This isn't my nose. It's my scalp and my forehead and my ears." He began examining my face in amazement.

I said, "So, Gabriel, can you please teach me how to cover up these scars?"

And then I added, "And, Gabriel, can you somehow make this fat, ugly nose look a little bit more refined and narrow? It's so fat and ugly and bulbous and doughy!"

That's how long my "eternal" gratitude lasted. Seven days! And that's how long that kind, gentle voice, that new guest that had entered my head, lasted!

God, please forgive me! Dr. Azizzadeh, please forgive me!

Just then I took out my iPhone to show Gabriel a photo of my old nose and I said, "You see how narrow and refined my nose was?"

Gabriel said to me, "First of all, put that photo away. It's history. And second of all, this nose you have now is so much softer, and it suits you so much better, because you're such a soft person, and that old nose was so bony. And anyway, this is your miracle nose. Can't you see that? So we're going to forget that old bony nose, okay? And, honey, we are going to make you POP!"

The guy working at the makeup counter had to remind the rabbi that she was blessed. And right then my angel Gabriel took a brush in his hand, and in three seconds all my scars were gone.

As I drove home from Gabriel, I remembered the teaching about the forty-two journeys: "Yes, even the steps you take backwards are your teachers." I had certainly regressed pretty far from my place of gratitude and kindness, and all it took was one week!

And that's why the next time I saw Dr. Azizzadeh I said to him, "Listen, I have to ask you a favor."

He said, "What can I do for you?"

"I'd like to see the picture you took of me," I said. "The one on the first day I saw you. I want to see what I looked like with my nose missing."

"Are you sure you're ready to see that?" he asked.

"Yes, I'm ready."

So he got up and he sat down behind his desk and he found the photo of me on his computer.

"Okay . . . are you ready?" he said.

So I started to walk toward his computer. And in that instant his computer shorted out. His screen went black. Dead. Nothing!

As God is my witness!

Actually, I don't even need God to be my witness on this one, because I have Dr. Azizzadeh as my witness!

For a second I thought, *Oh my God, is this a sign?*

He said it too! "Maybe you're not meant to see . . ."

But I said, "No, I *am* meant to see."

All along up to that instant I was too scared to look. I was afraid my face would be like a creature from a horror film.

But then Dr. Azizzadeh found the photo of me on his iPhone. I was bracing myself. I worried that I might cry or that I might get sick and vomit all over his office. I worried that I might regret what I was about to see. Could I go through with this? Would this image haunt me? But I looked at the photo. And I was so relieved to find that the sweet, gentle voice inside my head, the voice of my soul, was with me once more. Because even though a lot of my nose was missing, when I beheld the photo of my face, I saw me in my wholeness. And instead of revulsion, all I could see was the kindness in her eyes and all I felt was compassion for her.

I said to Dr. Azizzadeh, "God bless you. Thank you for showing me that photo. I needed to understand the true arc of this miraculous story."

What's the true arc of this story?

It is the arc of *all* our stories:

You are blessed and sometimes you can't see it. But the soul within you is here right now, like my angel Gabriel, to help you remember.

There is a kind voice in your head. She's always been there taking care of you and teaching you. She's your soul, and she's always showing you the way to your true calling and your holy destiny. Your soul has high and mighty powers to help you and lift you and change you. May you learn to hear her.

Experiences that you dread, that you never would have wished upon yourself, can also surprise you and illuminate your life in the most unimaginable way. And your soul is hoping you will be able to understand this.

You are loved more deeply than you know, you have no idea how deeply you are loved by the people in your life and by the One who created you. No idea how profound and powerful this love is. And your soul is here to help you feel it and to let it in.

Every single day a new light is shining on you, a light that's never been here before.

May we all be worthy, may we all be privileged, may we all be blessed to bask in its glow! Amen.

Seeing Your World to Come

NOT LONG AGO MY MOTHER appeared to me in a dream. She was sitting right beside me at a café, and I whispered to her, "So what's it like in heaven, Mom?" At first she pretended not to hear me, but I persisted, "Come on, Mom, tell me."

She said, "Nomi, the bathrooms are so lavish!"

"That's it?" I said.

She said, "Gorgeous bathrooms."

I said, "But what about the weather?"

She said, "Same as here."

I said, "Aren't there any differences between here and heaven?"

She said, "The bathrooms? Lavish!"

And that was it.

Perhaps my mom couldn't tell me the difference between this world and the World to Come because we're living in heaven and the sad part is: we can't see it. We can't see what's possible and what's available to us.

On New Year's Day I was having lunch with a dear friend and I asked her, "So did you make a resolution?"

She said, "I don't want to talk about it because my resolutions never come true!"

I started laughing, she started laughing too. I wasn't laughing at her, I was laughing at the idea of it. That's one of the funniest things I've heard in a long time. A resolution is not a wish you blow out on a birthday cake.

So often we confuse our prayers, our dreams, and our resolutions with wishes. Wishes are for genies, and you're not here to talk to a genie, you're here to stand in the presence of your Creator, the One who knows what your true capacities are.

One of my favorite biblical characters is Joseph the dreamer. Joseph understood that a dream isn't a wish. He knew that a dream had to be held on to even when his own brothers turned on him. Even in the pit Joseph stayed true to the high vision of his soul.

The rabbis say a dream is one-sixtieth of a prophecy, it's a seed. What does that mean? A prophet isn't someone who sees the future, or predicts what will be. A prophet is someone who has a dream. Now you might say, but we all have dreams. That's true. We all have glimpses of our lives as they can be, glimpses of the world as it can be, but we let those dreams dissolve.

A prophet sees the world as it can be and just can't let it go. A prophet is ready to take risks for that dream, to brave danger, is willing to suffer and bear the scars of that dream too.

We've all had dreams, glimpses of heaven, but most of the time the urgency passes and we drop back down to our normal routines. That's why our resolutions don't come true.

But a resolution is not what will happen *to* you, it's what will happen *through* you.

My favorite blessing in the entire Talmud is: "May you see your World to Come in this world." Your soul keeps trying to teach you this truth.

Every once in a while you can sense the Creator working through you. You play a tune, and you know your hand is being guided. You lift your voice to sing a melody, and you can hear the echo of angels. You put pen to paper and you realize the words aren't coming from you, you are simply here to take dictation. But then we lose that feeling and we forget our dreams and resolutions.

Slavery is not just the bondage of your body, it's the hypnotizing of your spirit until you no longer see that things can be different from the way they are now and you become habituated to lies: *I'm not strong enough, I'm not good enough.*

So what does it take to be free of whatever is keeping us locked up? It takes a cataclysm. A rumbling from within. An earthquake that shakes up everything you have come to know and accept about what is true. Suddenly the walls that confine you and the shackles that have bound you come crumbling down and you see a new truth.

The key to freedom is one word: "*veyadatem*," "and you will know it"—in your bones, in your heart, in your soul, in the depths of your being you will see and you will know!

And what will you know? That you are a child of God. Equal to all and slave to none!

That is what Dr. King meant when he said, "I have a dream." It's a vision that cuts through the lies like a laser to a truth that can no longer be denied or held back. A dream is a vision of heaven here.

Dr. King also understood that a dream has to be backed up with action. That's why he said: "The most dangerous type of atheism is not theoretical atheism, but practical atheism—that's the most dangerous type. And the world, even the church, is filled up with people who pay lip service to God and not life service."

Great leaders are those people who see heaven here. They see what's possible and they need to bring it into the light of day, to paint a picture of that world so others can see it. They need to teach it and repeat it until it becomes real.

In an archive I found a sermon Rabbi Marcus once gave about this very idea. He delivered these words more than seventy years ago, but they are as alive and true today as they were on the day he spoke them:

There is no man who ever lived who has not, at some time, dreamed of a fairer world, a more beautiful universe . . . No man has lived who, at some happy moment of dreaming, did not behold the promise of a higher existence. But soon the moment passes. So the dream passes away. The strivings of our economic life make great demands upon us . . . And so our dream world vanishes and we behold, once again, a universe which is real, genuine and, very often devoid of beauty and color.

There are, however, among men those who are endowed with greater vision than the average man . . . They have eyes which penetrate deeper and behold things in a more sustained manner . . . They have the power of taking this moment which is otherwise so short and fleeting and reshape it, recreate it into a form which is enduring and meaningful. The prophets are the men of vision . . .

Rabbi Marcus understood that turning a dream into a sustained vision and then bringing forth that vision into reality isn't something that happens to you from on high, and it doesn't happen overnight. It's a struggle, a daily struggle, to fight for what's right.

Prophecy is the very presence of God working through you, moving from subconscious to conscious experience. It's a taste of what can be.

Every dream we have for ourselves is only a reflection of the dream God has for us.

What has God planted inside your soul? How has God been working through you and blessing you? Start seeing your greatness, see beyond your limitations, see your power to grow.

Do you think I'm saying that if you just open your eyes you'll see that life is perfect and God is predictably present? No. Life can knock you down and God can feel far away. The conditions of our lives, the conditions of our world, may seem very far from heaven. Trials and tribulations can throw you. Challenges can throw you, but you must never let them own you.

I once read a commentary that said that hell isn't a place of fire and suffering. Hell is God opening your eyes and showing you the greatness that was yours to have and how far you are from where you could have been. If that is hell, then what is heaven? Heaven is when God opens your eyes and you see what is possible now.

What are you striving for?

Most resolutions people make are about gyms and diets. If only you could see what you could be resolving to repair and achieve. You were born with the power to see heaven, to bring your high vision into alignment with reality, to lift this world up.

In order for you to see a glimpse of the World to Come, it's important to have a vision of the World to Come. What's your vision of heaven?

One rabbinic commentary warns us, if you can't catch a vision of the World to Come then you're going to be a bench in the World to Come. I didn't say you're going to be sitting on a bench in the World to Come. You're just going to *be* a bench. Do you really want to be a bench so that other people can come sit on you in the World to Come?

You have the power to capture a vision of what heaven is.

The Promised Land isn't a far-off place. And heaven is not reserved for the dead. It's here, waiting for us to see it and to enter it.

So here are some deep questions to ask yourself if you want to learn how to see the World to Come in this world:

What does the world need from you? What does God want from you? What do your talents demand of you? What does your soul want from you?

What lies must you set right? What barriers must you break down? What are the veils standing in the way of that truth?

What have you been longing to overcome and break free of?

Like Joseph, you were born with the power to dream, to bring your soul's high vision into alignment with reality, to lift this world up.

What is your dream? The dream that rings forth from the very harmonic of your soul?

Heaven is here. May you see your World to Come in this world. Amen.

GAINING A HIGHER UNDERSTANDING
OF TIME AND ETERNITY

". . . A part limited in time and space."
—from Einstein's letter to Rabbi Marcus

Einstein insisted that we are all part of a whole, but he understood that our limited perception often prevents us from fully grasping this truth. No one can see the unity of all things with perfect clarity. We live our lives yearning to know eternity, but we get stuck in our own temporality. The one event that heightens this tension between soul and body, between our unity and our separateness, is death.

Neshama, the Eternal Force, is waiting to show you how to see time and eternity with new eyes, how to bridge earth and heaven. How to see the whole we are part of that encompasses all of creation.

Treasuring Blessings That Can Never Die

I GREW UP IN A home filled with food and love and laughter and music and stories. I was the youngest of four children and we were part of a tribe in Brooklyn, with my uncle Nat's family living on the floor above us, my uncle Ruby's family living next door to us, and my grandparents living above them. Nobody ever knocked on the door and nobody ever needed a key. Everybody was always barging into everybody else's home.

My parents were soulmates. They were constantly singing in harmony, walking hand in hand. As I grew, one by one my older siblings moved out and went off to college. And pretty soon it was just my mom, my dad, and me. It was quieter, but it was beautiful.

One day life was beautiful and then the next day my father was murdered. Now it was just me and my mom. As you can imagine, the two of us became unnaturally close, the way two broken hearts have to figure it all out together.

When I was in high school I tried so hard never to cry, I didn't want to add to my mother's sorrow. Instead, I threw myself into my studies. I was such a studious kid, such a nerd. I'd always work myself into a tizzy before an exam, and then I'd turn to my mom on the day of the test and I'd say, "Mom, bless me before the test. And bless my pen too." And she'd say, "Nomeleh, don't you know I'm a good witch. I know how it is, and I know how it will be." And I would take my blessed pen and scurry off to school.

Then it came time for me to go to college. Honestly, I don't know how she found the strength to let me go. How do you send your fourth child off when you have nothing at home but memories of a life that once was?

I don't know how I left, but I did.

And I hated it.

It was a culture shock to go from an Orthodox Jewish high school to Cornell University. It was so preppy. I'd never seen so many head-bands and Topsiders in my life. They kept saying that the ideal Cornelian was a scholar and an athlete. Some Greek ideal. Well, I was no athlete, and I didn't see myself as a scholar. So I started calling my mom every night, crying hysterically, "I want to go home. I don't like it here."

She was so strong. She'd say, "I want you to stay. Trust me, I'm a good witch." And then she'd bless me for my upcoming test.

And she was right.

After six months and fifteen pounds, I did learn to love college and I made new friends and I loved the learning. Though I never did get into athletics.

My mom was right about so many things. She knew my husband, Rob, was the right man for me even before I knew it. "Trust me," she said, "I'm a good witch. He's a keeper." And she walked me down the aisle at our wedding. Just the two of us. Me and my mom, hand in hand. And she gave me away again. It was hard for her to let me go and live so far away from home.

And then the widow with the broken heart became a bubby with a full heart and a full schedule of friends and grandchildren and volunteering and studies. And her bat mitzvah at age eighty.

At her seventieth birthday celebration, just when we thought she was going to make a speech, she turned around to me and she said, "Nomeleh, I want you to bless me."

All those years as a rabbi I spent giving blessings to others, all those years she'd been blessing me, and I had never blessed her. So I placed my hands on my mother's head, and I blessed her. How can I describe what passed between us? From that day on, it became our ritual. She'd call me every single night and ask me for her blessing. She had trouble sleeping, so I'd bless her. I'd say, "Mom, I bless you with peace, I bless you with sleep through the night, sweet dreams."

She had various ailments: her eyes, her legs, her feet, her asthma, her stomach. I'd call her, and I'd say, "Mom, how are your giblets doing?"

She'd laugh, we'd talk, and then she'd say, "I need my blessing."

And I would bless her. "I bless you with peace, I bless you with sleep through the night, sweet dreams."

I found myself saving her voice mails. People were constantly complaining that my mailbox was full, but I couldn't erase my mother's sweet messages: "*Shabbat Shalom* [good Sabbath]," "Happy Birthday," "Happy Mother's Day."

I'd say we spoke on the phone about six times a day. She wanted to know the details. If it was a Friday of Nashuva, she'd call first to bless me and wish me good luck, and then she'd ask, "What are you going to talk about tonight?" And then there were the wrap-up calls: "So, nu? How was Nashuva? How did it go? How was your sermon? Was it well received? How many people came?"

If I was traveling to speak out of town, I'd get a call in the taxi on the way to the airport. We'd talk and then I'd say, "I've got to go, Mom, I'm going through security." And she'd say, "Okay, call me on the other side." I'd call, we'd chat, I'd board the plane.

I'd say, "Mom, I've got to go, they've closed the cabin doors."

She'd say, "Okay, call me when you land."

We'd talk in the taxi on the way to my hotel, "Tell me about your hotel room. Is it nice? What are you going to talk about tonight?" And then the wrap-up calls. "So, nu? How did it go? What did you talk about? Was it well received? How was the crowd?" She enjoyed these wrap-up calls so much that I found myself telling little white lies:

"How was the crowd?"

"Packed!"

She'd say, "Standing room only?"

I'd say, "Yes, Mom, standing room only!"

"Were you a hit?"

"Yes, Mom, a big hit!"

"Was it a wow?"

"Yes, a definite wow."

I was invited to teach a session on prayer at a retreat for rabbis. At the end of my lecture, I said, "I want to teach you how to bless each other. We rabbis spend our lives blessing other people, but who blesses us?"

My colleagues said, "What are you talking about? How do we bless each other?"

"Me and my mom do it every single night," I said. "You can do this." And you should have seen how these grown men and women put their hands on one another's heads and melted into puddles of tears.

Afterward, my mom called for the reviews. "So, nu? How did it go with the rabbis? Were you well received? Was it a wow? Standing room only?"

And then, she was dying. The truth is, for a woman who was so intimately involved in the details of her kids' lives, her grandchildren's lives, her friends' lives, I don't know how she found the courage to let us go. I said to her, "Mom, bless me."

And she said, "Nomeleh, you've already been given the formula. All you have to do is live it."

And then I blessed her. "Mom, everything you needed to give, you've already given. You can go now." I stroked her hair, and I said, "I bless you with peace, I bless you with sleep." And I sang her a lullaby. After she slipped into unconsciousness, I whispered to myself, "Call me when you get through security."

WHEN SOMEONE YOU LOVE DIES, there are so many reflexes to retrain. You set the table for three, and then you remember, *Oh, there are only two settings now.*

For me, it was training myself to stop reaching for the phone. Ten times a day, I'd reach out to call my mom, and then I'd have to remind myself, *Oh, I can't call.* I'd think of something I needed to tell her, and then I'd have to sit on my hands. I'd have a Nashuva service and I'd find myself asking her questions to myself: *So, nu? How did it go? Was it a wow? Standing room only?*

With time, you stop reaching. When my mother died, a rabbinic mentor of mine said to me, "Naomi, the Kaddish that you say in April, it isn't the same Kaddish you say in November."

A friend of mine overheard this, and she asked me, "Are there really two different Kaddishes for different months?"

I said, "No, same Kaddish, but you're in a different place."

At first it's a Kaddish of anguish, of an open wound and an empty ache, and with each passing month it takes on a different tone and color.

Some days I said Kaddish like a robot. Some days I felt a tug. Some days I felt such a sweet feeling, sitting in the morning prayer service wrapped in my mother's prayer shawl, the one she wore at her bat mitzvah, saying Kaddish for her.

When someone close to you dies, the world says, "Get back to normal." But we all know better. No, you're not normal. Your soul knows that you need time to heal, take it. Time does heal. And somehow you learn to stop relying on those you lost for wisdom and comfort. You learn to stand on your own two feet. We learn to take care of ourselves. We learn to channel them: "What would he have said?" "What would she have told me to do?" But holidays come and old wounds reopen. We miss someone who should be with us, who should be sitting with us at our holiday table.

The world may expect us to be strong, but we don't have to be strong all the time. You don't always have to stand on your own two feet. Your soul is here to give you permission to reach out and to feel that tug and to remember sweet memories.

We don't need to contain ourselves, we don't need to refrain from reaching out. We can just let go and feel whatever it is that we need to feel. We can say what we need to say, hear what we need to hear. We can make time for sweet memories. For remembering those who cared for us, loved us, touched us, taught us. They all come to us, those we've loved and lost, whose souls and blessings will never leave us.

IT WAS AUGUST 25, 2011. It was my mother's birthday, and instead of celebrating with her I was alone in her apartment packing up her belongings, filling up boxes of dishes and books and knickknacks I would be shipping back to LA. I found it hard to leave behind even the most random, worthless objects. Each mug, each handkerchief was saturated with her very essence. Like a dog, I sniffed every sweater, looking for her scent. I slept there alone that night, tucked into my childhood twin bed, hugging the blanket my mom had crocheted for me when I was nine years old. And that night she visited me in a dream:

I walk into my mother's house, and there she is! Scurrying about. I'm dumbfounded. I don't want to insult her by reminding her that she's dead. She seems so oblivious to that fact.

I keep trying to pull my brother Danny aside to ask him to explain this. But I don't want her to overhear. I keep saying to myself, "But we buried her. I saw that." She's not a spirit or a vision. She's tangible. Skin and bones. And cooking and talking and hosting and enjoying us all.

Across the way, my dead aunt Sophie is there with a male attendant. She too has no idea she's dead. She's just aged and ailing and I wonder if she's going to have to die all over again.

I sneak Danny aside and I ask him how this is all possible medically, scientifically. He's a doctor. He says to me, "Nomi, sometimes the soul doesn't know it's dead."

I look at him and say, "That's a rabbinic answer. That's not a medical answer."

And then I thought for a moment and I said to him, "But her body is here, not just her soul. Her body! And it has substance."

Danny was groping for some explanation, something rational to say.

I kept trying to find a way to tell my mom I had a moving company coming in the morning to pack up all the stuff she'd left me. But I didn't have the heart to tell her she was dead. And I felt guilty taking away her belongings.

I kept saying, "Mom, I have something to ask you." I wanted to ask her if I could have some photographs. But I didn't ask.

And then she came right up to me and she said, "What is it, Nomeleh? You have a question for me?"

And suddenly I didn't want the photographs, I just wanted to hold her. I hadn't touched her all this time because I was too scared. And suddenly I just melted in her arms and began sobbing. And she just held me.

It was then that I realized she knew she was already dead. I cried long and hard and she held me and comforted me and let me weep.

May those we have loved and lost visit us in our dreams and in all our days. May their memory, their legacy, their love, and their light shine on us always. Amen.

Living on Soul Time

ONE DAY WHEN OUR KIDS were little, my husband, Rob, was rushing in the morning and he seemed particularly harried. He was driving the morning carpool and we packed the kids into their car seats and Rob drove off. A few minutes later he called me from the car and said, "Nomi, buy me some time." I felt so bad for him. I wanted to do anything to help him. But just then the reception went bad and I lost him.

I was thinking, *Who can I call? What meeting can I reschedule for him?* Finally I got Rob back on the phone. "Robby, what can I do for you? How can I help?"

He said, "Just buy me some time."

I said, "All right, all right, how? What can I do?"

Rob said, "Nomi! Time! In the farmer's market, you know, parsley, sage, rosemary—buy me some thyme!"

I started laughing. And then I went to the Venice Farmer's Market and had a deep philosophical conversation with the herb guy. I said to him, "Where's time?"

He said to me, "Time's over there."

I asked him, "How much is time?"

He said, "Well, it depends on how much time you want."

I said, "I want a lot of time," and I bought up all the time he had.

TIME . . .

It keeps spinning out of control. Every New Year I hear people saying to me, can you believe it's already another year? Where did the time go? Our years keep rushing by us, our weeks keep folding into one another. Our days are vanishing.

Just yesterday, my kids were in car seats, swinging on swings in our backyard and romping around the house in those adorable footsie pajamas. And I blinked my eyes and now they're both out of the house. My chirping nest is empty. How did that happen?

Every year during the countdown to Rosh Hashanah, I find myself staring at the moon each night in fear. When that last full moon of Elul (the last month of the Jewish calendar) is high in the sky, I know I'm in trouble, because I've got no sermons and Rosh Hashanah is exactly fifteen days away. Night after night I stare at that shrinking moon and I quote the Bible to it. I say, "Sun, freeze in the sky! Moon, stand still—don't move!" But the man in the moon keeps shrinking and smiling at me.

The Book of Psalms gives us such a powerful description of how fleeting our time is. It says, "Our days are like a passing shadow." The rabbis, of course, have a need to parse this description, so they ask: But what sort of shadow? Is it the shadow cast by a wall? Or is it the shadow cast by a tree? The answer is: no, it's the shadow cast by a bird flying overhead—*whoosh*, and it's gone.

How do we slow time down? Do we have the power to do such a thing? To slow down the clock so we can have more time, just a little more time with the people we love?

I began wondering about this problem when I was on a silent

retreat with thirty other rabbis several years ago. Yes, it's an oxymoron—rabbis and silence. But there I was, a week with no words. At first I was agitated by all the quiet, I wanted to catch up with old friends. But then I let the silence settle into me, and I let myself surrender to the silence.

I noticed I was breathing differently, slow and even. I was tasting my food differently. Everything was bursting with flavor. I saw the light in the room differently, and for the first time in my life I understood the words of the famous architect Louis Kahn, who taught about "the endlessly changing qualities of natural light, in which a room is a different room every second of the day." I heard the sounds of nature that I never notice, the chirping and the rustling. And I experienced something I haven't encountered in a long time: one single day felt like a week, like a month even—not because I was bored and staring at my watch and counting down the minutes until I could speak again. The day felt like a week because I had broken through to another dimension and touched something eternal. Time stood still.

That very night, I had a revelation. Suddenly a verse from the Psalms came to me, and I understood it finally in a way I'd never seen before: "Orech yamim asbiehu."

This phrase is usually translated as: "I will nourish you with length of days"—meaning, "I will bless you with a long life."

But now, in that moment, on that day that felt like a month, I was seeing what the words really meant. God wasn't promising us a long life. Plenty of great, holy people don't get to live a long life. Instead, God is promising us this: I will nourish you with *long days, orech yamim*. Long days.

Not long gray days when you're staring at the clock and can't wait for work to end. Long days that have color and shape. Days that feel full, days to feel deeply. To feel alive and in love. Where we feel whole and satisfied. Like we've actually *lived* the day and connected with the people we want to connect with instead of missing the day.

We've all had moments like that, glimpses. When time seems to stand still and your day feels rich and worthwhile. Moments when time gives way to eternity and you see your World to Come in this world.

Yes, we can break through from our temporal existence and taste heaven here.

MY MOM DIDN'T DRIVE, but she loved to take car rides. Whenever she'd visit me in LA inevitably she'd say, "Nomeleh, take me for a drive."

I'd say, "Where do you want to go, Mom?"

And she'd say, "Nowhere, just take me." We'd get in the car and go nowhere really. It's hard to explain to you what those rides were like. Just aimlessly driving and enjoying each other's company. Our rides were so magical. We'd talk and talk. And then we'd fall silent and just take in the beauty. We'd listen to music. And then we'd talk some more . . .

On the very last visit my mom made to LA before she died, I could see she looked frail and thin. Part of me didn't want to believe that she'd ever be gone. Her spirit was still as radiant as could be, perhaps more radiant than ever. But I was painfully aware of how precious our time together was.

During that visit my mom said, "Nomeleh, let's go for a drive." I was pretty busy, but I cleared my calendar and my mom and I drove with abandon, just like Thelma and Louise. We were listening to Barbra Streisand sing, "Nothing's gonna harm you, not while I'm around." I think I must have played that song ten times.

I got on the Pacific Coast Highway and with no plan at all I kept driving all the way to Santa Barbara. We stopped at a café and instead of eating there, my mom said, "Let's make a picnic." So we bought some takeout sandwiches and big gooey chocolate chip cookies and fresh-squeezed orange juice. And then we made a picnic on the lawn of the stunning courthouse building with its magical blue tiles. My mom was too tired to climb the stairs to the bell tower, but we had the best views anyone could ever have. What's a better view for a mother than the face of her own daughter?

She looked at me, I looked at her. Time stood still. The air was crystal clear. The sun, the grass, everything seemed so alive and vibrant.

Then my mom wanted to ride along the shore. Instead of driving, I thought we should take a bike. There was no way my mom could pedal a bike, so we rented one of those chariot bikes and I pedaled us along the bike path, surrounded by the water and the sand and those mountains. And when we drove home, we hit the Pacific Coast Highway just in time to watch the sun setting over the ocean in brilliant pinks and purples to the sound of Streisand singing, "Nothing's gonna harm you."

It was a perfect long day. A taste of Eden in this world.

That day remains with me, together with many other long days. And even though my mom is gone, those long, eternal days come to me and comfort me.

All I can tell you is, the regrets I have in my life are not about missed opportunities to advance my rabbinic career. My regrets are about wondering if I shared enough long days with my kids. And even though they're all grown up now, I pray that God grants me the opportunity to share more and more long days with them. Days that live on and on.

Once, a great Hasidic rabbi was dying. His disciples crowded around him and the great rabbi began to weep. His disciples asked him, "Rebbe, why are you crying?"

The rabbi replied: "My whole life is passing before me and I suddenly see—I had it all wrong! I was mistaken! The moments in my life that I thought were extraordinary were actually quite ordinary. And the moments that I thought were ordinary were the most luminous of all. I wish I had understood this!"

The holiest days aren't the showy ones—not the graduation and not even the wedding day. The holiest moments are those unexpected, ordinary times when you relax and let the magic in. Just sitting on the grass with your child doing nothing. Just holding someone's hand.

I've heard people say that it's bad to kill time. Shouldn't we make the most of every moment? But as I've grown older I've come to understand that we *need* to *kill* time. Smash the clock. Let go of your temporality and be available for something sacred and surprising to happen that you can't plan for.

I love the Yiddish word "schmoozing." You ask someone who just finished a conversation with a loved one: "So, nu? What did you talk about?" And they reply, "Nothing, we were just schmoozing." Just shooting the breeze.

We need more schmoozing.

We need to make time to fall in love a little bit every day. To fall back in love with the people we love. To fall in love with our friends. To fall in love with our work. To fall in love with a total stranger. To fall in love with God.

Our egos need goals. And I'm not suggesting that you should fritter away your days or ignore your responsibilities and ambitions. But trust me, your soul thirsts for encounters without goals. Meeting someone without an "ask" in mind.

The rabbis call this way of living *lishmah*. Doing something out of love for its own sake. Without any ulterior motive. Unconditional time. I pray that you give yourself the gift of long days with those you love.

Unconditional time, it's yours to have and to share. We can stop the clock and swim in Eden's waters together with the people we love. Break through the temporal to the eternal. Kill time!

IN 2012, MY FRIEND AIMEE was living in India and she came for a visit to LA. At a Sabbath dinner, she found herself sitting opposite the famous Jewish actor and singer Theodore Bikel. He was so charming with his stories and his magnetic presence, oh, and that voice of his. The timing of their meeting was all wrong. Theo was a widower still mourning the passing of his wife, Tamara, Aimee was living in India. And then there was the matter of their ages. Aimee was fifty, Theo was eighty-eight. But sometimes the wrong time is the right time. The temporal and the eternal intersect and we can see it.

They fell hard for each other.

Their relationship made *no* sense, and it made *perfect* sense. Aimee said, "God put a present in front of me, wrapped with a bow with my name on it. Was I going to ignore it? Run from it? Or open it and say, thank You, God."

Aimee moved to LA and within a few months she and Theo were married. It was a whirlwind romance. Faces glowing, souls intertwined.

Aimee and Theo were sure they had been soulmates in a previous time. They believed that before they were born into this life, their souls had made a pact to reunite at precisely the time when they both needed each other the most. This was that time. And they lived it with abandon.

One Sabbath, Aimee and Theo came over to our house for dinner. Theo was already quite ill, but he held court, telling stories and singing songs. Aimee was beaming with love. They both were.

For me, having Theodore Bikel over was like having Paul McCartney over for dinner. I so wanted to ask him to sign my records, but I was too shy to ask. I didn't want to seem like a groupie, but I was a groupie. I grew up on Theo's Yiddish and Hebrew songs. His music was my mother's milk.

NOT LONG AFTER THE PERFECT day I spent with my mom in Santa Barbara, I flew to Boston to be at her bedside. My mom asked me, "Nomeleh, play me some Yiddish music," and I put on Theodore Bikel.

I wish you could have seen how Theo's voice lit up her face in the hospital and helped her bear her pain. She closed her eyes and smiled, and I could see she was traveling to sweet long days when my parents were courting to those very songs, hand in hand.

Aimee said that when Theo was dying he too needed to listen to music. He wanted to hear *his* favorite musical artist: Theodore Bikel! As Theo prepared to leave Aimee for another world, they made a sacred vow that they'd find each other sooner in the next life.

At Theo's funeral, Aimee spoke about mapmaking, cartography. She said a crude way to measure a shoreline is by the mile. You miss so much that way, though. But if you measure by the yard, you start seeing the bends and the contours of that shoreline. And if you measure that same shore by the millimeter, you become intimate with even the smallest twists and turns.

Aimee said, "So Theo and I decided to measure by millimeters, and grew our shoreline as close to infinity as we could."

When Aimee spoke those words I knew she was talking about our God-given power to turn our brief stay in this life into long days.

We have the power to do this. To live full, rich days that have contours. Where our brief time with those we love plays on in slow motion and remains engraved in our memories. Days that don't blend together and vanish. We have the power to kill time and step into eternity and to see our World to Come in this world.

We can learn how to live on soul time.

Every day we're granted a special opening, where the channels between the temporal and the eternal are here for us to enter so we can experience moments of grace—sweet moments of grace.

Less than a month before his own death, Einstein's best friend, Michele Besso, died, and Einstein wrote these words of comfort to Michele's family: "He has departed from this strange world a little ahead of me. That means nothing. For us believing physicists, the distinction between past, present and future is only a stubborn illusion."

In the realm of the soul, past, present, and future are one.

Our souls are here each day to remind us that time and eternity are not cut off from each other. It's a separation that's not a separation. Your soul wants to show you what you've been missing and what you can still have in your life: long, nourishing days. No matter how brief they are—like the shadow of a bird flying overhead.

Every blessed day has a magical power all its own to change us if we let it, if we let go of our rational minds and let our souls do the seeing.

Our souls can teach us how to bless each day. Every day we're granted endless opportunities to pull back the curtain and touch another dimension and bless it. We are given the power to connect with those we've lost.

I'd like to ask you to do something sacred with me now. I'd like to ask you to close your eyes and welcome them. Picture a sweet moment with someone you've loved and lost. Try to picture them beside you. Look into their eyes. Let time stop. Just schmooze with them. See what they're wearing. Can you see their smile?

Take their hand and just sit in silence. Breathe in. See if you can remember their smell.

Just share a moment in eternity with them. Remember a lesson they taught you.

When you're ready, ask for your blessing.

And now offer them your blessing. Tell them what they meant to you, what you're grateful for. What they taught you. What you will always carry with you.

I offer you a memorial prayer I wrote. It is a conversation you can have with someone you've loved and lost. Bless them and may their blessings shine upon you always.

A Memorial Prayer

I haven't forgotten you, even though it's been some time now since I've seen your face, touched your hand, heard your voice. You are with me all the time.

I used to think you left me. I know better now. You come to me. Sometimes in fleeting moments I feel your presence close by. But I still miss you. And nothing, no person, no joy, no accomplishment, no distraction, not even God can fill the gaping hole your absence has left in my life.

But mixed together with all my sadness, there is a great joy for having known you. I want to thank you for the time we shared, for the love you gave, for the wisdom you spread.

Thank you for the magnificent moments and for the ordinary ones too. There was beauty in our simplicity. Holiness in our unspectacular days. And I will carry the lessons you taught me always.

Your life has ended, but your light can never be extinguished. It continues to shine upon me even on the darkest nights and illuminates my way.

I light this candle in your honor and in your memory. May God bless you as you have blessed me with love, with grace, and with peace. Amen.

40

Experiencing the Oneness

JERRY WAS EIGHTY-SEVEN AND I was his twenty-six-year-old rabbi. If at first he didn't know what to make of this "girl rabbi," it didn't take very long before we became quite close. Soon Jerry drafted me to come every Friday afternoon to his senior center, the Israel Levin Center, to lead Sabbath services. He said, "The old folks really need a shot in the arm."

Even though he was technically one of them, Jerry was so robust and fit that he seemed decades younger than his senior peers. And then Jerry asked me to lead a Passover Seder for the seniors. I already had a congregation that was more than a full-time job, but Jerry's circle of seniors became my second congregation.

When Rob and I got married, we invited my congregation to the ceremony, and when Jerry got the invitation he decided to spread the word to the entire Israel Levin Center. There were over seven hundred people at our wedding, and every time we play our wedding video I start laughing at the sight of my mother and me trying to somehow make it down the aisle with the Israel Levin women dancing and clapping in our path.

Not long after that, Jerry's health began to deteriorate. He stopped coming to synagogue, stopped going to the Israel Levin Center for lunch. I'd come by and visit him, we'd talk on the phone. He was always cheery and upbeat.

One day when I came to visit, Jerry took my hand and squeezed it with some urgency. His skin was paper-thin. He asked, "Rabbi, can I call you Naomi?"

"Jerry, of course you can," I said, "it's my name."

He said, "I've always loved the name Naomi . . . *Whither thou goest, I will go . . .*" And then he went on, "Naomi, I'm scared of dying. I thought as it got closer that I'd be more peaceful around death, but I'm not. I want to go out with dignity, but I'm terrified."

I held Jerry's hand and I said, "I've never met any person who welcomed death with perfect equanimity. Even Moses, who lived to the age of one hundred and twenty, pleaded with God for more time on earth."

Jerry said, "I didn't know that."

I said, "In one rabbinic tale Moses begged heaven and earth, the sun and the moon, to intervene with God on his behalf. He appealed to the mountains and the seas, but no one could help him extend his life span."

Jerry said, "It's a relief to hear this."

I continued, "Yes, even Moses wanted more time." Seeing how Jerry reacted to this rabbinic interpretation, I said, "If you like, when I come back next week I can share my favorite Jewish teachings about facing death, the ones that comfort me most."

"Yes, that sounds nice," Jerry said.

So I began collecting the Jewish teachings on death that calm and inspire me. Pieces from the Psalms, from the Talmud, and from the mystics as well. I cut and pasted and Xeroxed.

The next week, in the late afternoon, I went to Jerry's apartment. I turned on the light on his nightstand and began to teach him about the soul. We talked about how the soul comes from the place of eternity and is reluctant to enter this world and how God has to persuade her to descend. We talked about how the soul's descent is for the sake of an ascent, that it enters our World of Separation in order to fulfill a holy mission.

Then I read Jerry a passage from the Zohar about the soul's attachment to the body: "There is nothing more difficult for the soul than to separate from the body. No person dies before he or she sees the Divine Presence, and because of its deep yearning for the Presence the soul departs in order to greet it."

Jerry wanted to know more about the soul's reluctance to leave the body. I returned to the rabbinic account of Moses's death. I told him how God refuses to delay Moses's death and insists there is a boundary to every life. Once God gets Moses to agree to depart, God has to get the soul of Moses to agree too. This proves to be quite a challenge. God calls Moses's soul back home, saying, "Come, my daughter, it's time to go, don't delay. I will bring you to the highest heavens." But the soul refuses to leave.

She says, "God, I know You are Master of all souls, but I love Moses. Please don't make me leave him." In the end, the soul departs only when God personally draws her out from Moses with a kiss on the lips. Only then does she agree to return to the world above.

Jerry started smiling. He said, "So maybe fearing death isn't a weakness or a lack of faith. Could it be that my soul is caught between two worlds?"

"Exactly," I said.

A couple of weeks later, I told Jerry about two more Jewish end-of-life teachings that make death seem less terrifying. The first comes from the Zohar: "At the time of a person's death one is allowed to see relatives and companions from the other world."

Jerry said, "Do you believe this, Rabbi, I mean, Naomi? Do you think I will see my Florence's face before I go?"

I said, "I can't promise you this, but I can tell you that it's part of our tradition that such experiences and visions are possible."

And then I taught Jerry one more text about expanded vision at life's end. I told Jerry that a dying person is given an additional soul. I explained that when we receive this additional soul, we get to see the unity we were never able to grasp our whole life long. I imagine what we get to see is the higher perspective we've been seeking, a vision of heaven here that brings an overwhelming sense of well-being. A feeling of relief and release. And once you see the radiant Oneness, you are ready to make the transition into the next world.

Jerry was drawn to the idea that a dying person sees what he's been blind to all his life, and how this new way of seeing is a liberation.

Our discussions about death went on for many weeks, and Jerry's strength continued to decline. He was receiving hospice care now. One day when I came to see him Jerry asked me, "Is death painful?"

I said in front of his hospice nurse, whose name was Gloria, "I'm not a doctor or a nurse, but I can tell you what the Talmud says about how death feels."

Jerry said, "The Talmud tells you what death feels like?"

"Yes," I said. I could see Gloria was also very interested in our discussion. She was an Evangelical Christian and we invited her to listen in.

I shared a surreal Talmudic story with Jerry: Once a rabbi named Rava was sitting by the deathbed of his friend Rabbi Nachman. Rava asked Rabbi Nachman, "Come and visit me after you die." So Rabbi Nachman died and sure enough, not long after his death, Nachman appeared to Rava.

Rava asked his dead friend's soul, "Tell me what it's like, is death painful?"

Nachman said, "The moment of death is as painless and simple as removing a strand of hair out of a cup of milk." But then he added, "Still, if God were to ask me to return to the world of the living I would refuse, because the fear of death is so overwhelming."

Jerry began to tear up. He said, "You don't know what it means to me to know that fearing death isn't a sign of weakness."

I said, "Jerry, there's nothing weak about you. I'm terrified of death."

He said, "But you've got your whole life ahead of you."

"Nothing is guaranteed," I told him.

Jerry thought for a while about that Talmudic scene and asked, "Naomi, do you believe the dead can come back to communicate with the living?"

"Yes, I do."

The following week I told Jerry the following Hasidic tale:

When Rabbi Bunam died, one of his disciples came to comfort the rabbi's grieving son. The son wept before the disciple, "Who is going to teach me now?"

The disciple comforted the rabbi's son with this thought: "Up to now your father has taught you while wearing a coat; now he will teach you with his coat off."

Jerry said, "I never thought of my body as my soul's coat. That's a nice image. I like it." Gloria slapped her thigh in joy. She said she liked it too.

Several weeks later I came to see Jerry and he was lying in bed, quite pale and weak. Gloria left us by ourselves this time. There was a somber look on her face. Jerry whispered to me, "Naomi, does Judaism say anything about reincarnation? I've always been drawn to the idea of reincarnation and I was wondering, is it sacrilegious to think about it?"

"Jerry, it's not sacrilege," I said. "Jewish mystical texts teach us about the soul's reincarnation. These teachings are even in our daily prayers. In Hebrew it's called *gilgul*. In English we call it transmigration."

Jerry asked, "Where in our daily prayers does it talk about reincarnation?"

"In the daily bedtime Shema prayer, the same Shema a person recites at the moment of death. Every night we say: 'Master of the Universe, I hereby forgive anyone who angered or antagonized me or who sinned against me . . . whether through speech, deed, thought, or notion; *whether in this transmigration or another transmigration . . .'"*

Jerry said, "Oh my gosh. Why didn't they ever teach this to me when I was in Hebrew school? Forgive people for how they treated you in another life?" I could see Jerry was thrilled. His mind was starting to make connections, starting to make links and leaps, putting disparate thoughts and experiences together.

A few days later Gloria called to tell me that Jerry's end was near. I rushed over and Jerry seemed very placid, his face was at ease. He slipped in and out of consciousness. When he opened his eyes he saw me beside him and he whispered, "Rabbi, I'm ready to say the final Shema with you." I could see he was.

Just as he'd wanted it, Jerry was going out with dignity. He seemed to have found the peace he'd been searching for. We read the final confessional and the words of the Shema prayer, "Listen, Israel, the Lord our God, the Lord is One." Everything seemed to melt into oneness in that room at that moment. Time stopped. I could hear Jerry's belabored breathing. I could sense how the worry had departed from him. All that was left was love.

The teachings I shared with Jerry I offer to you.

May your soul's vision of oneness enter you and calm you and illuminate you. May it take its rightful place inside you. May you come to see your own eternity. Amen.

41

Giving Pleasure to the Soul

WHEN ROB AND I WERE about to be married, about a month before our wedding, I asked him to join me for a trip to New York. He was thrilled, thinking, *Great, we'll eat New York pizza, see family, go to a Broadway show.*

I said, "I want us to go to New York so we can invite my father to the wedding." I'd been feeling sad that my father wasn't going to be walking me down the aisle. Rob just looked at me. At that point, my father had been dead for thirteen years.

"What are you talking about?" Rob asked.

I said, "It's a Jewish tradition to invite deceased loved ones to the wedding."

Rob said, "Okay."

So we flew to New York and rented a car and drove from rush-hour packed Manhattan out to New Jersey, past the sprawling suburban homes until we reached the large cemetery with rows and rows of tombstones where my father is buried.

We stood before my father's grave in silence. Then I gathered up my courage, took a deep breath, and said, "Hi, Daddy, this is Rob. I love him. I'm sure that you're going to love him too. We're getting married on April fourteenth and we'd like to invite you to the wedding. We hope you can come."

SOMETIMES WHEN I LEAD PRAYER services at my spiritual community, Nashuva, I think about the biblical patriarchs and matriarchs—Abraham, Isaac, and Jacob, Sarah, Rebecca, Rachel, and Leah. I feel them watching over us. I wonder how much *nachas* they must be getting from watching Jews in the twenty-first century still passionately carrying on their legacy. How much *nachas* they must feel to know that we still remember them. That we even mention their names in our prayers today.

Nachas. I was talking to a friend of mine who is Catholic and I was telling her how much *nachas* I get from my children. She looked at me with a puzzled expression. "What's *nachas?*"

What's *nachas?* There's no word in the English language for this sacred experience. How do you put *nachas* into words?

Nachas is the unique experience of joy that a parent takes in a child, or that a teacher takes in a student, an aunt or uncle takes in a niece or nephew, a grandparent in a grandchild.

But *nachas* is not just joy. It's pride, it's pleasure, it's contentment. It's a spiritual feeling. A taste of heaven on earth.

The Yiddish word *nachas* actually comes from the Hebrew phrase *nachat ruach*, which means "ease of spirit." *Nachas* is that moment when the soul feels complete, when it rejoices in a job well done—having raised a child or a disciple well.

Nachas involves a sigh, a release, a sense of peace, and exhilaration and pride at the same time.

As we've already learned, sometimes parents deny their souls the gift of *nachas* because they never allow themselves to accept their children as they are. Because of that, they never get to experience deep *nachas* for the beautiful, unique souls that their children possess.

Of course, not everyone gets to be a parent or gets to experience the *nachas* of a parent. But every one of us is a child, and we all have the opportunity to give *nachas*. It takes so little to give a parent *nachas*. Just throw a crumb of appreciation. A little love. A little attention. As children we take so much for granted.

I remember spending those sleepless nights walking back and forth with my son when he was an infant, speaking to him in my mind, *There are so many things I'm doing for you right now and you'll never know it. You'll never know the sacrifice or the worry or the amount of space you take up in my mind and in my heart.*

As children it's so easy to forget.

It takes so little to give a parent *nachas*, but sometimes we are stingy with it.

I was explaining this to my Catholic friend, and she looked at me with tears in her eyes and she asked me, "Naomi, can a person give *nachas* to a parent after they have died?"

This is such a universal question. How many times have I felt it myself? I wish my mother could see how things are turning out for me. I wish my father could see how I am living out the Jewish legacy he gave me. I wish he knew Rob, I wish he could have danced at his children's weddings, I wish he could have had the *nachas* of bouncing eleven grandchildren on his knee.

How many times have people expressed this longing to me: I wish my grandmother were here to share this moment with me. I wish my mother could have been there when I gave birth. I wish my father could have known his grandson. If only my grandfather were here to see this. If only . . .

I looked at my Catholic friend and said, "I believe we can give *nachas* to the dead." And she just broke down. She told me that she hadn't been able to give love freely to her mother when she was alive. And now she had so many regrets.

I said to her, "*Nachas* transcends the grave."

You give *nachas* to deceased loved ones by remembering them. By telling them how grateful you are for all they gave you, for all the sacrifices they made for you. You give them *nachas* by living up to the values they sought to instill in you, by treasuring the legacy they left you, by sharing the wisdom they taught you with others. You give them *nachas* by keeping and carrying on your family traditions with pride.

There are many rabbinic and mystical texts that describe the intermingling of spiritual worlds. The rabbis describe an atmosphere that is saturated with spiritual flow. There are worlds of existence that our conscious minds have no access to that are interwoven with our own world. These spheres aren't far from us, they're here with us. Our minds can't sense them, but our souls know and see all.

To me, the greatest representations of the spiritual flow uniting all things are the paintings of Vincent van Gogh. Picture the painting *The Starry Night*. Can you see all those brushstrokes? How the heavens and the earth are connected by all those swirling channels? Streams flowing down and flowing up, eternally stirring and flowing and descending and ascending.

There are things we can't see with our eyes. Sounds we can't hear with our ears. People long gone whose presence is always with us, invisible but palpable.

Perhaps that's why my mother was able to tell me after my son's bar mitzvah and after my daughter's bat mitzvah, "I want you know that Daddy was here rejoicing today."

I said to her, "I know."

And that's why Jews have a practice of reciting a special memorial prayer for deceased parents before a wedding, because there is a tradition that the souls of deceased parents come under the wedding canopy with their children and experience *nachas*.

And that's why Rob and I stood before my father's grave a month before we were to be married and invited him to our wedding. Rob told me that naturally he was a bit resistant at first. He didn't believe it. He didn't expect anything to happen.

But on our wedding day as my mother and I proudly marched down the aisle hand in hand toward the wedding canopy, Rob sensed an invisible presence overflowing with *nachas*. I felt it in the depths of my soul. My father had come to give the bride away.

ALL OF US WHO HAVE loved and lost know the pang of gaping holes that nothing can fill. The empty seat at the holiday table, the hug, the kiss, the gentle words of assurance that we so wish we could have once more. But I believe with all my heart and soul that our loved ones are never far from us. Daily they are blessing us, guiding us, and taking pleasure in us.

We have the God-given power to offer the soul a gift. Allow it to give and receive *nachas* in this world and beyond. Allow your soul to teach you how to look upon your children and your disciples with awe. Allow your soul to take pleasure in the precious people that they are.

If your parents and grandparents and mentors are living, don't withhold your heart. Even if they frustrate you, even if they embarrass you. Share your joy with them, share your achievements, share your gratitude, share your love. Give their souls some *nachas*.

And if your loved ones have found a home in the realm of eternity, know in your heart that *nachas* transcends the grave.

May you be blessed to give and to receive the sacred soul pleasure of nachas. *Amen.*

42

Beholding Threads of Connection

IT WAS THREE YEARS AGO that I stumbled accidentally on a quote by Albert Einstein that stopped me in my tracks because it so captured everything I believe and everything I know to be true about the way we are all intimately connected to one another.

And then Rabbi Robert Marcus, who had helped so many children, but was unable to save the life of his own eleven-year-old son Jay, became part of my journey. In his heartbreak he'd reached out and written to Einstein seeking words of comfort, words to help him make sense of his own tragic loss. In return he received Einstein's powerful description of a world that is all one.

Over the past three years I've been searching the world for Buchenwald boys who could offer me any piece of information about Rabbi Marcus, who died in 1951.

But the one Buchenwald boy I most wanted to speak to, the one who I believed could really put Rabbi Marcus's story into context for me, was Elie Wiesel.

I so longed to interview Elie. I'd write, I'd call, I'd e-mail. His assistant always told me that his calendar was completely booked.

One friend of mine who knew Elie told me he was in poor health and that his mind might not be as clear as it once was. Perhaps Elie didn't remember Rabbi Marcus. Perhaps that was why I couldn't reach him.

Still, every few weeks I'd e-mail again requesting an interview.

I waited and reached out for three years and then, one day, I got a response! Elie wanted to speak with me. On the afternoon of our interview I was so excited my heart was pounding in my chest.

I still worried that Elie might not have much to tell me about Rabbi Marcus, but I was so grateful and honored to be able to speak with him.

Then I asked my first question: "Do you remember Rabbi Robert Marcus?"

Elie said, "Do I remember?"

He said, "I saw a soldier appear with a Star of David sewn onto his military uniform." Elie explained, "This meant a lot. Up to that moment, for us, a Star of David was a mark of death. And here suddenly it was a mark of freedom!"

That's not something you forget.

Then Elie told me about the power of that moment when Rabbi Marcus led the very first prayer service in the Buchenwald concentration camp. "We prayed all the time in Buchenwald," Elie said, "but this was different. It was a great happiness, surprising. It meant a great deal that we could pray with him."

Elie told me that he was in awe of Rabbi Marcus. He said, "Naomi, the distance from us boys to Rabbi Marcus was like the distance from the earth to the sun." Seventy years had passed, but his memories of that time had not faded.

And then I spoke with Elie about Judith, the young woman who took charge of his orphanage after liberation. I asked Elie, "What stood out for you about Judith?"

He said, "Her smile."

I asked him, "Could you feel her confidence?"

"Oh yes," he said, "absolutely, we all felt it. She came from a place of security and happiness. She created a safe place for us. Judith knew what we needed."

With kindness Elie allowed me to probe into those days with Judith. I asked him, "Did you know when you first arrived at Ecouis that you and all the boys had been diagnosed as damaged beyond repair?"

Elie replied in a voice filled with pain and understanding, "Yes, I was aware of that."

Elie told me about the day when Judith reorganized rooms by village. "It was a powerful moment," he said.

I asked Elie if he remembered Niny. It turned out that Elie too had a mad crush on the beautiful Niny.

Then I spoke with Elie about the day the boys argued over whether they should say the mourner's Kaddish for their families. Elie was one of the boys who stayed to recite the prayer for the departed. He told me that even from a distance of seventy years it was too difficult for him to speak about that day.

I said to Elie, "Judith told me she saw hope return to the boys. Did Judith give you hope?"

Elie said, "It's a very strong word, 'hope,' I'm not sure I'd use that word."

"What word would you use?"

"Hopefully, I'll find it. One day I'll find it."

Toward the end of our conversation I asked Elie the question I'd been longing to ask him: if he knew about a letter Rabbi Marcus had written to Einstein after the death of his son Jay. Elie told me he did not. I read Elie Einstein's letter to Rabbi Marcus and then I asked him, "What was the most important thing that got you through your worst times?"

Without missing a beat Elie replied, "Friendship . . . without a doubt, friendship."

Yes, friendship, of course! As Elie spoke I was beginning to see threads of connection. The way you can even be a friend to a total stranger. How Rabbi Marcus was there for Elie Wiesel and how Einstein was there for Rabbi Marcus. Strangers who reached beyond themselves to lift up and save another—people who rose above that "optical delusion of separateness."

We are all part of a whole.

You never know how a stranger is going to enter your life and save you and lift you and liberate you from the delusion that you are alone.

At that moment I was about to say thank you and hang up, but then I realized that I owed Elie Wiesel my gratitude, not for agreeing to do this interview, but for an act of kindness he bestowed upon me many years ago without even knowing it. I needed to thank him, and I might never have another chance.

So before I hung up with Elie I hesitated, but then I gathered up my courage because I just knew I had to tell him how he had saved my life.

I told Elie, "I need to tell you something. I assume you must hear this from so many people, how you've helped them, but I need to tell you what you did for me in my life."

"You cannot imagine how moved I am right now," Elie said. "Tell me what happened."

And so I began: "I grew up in Brooklyn. My father taught me, from the time I was a small child he began teaching me Torah and commentaries and how to pray too. He'd take me with him to synagogue every Sabbath and I would sit beside him and play with the strands of his prayer shawl."

I told Elie about my father's murder when I was fifteen years old and that I was an angry kid, so angry and lost and sad. I said I didn't have a plan for ending my life, but I didn't have any plan for living either.

I was only fifteen years old and I felt like I had come to the end of things. My father was gone. My mother wasn't the same woman anymore. The Sabbath wasn't the same. I wasn't the same. Prayer? How could prayer be the same? And what good was God anyway?

I said, "At that lowest point of my life, my mother saw that you were giving a lecture and she asked me to go with her. I didn't want to go, but she encouraged me and I went. It was a freezing-cold December night and we took the subway from Boro Park all the way up to the 92nd Street Y." I said, "I walked into this massive auditorium full of old people and I so didn't want to be there. We were sitting in the second-to-last row and I so regretted that I'd agreed to come to this thing. But then all of a sudden, the lights went down and you walked onstage and sat down at a desk with just a spotlight on you, and began speaking. At first I was daydreaming as you spoke, but then your words began to seep into my well-defended heart. Yes, your words were sinking in, the kindness of your voice. And your hands were performing some sort of ballet in the dark. It was as if your hands were doing a performance to the words you spoke all on their own. I remember being transfixed by your hands, and realizing it was the first time I experienced beauty since the day my father died. I was mesmerized. Watching and listening to you, a man who had been to hell and back, and seeing you offer beauty to the world gave me some sort of spark of hope. And somehow, that night, you opened a door for me to step through. That night was the beginning, a first step in many steps that would lead me back, bit by bit, out of the depths that had threatened to overtake me. Many years have passed and I have had many causes for joy. And I want to thank you for teaching me that there was hope in my future and that I would have cause to celebrate and to give thanks."

I said to Elie, "A man stands in front of an auditorium of two thousand people and he has no idea that he's opened a new door for some lost fifteen-year-old kid who is listening and taking it all in."

Elie said to me, "You cannot imagine how touched I am."

IT DOESN'T TAKE MUCH TO lift the veil that separates one person from the next.

You can't see it, you can't understand it, it can take a whole life-time for you to realize that we are all intimately intertwined with one another.

During the summer while I was recuperating from my reconstruction surgery, I came upon a story that so embodied Einstein's understanding of the way we are all interwoven into a single fabric.

The story was about a young bride-to-be whose father died and who had no one to walk her down the aisle on her wedding day. As I read on I remembered how naked I'd felt anticipating my own wedding day.

I skimmed the article and just began sobbing. So I reached out to this bride to get her story firsthand.

As I was preparing for our conversation I finally read the *New York Times* article that I had only skimmed earlier. I suddenly started to shiver, because I'd had no idea how closely my own life story paralleled Jeni Stepian's story.

Ten years ago, when she was twenty-three, Jeni's father, Michael, was murdered in a mugging. He was shot in an alley, and left to die there in the rain.

When we first spoke, I didn't want to tell Jeni about my own father's mugging and murder, I just wanted to hear her story. So I asked her, "Can you describe your father to me? Who he was to you?"

Jeni said to me, "My dad was a very generous, charismatic person, always reaching out to people. He was a people magnet, he talked to everybody, so social. He loved sports and being active, and his heart was so strong."

When Jeni's father was dying she saw that on his driver's license it said he'd chosen to become an organ donor, so the family decided to get in touch with an organization called Core, the Center for Organ Recovery and Education.

Jeni said, "My dad's death was so senseless, we wanted to honor him by helping somebody else. And soon the people at Core let us know they were able to use his heart."

She told me, "It helped us in our grieving to know that my dad's organs might save a life. We found out three or four days later that a man had received my dad's heart."

On that very same night that Jeni's father, Michael, was shot, there was a man named Arthur Thomas who was a college guidance counselor, married to his wife, Nancy, and a father of four chidren. He goes by Tom.

Tom's situation was very dire. I spoke with him too.

Tom told me, "Rabbi, my heart had weakened to the point of congestive heart failure and I couldn't walk more than ten steps without needing to stop and catch my breath."

When he went to see his cardiologist the doctor explained, "Tom, it's time for a transplant. Your heart's just not working properly."

Tom knew his situation was critical. He said he would suffer through horrible nights, petrified that he was about to die, always waiting to die.

Tom told me, "So they put me in the hospital. My other organs started to fail . . . And then one day I was lying in bed and my doctor comes and says: 'Good news! We think we have a heart for you.'"

The next thing he knew, Tom was taken into the operating room and the heart was flown in from Pittsburgh. The operation went smoothly.

Tom told me, "Rabbi, you won't believe this, but within just forty-eight hours I was walking around, talking to people."

He said, "Two weeks after the transplant I wrote the Stepians a thank you letter. And then I went back to work. I got a complete new lease on life."

Tom added, "Six months later I was skiing!"

Jeni told me that on December 24 of the year her father died, her family received a letter in the mail.

She said, "It was a very hard time. It was the first Christmas my dad was missing. When we opened the letter I read: 'Hello, my name is Tom, I received the heart from you and I just want to thank you. I was so sick for so long, waiting for so long for a heart.' "

Jeni said, "It was clear Tom spent a lot of time considering what he wanted to say."

She went on, "I was reading the letter and crying. It was great to know that this person who received my dad's heart was thriving."

I asked Tom to describe what he was feeling when he wrote that letter.

Tom said to me, "They made the decision to donate Michael's heart when they were in the worst possible pain, losing the key person in their family, and at that moment they decided to give life to a person they didn't even know."

Jeni told me that soon after receiving that letter a beautiful relationship began between Tom and her mom. They began talking on the phone every month, letters, cards, and flowers on her birthday and major holidays.

Jeni said, "Tom is so appreciative to have his life back, so very, very thankful."

I asked Tom what these ten years since receiving Michael's heart have meant to him.

He said, "Rabbi, the heart I received from Michael's family has given me the ability to grow older with my family and watch my children graduate from high school and then from college, and to be there alive to see two of my children get married. And I still ski! I'm living a normal life and none of that would have been possible without their generosity. I feel an obligation to live life to the fullest, to be kind to other people. I feel so wonderful to be alive."

And then Tom told me, "I do feel my heart when it beats. I used to think of it as *my* heart, but now I know it's *our* heart, I say, our heart is doing well."

And then Jeni met Paul, her soulmate. They fell in love, and soon they got engaged.

I asked Jeni, "What were you feeling when you realized your dad wouldn't be at your wedding?"

She said, "When I'd think about my wedding it made me sad that my dad couldn't be there walking me down the aisle."

She explained, "Every time I've gone to a wedding I've felt left out, sad. Someone stole that from me. I was jealous of girlfriends who had their dads still around."

And then Jeni told me, "I had a thought. Wouldn't it be awesome if Tom could come to my wedding to bring a piece of my dad with him? I wanted to invite him and have him walk me down the aisle."

Jeni didn't want to put Tom on the spot, so she wrote him this letter:

Tom this is Jeni, Michael's daughter. You have my dad's heart. And I'm so happy to have you in our lives. I recently got engaged, I'd like to know if you would come to my wedding if you're willing and walk me down the aisle.

She put her letter in the mail. Two days later Tom opened the envelope.

Tom told me, "When I received Jeni's letter I was stunned. I just needed to sit down. It was so beautiful. I knew I would do it the moment I read her request. It was this wonderful feeling of coming to the right spot with people. It was just perfect. It meant that her dad would be there for the wedding!"

He said, "I thought to myself, I'm so happy, I don't know how I'm not going to cry the whole time."

The day before the wedding Jeni met Tom for the first time in her life. Jeni and her sister and her mom, Bernice, and Tom and his wife, Nancy, all arranged to meet.

Jeni said, "When I saw him it was every emotion possible at once. I couldn't stop crying enough to talk."

She added, "All this time I kept wondering who this person will be. I read his letters, but to see him in person, living. I was blown away by every single part of that encounter. It was overwhelming."

And Tom told me, "It was such an emotional moment meeting Jeni. And then I took her hand and put it on my pulse so she could feel her father's heart beating."

Jeni described that exact same moment to me as well: "And suddenly he asked me if I wanted to feel his pulse on his wrist. I felt his pulse . . . and then I reached up and put my hand on his heart."

She said, "It was like a miracle, a dream come true, to complete so much that had been taken away, it was a final piece of closure and I was sobbing uncontrollably."

Then came the wedding day. What a day of celebration and rejoicing. And they both held it together that day as Tom took Jeni's arm and walked her down the aisle with pride.

Jeni said, "I just felt that my dad was just smiling down and I felt very at peace and very happy, like a little girl again living the dream of her wedding day. And I danced the father-daughter dance with Tom."

It was a Jessica Simpson song called: "You Don't Have to Let Go."

She said, "I chose it for my dad."

Jeni said, "Naomi, I feel like my dad, who was always larger than life, he needed more time and he gets to live on now. He had a bigger purpose, he knew he was destined for something bigger, and he gets to live on and have a second chance."

Jeni went on, "I've learned from this, you never know how someone will enter your life. So treat everyone like they're family."

As she spoke I was thinking of Einstein's "whole" and how beautiful and moving and healing it is when those walls of separation come down before our eyes and you realize the walls were never walls, just "optical delusions."

It was at that point in our conversation when I said, "Jeni, until I read the *New York Times* article more carefully this morning, I didn't know that your father was murdered. And I just want to tell you that my father was murdered in a mugging when I was in high school, I just wanted you to know that."

"Oh my, I'm tearing up," Jeni said. "You're the very first person I've ever spoken to who knows what I'm feeling. I have friends who lost parents, but it was always from illness, and I've always felt like no one understands what I've been through."

I said, "Jeni, I understand."

She said, "You don't know what this means to me."

And then she said, "Stories find you when you need them the most."

Yes, stories find you and suddenly you see, you are given a knowing, a vision of the world God wishes for us.

The soul within you understands that the veil of separation is a delusion. It's here to show you that the walls you see are not really walls at all, that boundaries that separate one person from another can come down in the most healing ways, so that we can be there for one another and comfort one another and strengthen one another and save one another.

Sefer Yetzirah, the Jewish mystical Book of Creation, teaches us: "Their end is imbedded in their beginning and their beginning in their end . . ." If you allow room for it in your heart, if you allow your soul to teach you, you can see how everything can come full circle, and how everything intermingles in ways of comfort.

When I spoke to Jeni I was still recuperating from my reconstruction surgery. I couldn't possibly see it yet, but soon I would come to understand how the story I've shared with you about my skin cancer and the doctor who restored me to wholeness, how this story would circle back on itself as well.

And so it was that exactly a month after my final reconstruction surgery, at 6:30 a.m., I found myself sharing a moment of prayer with my surgeon, Dr. Azizzadeh, as he prepared for surgery. But this time, he was the patient about to undergo surgery. As I was speaking to him and blessing him with healing I thought to myself, barriers that separate us do come down. And so do labels: doctor, patient, rabbi. Everything comes full circle.

And all that's left, all that's left . . . is soul.

THIS SUMMER IN LATE JUNE I was on a plane flying home with my daughter, Noa. Somehow we got bumped up to business class and we were both so happy, spreading out like royalty. We got cozy and comfortable and we magically entered one of those heart-to-heart mother-daughter talks.

We started reminiscing about my mom. All of a sudden Noa got really emotional and she told me, "Mom, I just don't think I've been the same person since Bubby died. I feel so lost without her." And she began sobbing. I was too.

I said, "You know Bubby is always with you, right?"

But I also didn't want to take away her right to feel sadness, so I told her, "I know how much you miss her. I miss her too. It's so empty without her."

Just two weeks after that flight came the whole unexpected crazy story with my nose and my first reconstruction surgery.

I got home from that surgery looking like hell, the elephant trunk, the hole in my forehead, blood dripping into my eye.

And that morning Noa came over, she's my baby. No matter how old she is, I try to protect her, I always will. No daughter wants to see her mom look the way I looked right then. I worried it might be too much for her.

But Noa came into my bedroom and she just crawled into bed with me. She's much taller than I am, she towers over me. So I was lying there and looking up at her. There she was mothering me, dabbing away the blood that was dripping into my eye with so much love and care. And right then it seemed as if our roles had reversed. She was the mother caring for me at that moment.

Suddenly I turned to her and said, "You know, Noa, I don't think you need to miss Bubby so much anymore, because I think Bubby decided to crawl inside you."

And we both wept.

Boundaries can melt. Veils that separate us from God, veils that separate us from our departed loved ones, veils that separate one person from another, those veils come down, and suddenly we are given eyes to see that we are all bound together in a great blessed magical oneness. Your soul is here to show you, it longs to help you see all the ways we are intertwined. Tom said, "I used to think of it as *my* heart, but now I know it's *our* heart." You don't need a heart transplant to teach you to feel "our heart" beating inside you. We are all One. Einstein told Rabbi Marcus that seeing ourselves as part of a whole brings peace of mind. And that is what Elie Wiesel was trying to explain when I asked him what gets us through our worst times: "Friendship," he reminded me, "without a doubt, friendship."

SADLY, ELIE WIESEL DIED NOT long after our intimate conversation. I will treasure the precious wisdom he shared with me always and the final words we spoke to each other:

He said, "Naomi, you found your way."

"You are a blessing," I replied.

"So are you," he said. "Don't forget that. Believe in that. More and more blessings."

More and more blessings to you, Elie, in this world and beyond.

And more and more blessings to you, reader. May you see connections and may you seek connections. The sacred threads that unite us all. Amen.

COMING FULL CIRCLE: THE LETTER

It was the letter from Einstein that sent me on a journey into the workings of the soul and how we can learn to welcome higher and higher levels of soul.

And it was the missing letter from Rabbi Marcus to Einstein that tugged at my soul. I wanted to understand what he was asking of Einstein. I longed to hear his question in his own words. I searched, but got nowhere. Perhaps I would never resolve the mystery of that missing letter. I would need to make peace with my questions, I told myself.

Little did I know that this story would circle back on itself as well, like the churning blessed stew I first taught my children about when they were young.

What opening are you seeking? Never lose hope. Doors can open when you least expect it. Stories can find you when you need them most.

I THOUGHT I HAD MADE my peace with the fact that Rabbi

Marcus's letter to Einstein would never be found. I thought I had learned all I needed to know about Rabbi Robert Marcus. I thought I could move on. Alas, I thought wrong. I couldn't get him out of my head. It felt like he was tugging at me, beckoning me to search deeper.

The search was not easy. I could not find Rabbi Marcus's children or his wife. I called the World Jewish Congress, but the person I spoke with told me no one there remembered this man who died in the 1950s.

And then I discovered a clue.

I was searching for photos of Rabbi Marcus on the Internet, and I came upon a comment written by someone named Fred Kahn, who mentioned that he had met Rabbi Marcus in Belgium after liberation in the fall of 1944. He described Rabbi Marcus as "an unsung hero."

Before long, I was on the phone with Fred. Fred is a child survivor who met Rabbi Marcus when he was liberated at the age of twelve. Fred told me about Rabbi Marcus's kindness, his nurturance, and his protection. He said that to this day he has saved several pieces of stationery Rabbi Marcus gave him.

I asked him, "Fred, do you know anything about a letter that Rabbi Marcus wrote to Einstein?"

Fred said, "Yes, Einstein wrote to Rabbi Marcus, but the original letter, no one knows what Rabbi Marcus wrote, and no one knows what happened to it."

But then Fred revealed something new. He said that when Rabbi Marcus died, his wife, Fay, was seven months pregnant, and a baby girl was born just two months after his death. They named the baby Roberta, after her father.

Fred said he'd been in touch with Roberta, and he gave me Roberta's contact information. My heart was racing with excitement. The moment we hung up I immediately began researching her name. I could see she was her father's daughter. Like her father before her, Roberta has dedicated her life to caring for others. I read about Roberta's deep commitment to social justice.

The next day I left a voice mail on Roberta's phone.

As I waited for Roberta's call, I found myself imagining the words that Rabbi Marcus wrote to Einstein, I wanted to understand what he was thinking and feeling. He must have written a truly powerful letter if his words inspired Einstein to reply with such poignancy. I assume Einstein was a pretty busy man.

So while I was waiting to hear back from Roberta, I tried to reach a woman named Alice Calaprice who had worked for the Einstein Archive at the Institute for Advanced Study, and who has written several books about Einstein. I found her name in the white pages and left a message on her phone saying: "I don't know if this is the right Alice Calaprice, but I'm a rabbi and I'm looking for the woman who is an expert on Einstein, because I have a question for you."

An hour later I got a phone call. "Rabbi, this is Alice Calaprice, how can I help you?"

I told Alice the story of Rabbi Robert S. Marcus and she said, "Oh yes, yes, yes, Einstein wrote a letter to him."

"Yes," I said. "I know all about *that* letter. What I'm looking for is the original letter, the letter that Rabbi Marcus wrote *to* Einstein."

"Well, let me see what I can find out," Alice said. "I'll get back to you . . ."

The next day I got an e-mail from Alice: "Rabbi, we're in luck."

And right there in front of me was the letter from Rabbi Robert Marcus to Albert Einstein. I printed it out and started reading . . .

Suddenly everything became clear to me. Why Einstein wrote what he wrote. How his words would offer comfort to a grieving father.

As I was reading with that letter in my hands I got a call. It was Roberta. The daughter born to Rabbi Marcus after his death.

We started talking. I told her that I'd been doing research about her father, of blessed memory, and how I'd been overwhelmed by his selflessness and devotion. She told me what a great man he was and how painful it was to have never met him or her brother Jay, whose untimely death so devastated her father.

She said, "My father died of a heart attack, but I can only imagine it was a broken heart that killed him. An irreplaceable loss, a beautiful child of such promise."

Then she said to me, "Rabbi, I so want to know what it was that my father wrote to Albert Einstein."

I started to tremble. I said, "I have your father's letter, it's in my hands right now. Would you like me to e-mail it to you?"

"No," she said. "Read it to me."

With tears streaming down my cheeks I began. As I read I imagined Rabbi Marcus's voice calling out from beyond the grave:

> Dear Dr. Einstein,
>
> Last summer my eleven year old son died of Polio. He was an unusual child, a lad of great promise who verily thirsted after knowledge so that he could prepare himself for a useful life in the community. His death has shattered the very structure of my existence, my very life has become an almost meaningless void—for all my dreams and aspirations were somehow associated with his future and his strivings. I have tried during the past months to find comfort for my anguished spirit, a measure of solace to help me bear the agony of losing one dearer than life itself—an innocent, dutiful and gifted child who was the victim of such a cruel fate. I have sought comfort in the belief that man has a spirit which attains immortality—that somehow, somewhere my son lives on in a higher world . . .
>
> What would be the purpose of the spirit if with the body it should perish . . . I have said to myself: "It is a law of science that matter can never be destroyed; things are changed but the

essence does not cease to be . . . Shall we say that matter lives and the spirit perishes; shall the lower outlast the higher?"

I have said to myself: "Shall we believe that they who have gone out of life in childhood before the natural measure of their days was full have been forever hurled into the darkness of oblivion? Shall we believe that the millions who have died the death of martyrs for truth, enduring the pangs of persecution have utterly perished? Without immortality the world is a moral chaos . . ."

I write you all this because I have just read your volume "The World As I See It." On page 5 you stated: "Any individual who should survive his physical death is beyond my comprehension . . . such notions are for the fears or absurd egoism of feeble souls." And I inquire in a spirit of desperation, is there in your view no comfort, no consolation for what has happened? Am I to believe that my beautiful darling child—a blooming bud that turned its face to the sun and was cut down by an unrelenting storm—has been forever wedded into dust, that there was nothing within him which has defied the grave and transcended the power of death? Is there nothing to assuage the pain of an unquenchable longing, an intense craving, an unceasing love for my darling son?

May I have a word from you? I need help badly.

Sincerely Yours,

Robert S. Marcus

I could hear Roberta sniffling. I could feel her tears on the other end of the line.

And then she said, "Thank you. A random call from a stranger and the missing piece of a puzzle has now found its place."

She added: "It's just what I thought my father would write."

I promised her I would keep in touch with her, and she promised to mail me more of her father's writings, and we hung up.

I was trembling.

I kept replaying Rabbi Marcus's letter in my mind. This man who'd protected and watched over so many children could not protect his own child. This man who had given faith to so many who had lost their faith, who had restored hope to so many who had lost their hope, now couldn't find hope himself. He had lost his way back to hope.

He was a rabbi in a spiritual crisis and as far as I could tell, he didn't turn to a rabbi for help. As political director of the World Jewish Congress, he had access to the greatest rabbinic minds of the twentieth century. Perhaps he did search for wisdom from a rabbinic mentor, but could not find the comfort he was seeking.

So instead he turned to the greatest scientific mind of his age and said, "Tell me there is an eternal soul. Tell me the soul is real." He needed to know that the soul survives, that death has no dominion over the spirit. *Don't tell me to believe. Don't ask me to have faith in it. I need to know it's a* fact. *A scientific fact.*

After everything his own eyes had seen, all the death he'd witnessed, only the assurance of a scientist could bring him comfort.

And that's when I turned and picked up Einstein's letter of comfort to Rabbi Marcus and I read it aloud to myself once more in its entirety:

Dear Dr. Marcus,

A human being is part of the whole, called by us "Universe," a part limited in time and space. He experiences himself, his thoughts and feelings as something separate from the rest, a kind of optical delusion of his consciousness. The striving to free oneself from this delusion is the one issue of true religion. Not to nourish the delusion but to try to overcome it is the way to reach the attainable measure of peace of mind.

    With my best wishes,

    Sincerely

    Albert Einstein

This was Einstein's letter of comfort to Rabbi Marcus. Was it personal? No, not really. Was it profound? I've been meditating on it every day for three years.

Einstein offered Rabbi Marcus and all of us a vision of heaven on earth. Did Einstein's words bring some measure of comfort to Rabbi Marcus's broken heart? I'd like to believe that Rabbi Marcus did receive solace from Einstein's words, but we'll never know for sure. I assume that if Rabbi Marcus wanted more straightforward words of consolation, he would have reached out to his rabbinic mentors and friends. But he turned to a man of science who searched for the Unified Field Theory and never quite found it, but never lost faith in the oneness of all things.

When you seek out a man like Einstein for inquiries about the soul, you are bound to get an answer that is out of the ordinary.

JUST TWO DAYS AFTER I spoke to Roberta she introduced me to her older sister, Tamara, the little baby girl Fay gave birth to in August 1944. Tamara is a petite woman in her late sixties, but the fire within her is mighty indeed. Tamara told me she met her father for the first time when she was two years old. She reminded me that she was only six when her father died, and she has only vague memories of him, but he was like a god in her eyes.

When I asked her what she remembered most about her father, this is what stood out. He smoked cigars, she told me, and in the evenings when he returned home from work he would delight her with a ring for her finger—the gilded paper ring from his cigar. Often it is the small gestures of love that live on—not the splashy offerings. A paper ring worth less than a cent is the image that remains imprinted on a daughter's heart.

I could tell Tamara is also cut from her father's cloth. She is a scholar who earned her Ph.D. in classics from NYU and served as chair of the classics department at Hunter College in New York City. Despite her focus on scholarship and rational thought, Tamara relayed the following story to me:

She said when her mother, Fay, was on in years and living in a retirement home her mind remained keen and sharp. One day when Tamara visited her mother, Fay told her with perfect clarity, "Jay visited me today."

Tamara asked her, "What did he say?"

Fay replied, "He said, 'I'm waiting for you, Mommy.'"

SIXTY-FIVE YEARS AGO A RABBI in pain turned to Einstein, a man of science, for spiritual wisdom and for solace. He was seeking a scientist's solution to a deep spiritual crisis. How do we make sense of senseless tragedy? Is our universe a cold and indifferent place? Is there hope? What is our comfort? What can we do when we feel like we are free-falling inside a vacuum of despair? Does the soul live on?

I stumbled upon a rabbi who saw that religion and science are not at odds with each other and who was not threatened by the insights science has to offer us. He was a man of God, seeking answers from the one man who knew more about the workings of this universe than any other human being alive in his day. A man who changed the way we understand time and space and matter. As Einstein aptly put it: "Science without religion is lame, religion without science is blind."

Einstein's answer to Rabbi Marcus was neither warm nor fuzzy. He never even said, "I'm so sorry for your loss." He didn't address the terrible agony that comes when a parent loses a child or when a young life is taken before its time. The truth is, in all the time I pored over Einstein's letter, I never stopped to read his thoughts as words of condolence. I read them as aspirations, as a way to see connectedness everywhere.

I found myself trying to imagine what it might have been like for me if I'd received Einstein's letter when my father was murdered. Would his words have comforted me? Would they have helped me to get over my devastating loss? Probably not. In his letter, Einstein never talks about love. He never mentions the dead. He never discusses the void, the emptiness, the loss. And he never speaks about memory or about what death cannot destroy. It would have been a disturbing condolence letter to receive. I think I would have probably been disappointed and upset.

Then again, I received so many disturbing gestures of comfort when my father died. People don't really know what to say in the face of tragedy. They offer platitudes. They reach for words in vain. Nothing can set death right. Nothing can. One thing I learned from all my research about Einstein was that he was a humanitarian who had difficulty with intimacy and connecting to the people who loved him, even his own sons. He was a man who lived in his head, not in his heart.

Several days later I thought about Einstein's letter to Rabbi Marcus again, and I realized that I was drawn to it from the start because it was bringing me comfort now in the face of my father's senseless murder so many years ago. It's not the sort of letter I could have understood in the days and weeks and months after my father's death. But from a distance of thirty-seven years, I see Einstein's words in the scheme of my life and the greater whole I have come to know in the intervening years. I can see now that my father has never left me. I couldn't see that then. I can see hints of eternity now that I had no access to then. I became a rabbi at the age of twenty-six and I've been a rabbi for twenty-six years. I've now spent half my life blessing souls as they enter this world, blessing souls as they unite under the wedding canopy, blessing souls as they enter the World to Come. I can taste Eden. I am full. The years and all the souls I've met and loved and lost have left their imprint upon me, and my soul has learned to speak more passionately about eternity and oneness. My heart has softened and my hands are open for receiving what life sends me day by day. I know who I am.

I love Einstein's phrase "true religion." I fantasize that someday all people across the globe will come together, not by denying our unique faiths, rituals, or traditions, but by raising our hands and voices in unity. The optical delusion of separation is tearing our world apart. We must learn to free ourselves from the cognitive walls that make us think we are strangers to one another. The walls that make us indifferent to the plight of people we don't know. I pray each day that we can learn to care, to act, and to expand our circles of compassion. I pray that you will join me. Together we can shatter the delusion of our separateness and create a world where the prophetic biblical verse comes to fruition in our time: "On that day God will be one and God's name will be one." One. All of us part of that whole.

I imagine Rabbi Marcus opening Einstein's letter and understanding that he would never be far from his beloved Jay because all things are connected in the One. Even when we feel far from those we have loved and lost, they are closer than we know. Time gives way to eternity, the boundary lines between life and death are nothing but a blur.

I prayed that Rabbi Marcus was able to see that Jay was with him, would always be with him.

And then I found another letter . . .

I LEARNED THAT MANY of Rabbi Marcus's papers and speeches from his years at the World Jewish Congress were housed at the

American Jewish Archives in Cincinnati. When I was lecturing in Ohio, I arranged to spend a day there looking through Rabbi Marcus's writings. I expected to be sifting through only a few files, but the librarian brought out a huge two-level cart packed with boxes. I was drowning and I only had one day to spend. The clock was ticking down.

I'm not an academic. I'm not a historian. This was the first time in my life I'd ever done this sort of research. And I have asthma, and the dusty pages were crumbling in my hands, making me wheeze. But alongside my panic I felt humbled and deeply honored to be holding pages that were written by Rabbi Marcus's own hand. I traced his script with my fingers.

I think the head archivist felt sorry for me. She began skimming the documents together with me, helping me weed through what was important and what could be set aside. Then she perused a file full of correspondences and said, "I think you're going to want to see this one." And she left me alone with the file.

I was standing up leafing through page after page. There were letters by Rabbi Marcus to political figures. Letters to the *New York Times*. Letters to rabbis and to colleagues. Intermingled with all these official documents I came upon a page with no address and no salutation at the top. It began this way:

"Today was Thanksgiving, my son, our first Thanksgiving without you and three months since you left us . . ."

I began to shiver, tears began streaming down my cheeks. I sat down and read on.

> Today we missed you, more than ever, my precious child—all of us, even Tammy. Sitting in the restaurant we felt your presence near and when we went to the movies to see "Ichabod and Mr. Toad" you were on the seat beside me . . .

. . . I see you swimming in every lake I pass and hear your voice calling to me from the distance asking me to come to you . . .

Since you have left me, dear child, I have dwelt for many hours on the meaning of immortality . . .

. . . I have sustained myself with the hope and consoled myself with the belief that somehow, somewhere we shall meet again. My unceasing love for you is immortal, my son; it is a stream direct from the fount of God and can never dry up; it must be satisfied in eternity; in that higher life to which death opens the door. I believe all this, my precious Jay . . .

. . . we shall once again be united in eternity, my darling. May God redeem my soul from the grasp of the grave as I know he has received you, my precious child, into the house of everlasting life and has breathed into you the breath of life eternal.

Sitting all alone in the archive, drenched in tears with that haunting, heartbreaking letter in my hands, surrounded by stacks of Rabbi Marcus's writings and teachings, I knew my search had come to an end. I felt emptied out and full. I realized all at once that Rabbi Marcus held the answer to the question about the soul that he'd posed to Einstein. He knew the "secret of the Upper World," it was already planted inside him.

The sacred words from the mystical Book of Creation came back to me: *Their end is imbedded in their beginning and their beginning in their end.* Everything comes full circle.

Buried quietly for decades, Rabbi Marcus's letter has now found new life. I can hear him reaching across time, sharing his teaching: Within us there lies a soul that is eternal and immortal. A soul full of wisdom and love that emanates from the Creator. A soul that links us together in life and can never be extinguished.

As I sat there, frozen in place, every stray sentence of the book I'd been writing for three years seemed to find its rightful place as well. Even a book has a soul, some message that never dies. Words seep in and penetrate our well-defended hearts and remain with us long after we close the cover and place the volume back on the shelf.

Rabbi Marcus knew the answer to the eternal soul he was searching for. What answer has been eluding you? What do you already know? Perhaps you've been searching for something you have not lost. There is a truth biding its time inside your soul that is longing to make itself known through you. Welcome it. And may you spread your wisdom and love far and wide.

Yes, Rabbi Marcus knew the answer to the eternal soul he was searching for. And soon his own soul would return to its Source. Fourteen short months after writing these words to Jay, Rabbi Robert Marcus, at the age of forty-one, joined his beloved son in that higher realm, the house of everlasting life.

May their memories be for a blessing, may their love be satisfied in eternity.

I DISCOVERED A QUOTE BY Einstein about the way we are all interconnected and it led me to a remarkable rabbi whose heroic story needed to be told. And the story of that rabbi and the letters he and Einstein shared has led me to you. It is the story of the soul that unites us all, the soul that never dies.

Dear Reader,
Within each of us, I believe, there lies a space that is holy, a space of purity and wisdom. Not even death can have dominion

over it. We all have access to it. It is the seat of God within each of us. The God who gives us strength to dream, who assures each and every one of us, *You are not alone, I am with you.*

I want to thank you for seeking the soul with me. Your soul is here for you. Tap into it, listen to it, welcome it. The Life Force, the Love Force, and the Eternal Force are within you, hoping to lead you to visions of the One and to the life that's already been planted inside you. If you are ready, if you nourish your starving soul and wake it from its dormancy, it will rise up and nourish you in life, in love, and in work. Mystical ascensions are available to you, you can glimpse a world that is more beautiful than heaven.

I believe we are part of a cosmic stew and it is near and far, it was and it is and it will be and time collapses in on itself and we are held together in a great oneness with all the living and all the dead and all the souls we've ever loved and who have ever loved us whose spirits illuminate our lives and light up the heavens. We can remember them, channel them, and welcome them into our consciousness and into our hearts and souls.

I believe with all my being that there is a higher dimension available to us not only in the next world, but right here where we are. Knowing your soul, aligning with your soul, and following your soul are the keys to entering heaven here. You have the power to experience expansive vision, you can free yourself from prisons of your own making, you can dream and find the power to act, you can learn to love and to forgive and to hear and heed the call of your soul. You can begin to see the oneness that has been evading you, to see beyond the delusion of your separateness.

Let your soul be your guide.

May you come to experience the "Me within me." May you be blessed with eyes to see the oneness your soul has been longing to show you. Know who you are. The seal of the Creator is on you. May you see your World to Come in this world. May you experience long days full of meaning and may you live to give nachas, *deep soul pleasure, to the Creator who dreamed you into being.*

And may God smile and sigh a deep sigh of relief and laugh with pure joy upon seeing your soul fulfill its call. Amen.

Acknowledgments

My agent, Esther Newberg, has been my rock, my guardian, my champion, and my advocate for the past twenty years. I adore her and trust her always, there would be no book without her. My gratitude to my publisher, Bob Miller, for his unwavering support, his guidance, and his faith in this project from day one. And many thanks to my editor, Whitney Frick, for her insight and encouragement and for wisely steering me back to the soul. Thanks to Jasmine Faustino, senior associate editor, for all her indispensable input and help. Special thanks to my dear friend Dan Adler who first introduced me to Bob Miller many years ago and who is always supporting me with his mysterious, magical powers and his love.

I have no words to thank Roberta Leiner and Dr. Tamara Green for sharing their homes, their hearts, their stories, and their precious legacy with me. Their beloved father, Rabbi Robert S. Marcus, of blessed memory, was a man of greatness. His life and teachings inspire me daily. I pray that his legacy, his passionate dedication to social justice, and his words from the heart will inspire and illuminate the lives of many others.

Any acknowledgment would be incomplete without thanking Albert Einstein, whose letter to Rabbi Marcus has been a deep and lasting comfort to me. It led me on a three-year journey and inspired me to write this book, may his memory be for a blessing. I understand very little of Einstein's attempts at a Unified Field Theory, but his hopes for a Unified World give me hope every day.

I am indebted to the Buchenwald boys, who generously shared their stories with me for this project. I am forever grateful to Elie Wiesel for offering me his time, his heart, and his memories. Sadly, Elie Wiesel and Naphtali Lau-Lavie passed away prior to the publication of this book, may their memories be for a blessing. My gratitude to Henry Oster, Perry Shulman, Szaja Chaskiel, and Robert Waisman. And to the members of Kibbutz Buchenwald / Kibbutz Netzer Sereni: Avraham Ahuvia, of blessed memory, who passed away prior to the publication of this work, David Rosen, Tzvia Shoham, Kibbutz Archivist, Simcha and Neomi Appelbaum, Mali Lamm, and Shmuel Goldstein, husband of Sarah (Feig) Goldstein, of blessed memory.

Thank you to all those who shared their powerful stories with me and appear in this book: Roberta Leiner and Dr. Tamara Green, Carol Taubman and Dr. Helene Rosenzweig, my guardian angels, Rabbi Stuart Geller, Alan Golub, Ibolya Markowitz, Laurie Goldmith-Heitner, the amazing Judith (Feist) Hemmendinger, Dr. Alan Rabinowitz, Scott Tansey, Dr. Ruth Westheimer, Elaine Hall, Neal Katz, Byrdie Lifson Pompan, Dr. Babak Azizzadeh, Naomi (Salit) Birnbach, Jeni Stepian Maenner, Tom Thomas, Rachel, Jerry, of blessed memory, Aimee Ginsburg Bikel and the great Theodore Bikel, of blessed memory, and Louis Sneh and his beloved Dina Sneh, of blessed memory. And my gratitude to Fred Kahn, who led me to Roberta Leiner.

A world of thanks to my dear friend Rabbi Stewart Vogel who generously read multiple versions of this manuscript and advised and encouraged me through times of uncertainty. And to Rabbi Toba

August, my study partner, who also read multiple versions of this manuscript and graced me with her wisdom and love.

The following friends and colleagues read this manuscript and left their invaluable imprint upon it: Rabbi Burton Visotzky, Teresa Strasser, Rabbi David Wolpe, and David Suissa. Dr. Ginger Clark listened to many chapters aloud and always led me deeper. The amazing Don Was meditated with me on Music and Soul. Rabbi Moshe Re'em weighed in on Love and Soul. My niece Sari Thayer brainstormed with me on Learning and Soul. Barry Michels guided me through writer's block, God bless you, and God bless my shadow.

Thanks to the Hevraya at IJS and to my teachers, Rabbi Jonathan Slater, Dr. Melila Hellner-Eshed, and Rabbi Sheila Peltz Weinberg.

The following people were indispensable sources of help in my research: Dr. Michael Berenbaum, Patricia Glaser, and Sheri Kaufer. Professor Hanoch Gutfreund, academic director of the Albert Einstein Archives. Chaya Becker, assistant to the curator, Barbara Wolff, and Dr. Roni Grosz, curator of the Albert Einstein Archives. The incredible Dr. Kip Thorne, Feynman Professor of Theoretical Physics, Emeritus, Caltech. Dr. Gary Zola, executive director, the Jacob Rader Marcus Center of the American Jewish Archives, Dr. Dana Herman, managing editor and academic associate of the AJA, and Elisa Ho, associate archivist. Margo Gutstein, archivist at the Simon Wiesenthal Center, William C. Connelly at the United States Holocaust Memorial Museum, Karin Dengler and Timorah Perel at Yad Vashem, Miri Hakim at Mikve Israel. Many thanks to Alice Calaprice, who located Rabbi Marcus's letter to Albert Einstein for me. Yossi Cohen, archives manager, Israel State Archives. Marissa Poock, Elie Wiesel Foundation. Susan Edel at the Magen David Adom Tracing Service, Serena Woolrish at Allgenerations.com, Sherly Postnikov, location specialist at HIAS, Eric Arnold Fritzler, archivist at American Jewish Historical Society, and National Jewish Welfare Board Military Chaplaincy Records. Gunnar Berg, YIVO archivist. Sima Borsuk, social worker,

Geriatric and Holocaust Survivors' Programs Pesach Tikvah. Eve Kahn, the *New York Times*. Yael Kaufman at Atlit Detention Camp, Clandestine Jewish Immigration Information and Research Center. Jonathan Kirsch, Baruch Weiss, Dr. Chana Kronfeld, Dr. Esther Dreifuss-Kattan, Barry Fisher, Professor Kenneth Waltzer, who led me to several Buchenwald boys, Dr. Alex Grobman, Ted Comet, Albert Weber, and Tom Sawicki. Martin Barr, William and Gladys Barr, and Phyllis Lasker, of blessed memory. My gratitude to Rabbi Amichai Lau-Lavie and Joan Lau-Lavie.

Many thanks to Arielle Eckstut, the Book Doctor, and to Alexandra Romanoff, who both offered important editorial advice.

My Nashuva spiritual community and its leaders are true blessings to me. With you, Judaism has come alive, we've created something remarkable together.

Special thanks to Brett and Rachel Barenholtz, Dr. Helene Rosenzweig and Dr. Richard Bock, Carol Taubman and Norman Manrique, Carin and Mark Sage, Andrea Kay, Julie Drucker, Jon Drucker, Dina Shulman, Jennifer Krieger and Dr. Lauren Krieger, Laurie and Stan Weinstock, Ed Greenberg and Jane Kagon, Holly and Harry Wiland, Lori Brown and Tom Beaulieu, Phil and Brenda Bubar, Laurie Berger, Bill and Ethel Fagenson. And to the Nashuva Band for restoring my soul and filling my life with beautiful music and prayers to God: Jared Stein, Justin Stein, Andrea Kay, Ed Lemus, Bernadette Lingle, Fino Roverato, Jamie Papish, Alula Tzaddik, and Avi Sills.

My parents, George and Ruth Levy, of blessed memory, are with me always. I give thanks to God for loving parents who guided me, believed in me, supported me, and taught me day by day. Their love, their legacy, their wisdom, and their light are forever shining upon me and lighting up my way. I thank my siblings, whom I can always count on: Dr. Miriam Levy, Dr. Daniel Levy, and David Levy. My in-laws, Sari and Aaron Eshman, are true inspirations in my life, offering their love, their support, and their amazing energy every day. I thank my brothers- and sisters-in-law and all my nieces and nephews and cousins. I remember my departed relatives with gratitude and love.

My husband, Rob Eshman, is my soulmate. When my mom first met Rob even before we were dating, she told me, "He's a keeper." I listened to her, and I've kept him for twenty-five years, and may God grant us many, many more years together in health, in fun and in laughter, in blessings and in love. Rob is my first and my last editor and everything in between. His influence on this book is everywhere, with each read he's lifted me and this work higher. He's given me his heart, his wisdom, his ear, his criticism, his constant encouragement, his patience, and his love. And he still woos me with his amazing meals every single day of our lives together.

How amazing is it when you get to the point in life when you can turn to your kids for help, support, and advice. Our children, Adi and Noa, are God's gifts to me. They are my lights, my mentors, my greatest blessings, and my comfort. They both read this book, offered their insights and their edits, and they both made it better. They make me better all the time.

Whole and complete, this work is my prayer to God, Soul of Souls, Creator of all.

Purim! 14 Adar 5777
March 12, 2017
Venice, California

Notes

Chapter 2: Einstein and the Rabbi

13 *"A human being is part of"*: Albert Einstein to Robert Marcus, February 12, 1950, Albert Einstein Archives, Hebrew University of Jerusalem, AEA 60-426.

15 *"Dear Son"*: Letters by Rabbi Robert Marcus in this chapter and much of the biographical material are from Rabbi Robert S. Marcus personal papers. Courtesy of Roberta Leiner and Dr. Tamara Green.

16 *"You are free!"*: As told to me by Judith Feist Hemmendinger.

16 *"Have found 1000 Jewish children"*: Judith Hemmendinger, *Survivors: Children of the Holocaust* (Bethesda, MD: National Press, 1986), 13.

17 *"With tears streaming down his face"*: Margalit Fox, "Rabbi Herschel Schacter Is Dead at 95; Cried to the Jews of Buchenwald: 'You Are Free,'" *New York Times,* March 26, 2013.

18 *"They have cows"*: Rabbi Robert S. Marcus personal papers.

19 *"My kids had been brought"*: Reports, 1944–1945, World Jewish Congress Records, MS-361, Box B39, File 4, American Jewish Archives (AJA), Cincinnati, Ohio.

20 *"The New Year was ushered in"*: 1950, World Jewish Congress Records, MS-361, Box B39, File 8, AJA.

Chapter 3: Finding the Me Within me

25 *"something deeply hidden"*: Walter Isaacson, *Einstein: His Life and Universe* (New York: Simon & Schuster, 2007), 13.

Chapter 5: Encountering the Three Levels of the Soul

34 *Three Levels of the Soul*: For an in-depth discussion of the soul, see Isaiah Tishby and Fischel Lachower, *The Wisdom of the Zohar: An Anthology of Texts*, vol. 2, trans. David Goldstein (Portland, OR: Littman Library of Jewish Civilization, 1989).

Chapter 6: Giving the Soul What It Wants

45 *"If all the delights"*: C. G. Montefiore and H. Loewe, eds., *A Rabbinic Anthology* (Philadelphia: Jewish Publication Society of America, 1960), 314.

Chapter 7: Meditating Is Medicine for the Soul

56 *a person who feels complete*: Adin Steinsaltz, *The Thirteen Petalled Rose: A Discourse on the Essence of Jewish Existence and Belief* (New Milford, CT: Maggid Books, 1980), 99.

Chapter 11: Restoring the Soul in Nature

76 *"The most beautiful thing we can experience"*: Alice Calaprice, ed., *The Ultimate Quotable Einstein* (Princeton, NJ: Princeton University Press and the Hebrew University of Jerusalem, 2011), 330.

77 *"When a person returns"*: Rabbi Nachman, *Outpouring of the Soul: Rabbi Nachman's Path in Meditation* (Jerusalem: Breslov Research Institute, 1980), 50.

77 *"Master of the Universe"*: Translated by Rabbi Shamai Kanter.

Chapter 13: Stepping Back to Gain a Wider Perspective

89 *George Harrison said*: The Beatles, *The Beatles Anthology* (San Francisco: Chronicle Books, 2000), 339.

90 *"Look, this is the manuscript of a scientific book"*: Viktor E. Frankl, *Man's Search for Meaning* (Boston: Beacon Press, 2006), 14.

90 *"How should I have interpreted such a 'coincidence'"*: Ibid., 115.

Chapter 15: Seeing Through the "Truths" We Tell Ourselves

104 *Aaron was one of Rabbi Marcus's Buchenwald boys*: As told to me by Judith Feist Hemmendinger. The story also appears in Judith Hemmendinger and Robert Krell, *The Children of Buchenwald: Child Survivors of the Holocaust and Their Post-War Lives* (Jerusalem: Gefen, 2000), 76.

Chapter 16: Glimpsing the Tapestry

108 *Seventy years later, the* New York Times *recounted the tale*: Eve M. Kahn, "A Pilot and Holocaust Survivors, Bound by War's Fabric, Are Reunited in Brooklyn," *New York Times*, November 8, 2015.

110   *Einstein loved to escape into his thoughts there*: For a description of Einstein in Caputh, see Isaacson, *Einstein*, 359–360.

110   *"The sailboat, the sweeping view"*: Ibid., 360.

110   *"The most beautiful emotion we can experience"*: Ibid., 387.

111   *"Take a very good look at it"*: Ibid., 401.

111   *"Because of Hitler"*: Ibid., 403; and Albert Einstein Archives, AEA 50-834.

112   *"Life is a great tapestry"*: Calaprice, ed., *The Ultimate Quotable Einstein*, 230.

Discovering the Power to Act

113   *"The body without the spirit is a corpse"*: Abraham Joshua Heschel, *Moral Grandeur and Spiritual Audacity: Essays*, ed. Susannah Heschel (New York: Farrar, Straus & Giroux, 1996), 112.

113   *"Our legs uttered songs"*: Scott A. Shay, *Getting Our Groove Back: How to Energize American Jewry* (New York: Devora, 2007), 247.

Chapter 17: Breaking Free of Old, Familiar Patterns

117   *"I held him close and would not let him go"*: I was inspired here by a commentary in Rabbi Sholom Noach Berezovsky, *Sefer Netivot Shalom* [Paths of Peace], vol. Devarim, in Hebrew (Jerusalem: Machon Emunah Ve-Daat Yeshivat Bet Avraham Slonim), 78.

Chapter 23: Finding a Soulmate

164   *"From every human being there rises a light"*: Anita Diamant, *The New Jewish Wedding* (New York: Simon & Schuster, 1985), 109.

Chapter 26: Parenting with Soul

176   *So what secret of the Upper World*: See Berezovsky, *Sefer Netivot Shalom* [Paths of Peace], vol. 182–184.

176   *But in high holy matters there is a knowing*: My thoughts on the soul's instincts were inspired by a teaching of Rav Kook's found in Chanan Morrison, *Gold from the Land of Israel: A New Light on the Weekly Torah Portion from the Writings of Rabbi Isaac HaKohen Kook* (Jerusalem: Urim, 2006), 142.

Chapter 27: Heeding the Call of the Soul

183   *"Our strongest gifts"*: Parker J. Palmer, *Let Your Life Speak: Listening for the Voice of Vocation* (San Francisco: Jossey-Bass, 2000), 52.

183   *the word "vocation"*: Ibid., 4.

184   *"Sweetest, Returned to headquarters"*: Rabbi Robert S. Marcus personal papers.

Chapter 28: Knowing You Are the Right Man for the Job

185 *Knowing You Are the Right Man for the Job*: The information in this chapter stems from six interviews I conducted with Judith Feist Hemmendinger and from Hemmendinger and Krell, *The Children of Buchenwald*.

186 *The experts who observed these boys*: For a description of the boys in Ecouis, see ibid., 28–32.

187 *"The Chaplain returned to us our souls"*: Ibid., 31.

188 *"The boys were born psychopaths"*: Ibid., 33.

189 *to heal the way the boys approached food*: For a description, see ibid., 35–36.

190 *to stop the fighting*: For a description of how Judith rearranged the rooms, see ibid., 35.

190 *"How awful and disgraceful"*: Ibid., 37.

190 *"But you have been in Auschwitz yourself!"*: Ibid.

191 *"What would your parents have done?"*: Ibid., 70.

192 *"My two brothers received me very well"*: Ibid., 81–82.

194 *Can you imagine that reunion?*: For a description of the reunion, see ibid., 91–94.

194 *"Tonight's gathering serves as a continuation"*: Ibid., 92–93.

195 *"Dear Judith"*: Ibid., 10–12.

Chapter 29: Feeling the Soul's Tug

199 *the word "decide"*: Roy F. Baumeister and John Tierney, *Willpower: Rediscovering the Greatest Human Strength* (New York: Penguin Books, 2011), 86.

200 *meeting the soul is like encountering a deer*: Palmer, *Let Your Life Speak*, 7.

202 *our ears can't hear the call*: I was inspired here by a commentary in Berezovsky, *Sefer Netivot Shalom* [Paths of Peace], vol. Vayikra, 12–15.

203 *"It will also happen sometimes"*: Rabbi Kalonymus Kalman Shapira, the Piaseczno Rebbe, *Hachsharat Avrekhim 9:3*. Translation from Yitzhak Buxbaum, *Jewish Spiritual Practices* (Lanham, MD: Jason Aronson, 1990), 484–486.

Chapter 30: Turning Your Weakness into Your Strength

205 Time *magazine described him:* Bryan Walsh, "The Indiana Jones of Wildlife Protection," *Time,* January 10, 2008.

209 *the area of your life where you are most blocked*: See Berezovsky, *Sefer Netivot Shalom* [Paths of Peace], vol. Devarim, 127.

Chapter 32: Defeating the Soul's Adversary

217 *with a hole in his pocket*: See Berezovsky, *Sefer Netivot Shalom*, holiday vol. B, Shavuot, 352–354.

220 *"Come with me on this journey"*: When I was suffering from writer's block, I learned this truth from my friend and teacher Barry Michels.

Chapter 35: Perceiving the Forty-Two Journeys of Your Soul

246 *Forty-Two Journeys of Your Soul*: For the analysis of the forty-two journeys that the chapter is based on, see Berezovsky, *Sefer Netivot Shalom* [Paths of Peace], vol. Bamidbar, 175–184, and vol. Shemot, 280–281.

Chapter 37: Seeing Your World to Come

261 *"The most dangerous type of atheism"*: *A Knock at Midnight: Inspiration from the Great Sermons of Martin Luther King, Jr.,* ed. Clayborne Carson and Peter Holloran (New York: Warner Books, 2000), 15.
262 *"There is no man who ever lived"*: Speeches, 1937–1946, World Jewish Congress Records, MS-361, Box B39, File 9, AJA.
263 *a bench in the World to Come*: I expanded on Berezovsky, *Sefer Netivot Shalom* [Paths of Peace], vol. Bereshit, 260.

Chapter 39: Living on Soul Time

276 *I understood the words*: Michael Kimmelman, "Decades Later, a Vision Survives," *New York Times,* September 12, 2012.
278 *"ordinary were the most luminous of all"*: I expanded on ibid., vol. Bamidbar, 198.
281 *"He has departed from this strange world"*: Isaacson, *Einstein,* 540.

Chapter 40: Experiencing the Oneness

286 *"There is nothing more difficult for the soul"*: Paraphrased from Tishby and Lachower, *The Wisdom of the Zohar,* vol. 2, 851.
286 *"God, I know You are Master of all souls"*: Paraphrased from Hayim Nahman Bialik and Yehoshua Hana Ravnitzky, eds., *The Book of Legends, Sefer Ha-Aggadah: Legends from the Talmud and Midrash,* trans. William Braude (New York: Schocken Books, 1992), 104.
286 *"At the time of a person's death"*: Simcha Paul Raphael, *Jewish Views of the Afterlife,* 2nd ed. (Lanham, MD: Rowman & Littlefield, 2009), 290.
287 *dying person is given an additional soul*: Ibid., 287.
288 *"Up to now your father has taught you"*: Martin Buber, *Tales of the Hasidim: The Later Masters* (New York: Schocken Books, 1947), 269.

Chapter 42: Beholding Threads of Connection

300 *young bride-to-be whose father died*: Katie Rogers, "Bride Is Walked Down the Aisle by the Man Who Got Her Father's Donated Heart," *New York Times,* August 8, 2016.
305 *"Their end is imbedded in their beginning"*: Aryeh Kaplan, *Sefer Yetzirah: The Book of Creation; In Theory and Practice,* rev. ed. (Boston: Weiser Books, 1997), 57.

Coming Full Circle: The Letter

312   *"Dear Dr. Einstein"*: Robert S. Marcus to Albert Einstein, February 9, 1950, Courtesy of the Albert Einstein Archives, Hebrew University of Jerusalem, AEA 60-423. With permission from Roberta Leiner and Dr. Tamara Green.

314   *"Dear Dr. Marcus"*: Some of you Einstein experts may be familiar with a second Einstein letter that begins exactly like this one, but ends by speaking about widening our circles of compassion. For some time I thought this second letter was a corruption of the first. But Barbara Wolff at the Albert Einstein Archive in Jerusalem explained to me that Einstein actually penned this second letter to another grieving father and "plagiarized" himself. It turned out that there was another parent who lost a child and wrote to Einstein for comfort exactly nineteen days after Rabbi Marcus had written to Einstein. By some awful coincidence, the author of the second letter was also a grieving rabbi. Like Rabbi Marcus, Rabbi Norman Salit was a prominent rabbi in New York City, and he too had received a degree in law from NYU. Rabbi Salit's sixteen-year-old daughter Miriam died of encephalitis just a month after Rabbi Marcus's son Jay died. Rabbi Salit was desperately trying to provide solace to his surviving daughter, who was nineteen years old, but he couldn't seem to offer her the words of comfort she needed to hear. It was she who asked her father to write to Einstein on her behalf. I located Rabbi Salit's surviving daughter. Her name is Naomi (Salit) Birnbach. The two Naomis got together in Manhattan. We sat down in a café and I asked Naomi to tell me about the request she made of her father. She said, "Einstein was the smartest man in the world and I was baffled by my sister Miriam's illness and death." She told me Einstein was the only person she could think of to address her sister's senseless death.

316   *"Science without religion is lame"*: Isaacson, *Einstein*, 390.

319   *"Today was Thanksgiving"*: Publications, 1932–1933; 1943–1950, World Jewish Congress Records, MS-361, Box B41, Folder 2, AJA.

Bibliography

Baumeister, Roy F., and John Tierney. *Willpower: Rediscovering the Greatest Human Strength.* New York: Penguin Books, 2011.

The Beatles. *The Beatles Anthology.* San Francisco: Chronicle Books, 2000.

Berezovsky, Sholom Noach. *Sefer Netivot Shalom* [Paths of Peace]. Jerusalem: Machon Emunah Ve-Daat Yeshivat Bet Avraham Slonim.

Bialik, Hayim Nahman, and Yehoshua Hana Ravnitzky, eds. *The Book of Legends, Sefer Ha-Aggadah: Legends from the Talmud and Midrash.* Translated by William Braude. New York: Schocken Books, 1992.

Buber, Martin. *Tales of the Hasidim: The Later Masters.* New York: Schocken Books, 1947.

Buxbaurm, Yitzhak. *Jewish Spiritual Practices.* Lanham, MD: Jason Aronson, 1990.

Calaprice, Alice, ed. *The Ultimate Quotable Einstein.* Princeton, NJ: Princeton University Press, 2011.

Carson, Clayborne, and Peter Holloran, eds. *A Knock at Midnight: Inspiration from the Great Sermons of Martin Luther King, Jr.* New York: Warner Books, 2000.

Diamant, Anita. *The New Jewish Wedding.* New York: Simon & Schuster, 1985.

Fox, Margalit. "Rabbi Herschel Schacter Is Dead at 95; Cried to the Jews of Buchenwald: 'You Are Free.'" *New York Times,* March 26, 2013.

Frankl, Viktor E. *Man's Search for Meaning.* Boston: Beacon Press, 2006.

Hemmendinger, Judith. *Survivors: Children of the Holocaust.* Bethesda, MD: National Press, 1986.

Hemmendinger, Judith, and Robert Krell. *The Children of Buchenwald: Child Survivors of the Holocaust and Their Post-War Lives.* Jerusalem: Gefen Publishing House, 2000.

Heschel, Abraham Joshua. *Moral Grandeur and Spiritual Audacity: Essays*. Edited by Susannah Heschel. New York: Farrar, Straus & Giroux, 1996.

Isaacson, Walter. *Einstein: His Life and Universe*. New York: Simon & Schuster, 2007.

Jacob Rader Marcus Center of the American Jewish Archives (AJA) World Jewish Congress Collection (MS-361).

Kahn, Eve M. "A Pilot and Holocaust Survivors, Bound by War's Fabric, Are Reunited in Brooklyn." *New York Times*, November 8, 2015.

Kaplan, Aryeh. *Sefer Yetzirah: The Book of Creation: In Theory and Practice*. Rev. ed. Boston: Weiser Books, 1997.

Kimmelman, Michael. "Decades Later, a Vision Survives." *New York Times*, September 12, 2012.

Rabbi Robert S. Marcus personal papers courtesy of Roberta Leiner and Dr. Tamara Green.

Montefiore, C. G., and H. Loewe, eds. *A Rabbinic Anthology*. Philadelphia: Jewish Publication Society of America, 1960.

Morrison, Chanan. *Gold from the Land of Israel: A New Light on the Weekly Torah Portion from the Writings of Rabbi Isaac HaKohen Kook*. Jerusalem: Urim, 2006.

Rabbi Nachman. *Outpouring of the Soul: Rabbi Nachman's Path in Meditation*. Jerusalem: Breslov Research Institute, 1980.

Palmer, Parker J. *Let Your Life Speak: Listening for the Voice of Vocation*. San Francisco: Jossey-Bass, 2000.

The Papers of Albert Einstein. Albert Einstein Archives. Hebrew University of Jerusalem.

Raphael, Simcha Paul. *Jewish Views of the Afterlife*. 2nd ed. Lanham, MD: Rowman & Littlefield, 2009.

Rogers, Katie. "Bride Is Walked Down the Aisle by the Man Who Got Her Father's Donated Heart." *New York Times*, August 8, 2016.

Shay, Scott A. *Getting Our Groove Back: How to Energize American Jewry*. New York: Devora, 2007.

Steinsaltz, Adin. *The Thirteen Petalled Rose: A Discourse on the Essence of Jewish Existence and Belief*. New Milford, CT: Maggid Books, 1980.

Tishby, Isaiah, and Fischel Lachower. *The Wisdom of the Zohar: An Anthology of Texts*. Vol. 2. Translated by David Goldstein. Portland, OR: Littman Library of Jewish Civilization, 1989.

Welsh, Brian. "The Indiana Jones of Wildlife Protection." *Time*, January 10, 2008.